# THE
# ALCOHOLISM
## AND
# ADDICTION
# CURE

---

CHRIS PRENTISS

POWER PRESS

LOS ANGELES, CALIFORNIA

*The Alcoholism and Addiction Cure* is also available in a 10-CD audio version, read by the author.

Library of Congress Control Number: 2005907002

ISBN: 978-0-943015-44-6 (paperback)
ISBN: 978-0-943015-54-5 (hardcover)

10 9 8 7 6 5 4 3

For information, address:

Power Press
6428 Meadows Court
Malibu, California, 90265
Telephone: 310/392-9393
E-mail: info@PowerPressPublishing.com
Website: www.PowerPressPublishing.com

For foreign and translation rights, contact Nigel J. Yorwerth.
E-mail: Nigel@PublishingCoaches.com

For information on the Passages Addiction Cure Center in Malibu, California, contact:

Telephone: 310/589-2880 (toll free in the U.S. 888/777-8525)
E-mail: chris@passagesmalibu.com
Website: www.passagesmalibu.com

Cover design: Nita Ybarra
Interior design and production: Robert S. Tinnon Design and Media Works

*I know your struggle, I know your heartache.*
*I have seen the rending of families, the suffering,*
*the tragic endings, and I have seen the wonder*
*of transcendence over it all.*

*This book is dedicated to you who seek freedom*
*from dependency for yourself or a loved one.*

# CONTENTS

Acknowledgments    ix

**Chapter One**  My Pledge to You    1

**Chapter Two**  Healing the Underlying Causes    11

**Chapter Three**  To Hell and Back    43

**Chapter Four**  Changing the Treatment Paradigm    129

**Chapter Five**  The Four Causes of Dependency    145

**Chapter Six**  Believing a Cure Is Possible for You    159

**Chapter Seven**  Creating Your Holistic Recovery Program    175

**Chapter Eight**  Your Personal Philosophy    279

**Chapter Nine**  The New Chapter in Your Life    315

Notes    329

Index    333

# ACKNOWLEDGMENTS

I HEREBY ACKNOWLEDGE THE PRODIGIOUS EFFORT PUT FORTH on behalf of this book by Nigel J. Yorwerth and Patricia Spadaro of PublishingCoaches.com in Bozeman, Montana. Their meticulous editing, proofing, organization of the material, and shepherding of the book through all its stages was exemplary in every way. They brought their own particular wisdom to bear in a gracious and unobtrusive manner, for which I am grateful.

I wish to thank Jessica Cail for her diligent efforts in research and in providing substantiation of factual information presented in this book.

I also wish to acknowledge the editing effort of Monica Faulkner. Monica makes every writer look professional.

I also wish to acknowledge Robert S. Tinnon for his precise layout and design of the interior of the book.

I also wish to thank Nita Ybarra for her clean and uncluttered cover design.

I thank those wonderful therapists at Passages Addiction Cure Center for their dedication to healing, to being the best they can be, and for their loyalty and expertise. I also thank the doctors and therapists who have made such a wonderful contribution to this book.

And lastly, I thank Pax. Without him, none of this would have ever happened. He is a constant reminder to everyone who comes to Passages and to everyone who reads this book of the tremendous growth and possibility for greatness that exists within every dependency. Seneca, a Roman philosopher who lived in the first century A.D., said, "Gold is tempered by fire, brave men by adversity." Certainly Pax was tempered in the fire, and certainly everything was burned away that was not pure. What is left is a shining example of the potential in each of us to surmount even the greatest adversity.

CHAPTER ONE

# MY PLEDGE TO YOU

**cure** *n.* **1)** Restoring to a
sound or healthy condition.
**2)** A healing.

WITHIN THE COVERS OF THIS BOOK, I WILL SHOW YOU how you can cure your alcoholism or addiction. Here, at the outset, I want you to notice that I do not mince words. I do not say "however," "maybe," "although," "perhaps," or use other qualifying terms or conditions. By reading this book, you *will* learn how to cure your alcoholism or addiction.

That statement is based on the results we achieve at Passages Addiction Cure Center in Malibu, California, the world's most effective center for the treatment of substance abuse. At Passages, we assist people every day to cure themselves. *We* don't cure *them*—we assist them to cure themselves. By learning how to activate your mental and physical resources, and by getting qualified help, you too can cure yourself or help bring about a cure for your loved one.

**Note:** I wrote *The Alcoholism and Addiction Cure* as if you are the one seeking a cure, even though you may be reading this to learn how to cure a loved one.

1

Although you and I have never met face-to-face and gotten to know each other, I consider you my friend. If we meet, you'll find that we share similar experiences, particularly with regard to dependency. You or your loved one are treading the same ground that I trod with my son Pax, who was dependent on heroin, cocaine, and alcohol for ten years.

You and I have felt the same despair, suffered the same hardships, experienced the same losses, seen the same rending of friendships and family, watched ourselves or our loved ones relentlessly spiral downward, and had our hearts broken and our spirits dashed. The difference between us, if there is a difference, is that Pax has come out the other side whole, healed, and cured, while you or your loved one is still caught in the grip of the powerful, soul-sucking vortex of dependency on addictive drugs, alcohol, or addictive behavior.

Pax began using marijuana when he was fifteen, along with an occasional beer. I did what I could to deter him from that behavior, but he continued. At the time, I was unknowledgeable about how that seemingly harmless behavior could escalate into hard drug use. When Pax was eighteen, he came home from school one day and began crying. He told me he was hooked on heroin.

For the next six years, I battled heroin for Pax's life. Pax wanted to quit but he couldn't. He didn't know how. He went to thirty-day programs, sixty-day programs, and ninety-day programs. Nothing worked. He was clean forty times or more. Each time he relapsed, I would ask "Why?" Each time, he did not know the answer beyond saying it was the incredible high. It was as if he was powerless to resist the temptation. I never knew from one day to the next if I was ever going to see him again, and I was constantly afraid I would lose him. Several times I almost did lose him.

We went to drug therapists, alcohol therapists, psychologists, psychiatrists, addiction specialists, and counselors of every sort. As I look back on those sessions, I remember asking myself why none of them were seeking to discover *why* Pax was using heroin and other drugs. They all had suggestions for rehab, meetings, twelve-step programs, and more counseling, but not one of them initiated any investigation into what might be a probable cause of his substance abuse. In nearly every case, their suggestions were directed to creating an environment where he would be less apt to use heroin, and they advised me to punish him for his bad behavior. I learned firsthand, however, that punishment doesn't work as a means to correct substance abuse, even when someone is facing death.

At one point during Pax's odyssey, a gang of drug dealers drove him into the desert to kill him because he had stolen drugs from them. They forced him to dig his own grave. Somehow, he talked them out of doing that by convincing them that he could get the money. The day after that harrowing experience, his jaws were broken in two places and wired shut from being kicked in the face by another drug dealer who wanted money from him. He came home from the hospital, his teeth pointing in all directions, barely able to speak. And through his teeth he was sifting food—and smoking heroin and using cocaine. At one point, determined to break the cycle of drug use, I took him away with me to an isolated cabin in the Big Sur mountains on the coast of California. I kept him absolutely clean for nine months. The first week we left Big Sur, he used heroin, cocaine, and alcohol.

I believed that Pax was turning to heroin for a reason. I did not know what the reason was, but I believed there was one. In his drug-free days before he became dependent, he was athletic, outgoing, happy, and a good student, even achieving a student-of-the-month award. He wanted to stop using heroin and cocaine and return to a normal life, but he was unable to stop. The day Pax discovered the "why" behind his dependency was the last day he ever used drugs or alcohol. In that moment, he was able to free himself of his addiction.

Today, Pax is whole in every way—healthy, happy, prosperous, clear-minded, completely cured, and helping others to achieve the same freedom that he has achieved. It was Pax's idea to open Passages Addiction Cure Center. He said, "Look, we know how to do it, let's do it." Together, Pax and I founded and are now codirectors of Passages, where we work side by side every day. I see him, and I'm proud of him and of what he has accomplished and is accomplishing. He has been reclaimed from the land of the dying, from an addiction to alcohol and addictive drugs that was so powerful that at times it seemed impossible to save him. Yet save him we did. All credit to him and to the generous and loving Universe of which we are all a part.

So, I feel close to you, even though we haven't met. I have no axe to grind here, no hidden agenda. I want to help you. I *can* help you, if you will let me. But to do so, you must come to see me as a friend who has your best interests at heart—a friend who has traveled the same road that you or your loved one is now traveling and who has reached the best destination possible: a completely reclaimed life.

## Giving Back

During our journey to hell and back, Pax and I learned many things about the world of alcoholism and addiction. We researched everything we could find about treatment programs, alcoholism, and addiction, and we learned by experience what did and did not create lasting recovery, both in Pax's life and in the lives of others in treatment. When nothing else worked, we created a holistic, hand-tailored program that saved Pax's life. At

Passages Addiction Cure Center, he and I use what we learned curing him to help others discover the roots of their addiction or alcoholism and break free.

I've written this book to give you hope and to share with you what works. By following the guidelines on these pages—the same guidelines we use at Passages—you will look at alcoholism and addiction in a revolutionary new way, and you will be able put together your own personalized, holistic treatment program with the support of health professionals where you live.

I want you to know that I am intimately involved in the lives of people who come to Passages for help, with those who, like you, have become dependent on drugs, alcohol, and other addictions. During their time of healing at Passages, I learn what life is like for them. I talk with them about their lost dreams and their shattered lives, and I talk with them about a return to good times. I assure them that they will achieve a complete cure. I ask them how they're feeling, whether they're sleeping well, and whether they have any concerns. We become friends.

I also talk every day with members of our team of therapists. I ask them about each client's progress, about who needs more work, about who has concerns that need to be met, and about who's making the leap into the hyperspace of believing that they're cured. Every Thursday, I participate in the weekly treatment team meeting where we discuss each client's progress and decide what his or her most important next steps are during the following seven days. We decide short-term and long-term goals. We plan carefully, knowing that our clients' lives are at risk. All the therapists come to know each client intimately, and we all seek the same goal: to discover the cause of their dependency so we can help them to heal themselves.

We're involved in the deepest parts of our clients' psyches. We learn their hidden fears, their pain, their hopes, their heartaches, their losses, their deepest sorrows, their embarrass-ments, their traumas, the times they were raped, beaten, humil-iated, forced to do unnatural acts, lied to, betrayed, and all the thousand-and-one heartaches and sorrows that come to us all. We learn of what they've done to others, and of the guilt, remorse, and pain they are carrying. We offer them safe passage through to the other side of guilt and remorse where healing occurs. That's where our name, Passages, came from.

I also return the phone calls from people who want to come to our program or who have a loved one they want to send to Passages for healing. I tell them about our program. They relate the stories of their lives or the lives of their loved ones. I ask them what their world was like before the crushing effects of addictive drugs and alcohol devastated their lives. That's when I hear about the good times, the times before they or their loved one became dependent on addictive drugs or alcohol. If I'm talk-ing to the person who has become dependent, I hear of their yearning for a return to how they used to be before they became substance abusers. If I'm talking to someone whose loved one has become dependent, I hear of their yearning to get that loved one back. That's what everyone wants: to get back the loved one who is lost to dependency or, if the caller is the one who is addicted, to get back to a state of normalcy.

One mother whose son went through the Passages program about three years ago said that during the twelve years of his drunkenness, all she ever hoped for was to get him back. She said that was what we did for her: we gave her back her son. At graduation ceremonies at Passages, when the parents and friends of those graduating speak, the most common comment is "Thank you for giving me back the person I love." At Passages Addiction Cure Center, that's what we do best. It's what we're known for—returning people to the condition they were in before they began using addictive drugs or alcohol, but freed from the underlying conditions that caused them to use those substances in the first place. In most cases, their condition is better than it ever was before.

## Emerging from a Long, Dark Journey

Because many people have learned that life is tough, that dreams can't be fulfilled, and that tragedy strikes, because they may have been told the lie repeatedly that alcoholism and addiction are incurable diseases, and because they have experienced relapse many times, they don't believe that a complete cure is possible. In their first few days at Passages, I see them cautiously moving forward toward that belief as though they are inching out onto a frozen pond where the ice may not support their weight. They're hesitant, almost afraid to believe they will be well again.

As the treatment progresses, they gain confidence from the therapists and from the other clients who have been in the program a little longer than they have. Within a week, they're fully into the program, and the change is becoming apparent. They talk to me because they trust me and know that I want to help them. I hold a vision in my mind of what they were like in their best moments before addictive drugs and alcohol took over. I hold that vision strongly, and they sense that vision and begin to believe in a return to that condition.

From the moment they walk through the door, I hold the intention clearly in my mind that they will return to a state of perfect balance, perfect health, and renewed zest for life. I see them being transformed as they work with our team of therapists, each one of whom holds the same vision of a complete cure. I see the miraculous, nearly unbelievable change as they emerge from their long, dark sojourn through the land of dependency.

I lead a metaphysics group every Tuesday morning where we talk about spirituality and personal growth. I tell them about our Universe, about how it works, and about their place in it. I tell them about Universal law and how it affects them. They learn how their thoughts and emotions not only affect their bodies but actually create their bodies, their health, and their very lives. They learn that they actually *are* the Universe, a part of it, and that, as the Universe is eternal, so too are they. In a relaxed state of mind, they are introduced to their perfect self-images. They begin to see themselves differently. They lose that horrible image of themselves as incurably diseased alcoholics and addicts and they replace it with one that is pure, bright, virtuous, whole, healthy, and forever free of addictive drugs and alcohol.

I see their smiles come as their confidence begins to grow, as they come to understand a new way of life, and as they begin to transcend all that was holding them back from a life of sobriety, happiness, and the fulfillment of their dreams. I see the relief wash over them as they learn to see all the hurts from the past in a new light, as rape, incest, betrayal, physical and mental trauma, and all the other indignities to which they've been subjected take on a new meaning. They begin to place those events where they belong—in the past, where, though painful and even disastrous, they were an essential part of their lives from which they can learn and grow. I see the hurts from those personal injuries, the anger, the rage, the sadness, and the humiliation, dissolve in the light of a new way of seeing.

I provide one-on-one consultations with those who want them or who I believe need them. As the weeks progress, I see them begin to nod in agreement as I describe how they relate to the Universe and how what has happened to them was part of a natural unfolding that will ultimately come to benefit them. I talk to them after they've had a particularly good session with one of our therapists, and I see their awakening taking hold, their smiles reappearing, their heads lifting, their shoulders squaring, and their determination returning.

I also talk to our clients when they are ready to graduate, after their healing has been accomplished. I watch them as they emerge into the clean air and bright sunshine of freedom, as they return to complete sobriety without fear of relapse. I hear the profound gratitude and wonderment in their voices as they prepare to depart. I talk with the counselors who talk with them after they've left Passages and returned home. Sometimes I call them after they've gone home, or they write to me, send me e-mail messages, or call me on the telephone, and I hear in their voices the pride they feel in their new life. I hear them affirm, "It's just the way you and the team said it would be."

I received this note from a husband whose wife went through the Passages program: "Words cannot express the gratitude I feel for you and your staff at Passages. You have given me back my wife who was lost in drunkenness all those miserable years. I still find it hard to believe. When I checked her in, I felt hopeless, even after your great assurances that all would be well. She's only been home six months, but it's as if she's been reborn—I'm more grateful than I can say."

Another family member of a graduate wrote this note to Pax and I from England: "I am writing to tell you that Clarence is doing wonderfully well. I wish we had a Passages in England, but we don't. I believe there is no place like Passages anywhere else in the world. I'm thanking you for our entire family. He was lost to us for so many dreary years. It's a miracle. From the dead to the living. He's jolly, happy, and a love to be with. His drunken binges are a thing of the past. I don't know how you did it, but you did. I love you both for what you have done for my dear husband at Passages. It's been a year now since he's returned, and we have confidence that his past will remain in his past and will not return to haunt our future. Please give my love to all your wonderful therapists."

I've written about my involvement with the clients at Passages Addiction Cure Center because I want you to know that I am on the frontline, in the trenches with our therapists. It is essential, vitally essential, that you believe what I am going to write about the curing of your dependency because it is the major factor in achieving your cure. As you believe, so it will be for you. Your thoughts, your emotions, and what you believe will be the key factors in returning you to permanent sobriety and the fulfillment of your lifelong dreams. It is not just the curing of your dependency that I want you to accomplish, but the fulfillment of your most cherished desires and the satisfactory completion of your soul journey.

I suggest you read all of this book before you put into use the three-step program that will cure you of your dependency. Open your mind and your heart to the following pages, for on them are printed the words that will guide you or your loved one to a life completely free of dependency on alcohol and/or addictive drugs. Trust the words, for they have guided thousands of people just like you and Pax to a complete cure.

Pax and I have also created a website with additional resources—www.TheAddictionCure.com. The website was originally intended for people who saw me on television and wanted to order this book, but we have greatly expanded the website to include an informative monthly newsletter, tips from Pax to help you with your program, and a way to obtain supplements that will help you with your detox procedure and return your body and brain to a state of health and well-being. On the website, you can also ask questions of Pax, me, or our therapists.

## CHAPTER TWO

# HEALING THE
# UNDERLYING CAUSES

I HAVE VISITED MANY DIFFERENT TWELVE-STEP MEETINGS where recovering alcoholics and addicts meet to provide comradeship and support to each other. At those meetings, when the members take turns speaking to the group, I hear in their speeches and conversations the struggles of members who only have a year or two of sobriety. At the last meeting I attended, a member was receiving his one-year chip for having maintained his sobriety for twelve months, and he gave a little speech to the hundred and fifty of us in attendance. His speech was filled with emotion and gratitude as he told us an impassioned story of how he was maintaining his sobriety each day.

"When I awaken each morning," he said, "the first thing that happens is that my knees hit the floor and I'm begging God for another day of sobriety. The second thing I do is call my sponsor to get a program for that day's activities. I call my sponsor for support five more times during that day, and after dinner I go to an AA meeting, and before I get into bed that night my last act is to drop to the floor and thank God for another day of sobriety. Staying sober is what I work at all day long."

I was moved by his passion, by his sincerity, and by his powerful drive. I felt tremendous respect for that courageous young man who was winning his struggle to remain sober. However, I couldn't help but think to myself, "That boy needs treatment!" Was he living a relaxed, calm life, free of the fear of relapse? Every day, every hour of every day, he was struggling to remain sober, with the dark specter of relapse hovering over him like the wings of a living, evil force.

In contrast to that young man's condition, I thought of two graduates of Passages with whom I had spoken that morning. One had just completed four months of sobriety, while the other had completed two-and-a-half years and had recently married. Both had called to say hello and to reconnect with us. Both were out in their respective communities lending assistance to others who were still struggling to become sober. Both reported that they had become more productive in their line of work than ever before. Neither was struggling to stay sober. Being sober was a natural part of their lives. They are the product of an entirely new point of view in treatment therapy, a new paradigm.

## A New Paradigm

A paradigm is a system, model, pattern, or example. In this case, the paradigm deals with a belief system—one that comprises everything generally held to be true, and one that you might believe to be true, about alcoholism and addiction.

For centuries the fundamental belief held across most civilized cultures was that alcoholism was a moral failing or demonic possession. Those who drank alcohol to the point that it interfered with work and social life were shunned. For people who were not such heavy drinkers, the answer naturally appeared to be moderation of drink. They believed that those who could not abstain clearly demonstrated a weakness of moral fiber. Alcoholics were, and in large part remain, objects of scorn. The lies, deceptions, disappointments, and heartbreak that surround the alcoholic's plea, "Give me one more chance—next time it will be different," have been around for centuries.

Much of the world still labors under those concepts. In 1874, Benjamin Rush first described alcoholism as a disease. In 1935, two pioneers in the field of alcoholism set about to create a fellowship where alcoholics could support each other in recovery. Primarily interested in keeping their own fledgling sobriety going and helping others to do the same, Bill Wilson and Robert Smith, M.D., cofounded Alcoholics Anonymous (AA).

Wilson and Smith's novel concept was the *biological* aspect of alcoholism; they described alcoholism as an *allergy* of the body. One of their first successes was to change the prevalent view of alcoholism from a moralistic failing to a medical illness. Just as people were not responsible from a moral standpoint for contracting tuberculosis or cancer, neither were they morally responsible for their alcoholism. The trouble was, and still is, that while AA did a wonderful thing in eliminating the degrading concept of *sinner*, they replaced it with the equally degrading concept of *alcoholic*.

In 1956, the American Medical Association (AMA) named alcoholism as a disease. Throughout the world today, the existing primary paradigm regarding alcoholism and addiction is not only that they are diseases, but also that they are incurable. We're told that even if we were to stop abusing substances, the disease would continue and we would be addicts or alcoholics forever. It is that belief that is primarily responsible for the stagnation that has existed for the past seventy years or so in the treatment of alcoholism and addiction. It is that paradigm that has given birth to those two terrible, and untrue, slogans "Once an alcoholic or addict, always an alcoholic or addict" and "Relapse is part of recovery."

It is my intention to change that paradigm in your mind, and perhaps throughout the world. Innovators in any field who have brought about revolutionary changes report that long-standing paradigms are exceedingly difficult to eradicate and replace with new paradigms. However, eradicate and replace we must if we are to survive.

In the early part of the twentieth century, there was a paradigm regarding the four-minute mile. It was said, and almost everyone believed it, that it was impossible for a human to run a mile in under four minutes. Doctors of that era said that the human physiology would break down and kill a runner before that could be accomplished. Engineers said that the aerodynamics of the human body made it impossible for someone to run a mile in under four minutes.

It seemed that that belief must be true because no matter how many thousands of runners attempted it, they all failed. That's the power of a paradigm. It cripples everyone who believes in it, and makes it seemingly impossible to break through to the other side. Yet on May 6, 1954, Roger Bannister ran a mile in 3 minutes, 59.4 seconds. He broke through the existing paradigm. *Six weeks later*, John Landy, an Australian, ran the mile in 3 minutes, 58 seconds, and by the end of 1957, sixteen more runners had run the mile in less than four minutes.

Today, many runners regularly run the mile in less than four minutes, and one man, John Walker, has done so more than a hundred times. The current world record is 3 minutes, 43.13 seconds, held by the Moroccan Hicham El Guerrouj, who established it July 7, 1999. Once the old paradigm was smashed and a new paradigm was created, running the mile in less than four minutes became a common occurrence. It's not that the runners were faster or stronger—it's that they knew it could be done. That's what happens to a paradigm when a hole is blown in it; everyone pours through the gap in the new way of thinking.

Now it is your turn to end your existing thought paradigm about alcoholism and addiction and you. *You are not an alcoholic or an addict. You are not incurably diseased. You have merely become dependent on substances or addictive behavior to cope with underlying conditions that you are now going to heal, at which time your dependency will cease completely and forever.*

## Alcoholism and Addiction Are Not Diseases

When Pax and I were doing what you are now doing, searching desperately for help, we talked to psychologists, psychiatrists, interventionists, drug and alcohol counselors, and addiction specialists. They would tell us that rubbish that alcoholism and addiction were incurable. At first, we relied on their judgment because they were the experts, and as a result Pax and I suffered great hopelessness and despair (although in my heart I never believed it, and I would tell Pax that they were wrong because I didn't want him to feel there was no hope). As the years passed and I gained more insight, information, and experience with Pax and others who were addicted, I came to understand that alcoholism and addiction were not diseases at all but responses to underlying conditions. Then, every time I heard someone hand out the same "disease" line, I would get so mad that I would feel like spitting nails.

After several years of hearing that, I wanted to get up and shake people who were repeating those statements and ask them to wake up and think. We heard the same thing from nearly everyone we spoke to. It's as if they had all gone to the same school and learned it from the same teacher. It made me feel as if I had gone back to the Dark Ages and that next they were going to recommend bloodletting as a remedy.

Today, having healed hundreds of people just like you and Pax, I can write with complete certainty that alcoholism and addiction are not diseases.

If alcoholism and addiction are not diseases, what are they? The short answer is that they are names used to describe the states in which we find ourselves after we've used alcohol or addictive drugs for a long enough period of time to have developed a dependency on them, meaning that we can't permanently discontinue their use without help.

Alcohol and drugs are not the problems; they are what people are using to help themselves cope with the problems. Those problems always have both physical and psychological components—anything from anemia, hypoglycemia, or a sluggish thyroid to attention deficient disorder, brain-wave pattern imbalances, or deep emotional pain. You will be reading later about the steps to recovery that address these causes, but foundational to them all is this key premise: *when the underlying problems are discovered and cured, the need for alcohol or drugs disappears.*

I would like to see the word *alcoholism* eliminated from the English language as well as the labels *alcoholic* and *addict*. There is a stigma attached to them. The word *alcoholism* alone has a whole world of grim meaning attached to it. We've been inundated with studies of alcoholism, theories about alcoholism, lectures about alcoholism, stories of alcoholism, and essays on alcoholism, when all that has really happened is that people have become dependent on alcohol to cope with their underlying conditions.

Alcohol is just a quick and easy way to change ordinary, everyday reality from unbearable to bearable. All it takes is a short trip to the liquor store and a few drinks. People who are dependent are merely using alcohol as a crutch to get through the day. Yet doctors and scientists are still treating "alcoholism" as if it is the problem, when it has nothing at all to do with the problem. They might as well be studying "scratchism" for people who have a chronic itch.

Suppose you had a chronic itch and scratched it regularly throughout the day. Would you have "scratchism"? Would you be a "scratchaholic"? Of course not. What if you had a constant headache, and to cope with it you took aspirin several times each day. Would you suffer from "aspirinism," and would you be called an "aspirinaholic"? More important, if you sought help for treatment of those ailments, would you be treated for "scratchism" or "aspirinism"? Of course not; you would be treated for the underlying conditions that led you to scratch or use aspirin—perhaps poison ivy or stress.

## All Dependency Is a Symptom, Not a Problem

It's much easier to cure someone of a dependency than to try to cure an "alcoholic" who has "the incurable disease of alcoholism." The same is true for curing an "addict." A woman from Australia came to us with a severe drinking problem. While she was in treatment, we learned that her husband had forced her to participate in strange and demeaning sexual practices and that in some of those practices he would beat her. Her self-esteem had been trampled, she had become demoralized and humiliated, and she didn't know what to do about it. She became a heavy drinker and was hospitalized several times. Her psychiatrist suggested a treatment center. Because she was a prominent figure in Australia, they looked for a center outside the country and found Passages.

After some cautious and gentle probing, we were able to uncover the cause of her misery and shame. We were also able to help her find the courage to resolve that she would never let her husband abuse her again. We then brought her husband in for counseling and learned that he actually thought she secretly

enjoyed his strange sexual practices and physical abuse. When he
learned otherwise, he was ashamed of what he had done, and
because he truly loved his wife, he promised that he would never
harm her or subject her to that strange behavior again. They are
both happier than ever before, and neither one uses alcohol.

I received this letter a year after she had been in treatment:

My Dearest Chris:
Twelve months have passed since I returned to Australia
from Passages, twelve blessed months of peace and love.
I had thought for several years before going to Passages
that life had played a terrible trick on me, that it was not
worth living, and I contemplated taking my life as a way
out of my heartbreaking situation. I am such a prominent figure here 'down under' that I could not take the
chance of seeking help here, and that turned out to be
the greatest blessing of all. There is no place in Australia
that offers even a small percentage of what you and Pax
have put together in Malibu. Your staff is beyond com-
parison. I cannot imagine how you assembled them all
under one roof. I am not particularly religious, but I am
deeply spiritual, and surely, if there is a God, I suspect
that God lives in Malibu and watches over you and your
wonderful facility.

Not only has there not been a recurrence of those
terrible events of my past, but my husband has gone to
the greatest lengths to show me that he truly loves me.
He speaks of Passages reverently, as if it was he who
went there for a month instead of me. I cannot express
my gratefulness in words . . . there are none that are
adequate, but suffice it to say that I think of you and
your staff every day. I am in regular contact with eight
out of the eleven others who were in my group, and two

have been here to visit me. We all feel the same about
you and Passages. You and Pax are our personal heroes.
Your dedication to creating and maintaining the finest
facility in the world is totally appreciated, and we, for a
few, believe you have done exactly that. I send this letter
along with my love. Please say hello to everyone there.
I will be at the reunion this July.

Your friend, Emily

If I were to create a word that more accurately describes
alcoholism and addiction, I would say it was *dependencyism*.
Sounds silly, doesn't it? Yet it's no sillier than the word *alcoholism*. The reason the word *alcoholism* no longer sounds silly to
you is because you're used to hearing it, reading it, and thinking
about it. The reason *dependencyism* sounds silly is because this is
the first time you've seen it in print.

Imagine this conversation:

"What's wrong with you?"

"Oh, I have dependencyism."

"Dependencyism? What's that? Is it contagious?"

From here on, you'll see that I frequently refer to both alcoholism and addiction as "dependency." Dependency can be to
alcohol, addictive street drugs, addictive prescription drugs, or
even certain behaviors. I'm not going to deal specifically with
dependency on sex, gambling, food, cutting, or any other behavior that you may have chosen to help you cope with your life, but
in nearly every case, what applies to drug and alcohol dependency applies to other dependencies as well.

Reading this book will open your mind to new ways of
thinking that will cause you to see your dependency, and perhaps your entire life, in a whole new light. It will help you
understand that *all dependency is a symptom, not a problem.*

Seeing your dependency in that new light will enable you to heal yourself more quickly and more effectively than ever before—and permanently.

## The Self-Punishment Syndrome

The following story about Carla is a good example of how core issues always underlie dependencies. Carla, a beautiful twenty-two-year-old girl, was dependent on alcohol and drugs and regularly cut herself. She was completely cured of cutting herself before she left Passages. Her cure began when I told her why she was doing it. I explained to her that from a very young age, we learn how to make things right for ourselves. As a child, when we did something wrong we were punished, and then the one who punished us let us know that once we had paid for our wrongdoing, everything was okay. Also, the punishment made us feel that somehow we had atoned.

As we grew to adolescence, those lessons continued. When we did something wrong in school, we were punished, and the punishment made everything okay again. Our friends treated us the same way—when we did something wrong, they punished us by not being our friend until we made it up to them in some way (that was our punishment), and then everything was okay. Our penal system works the same way. When we do something wrong, we're punished, and then it's okay.

I also told Carla that sometimes if we do something wrong that we're sorry for and there is no one around to punish us, we punish ourselves. We repeat the pattern we learned—we hurt ourselves to make ourselves feel okay. Some of us even continue to punish ourselves to feel okay long after the incident is over. When most people do something wrong to someone, they just feel bad for a while and once they've "atoned" in some way or vowed never to do it again, they don't feel as if they have to keep punishing themselves. Some people, however, carry the hurt around and keep punishing themselves for many years, particularly those who feel they are responsible for having seriously hurt another in some way. These individuals may have completely forgotten the original incident, but the punishment continues, and their dependency on substances and aberrant behavior begins as a way to punish themselves so they can once again feel okay.

I knew from the treatment team that Carla had done something to someone years before that she believed had resulted in that person committing suicide. Carla was still suffering because of it. So I asked her why she was cutting herself.

"I don't know," she replied.

"Does it hurt?"

"Yes, and I'm afraid because recently I've been feeling as if I want to cut more deeply with the razor blade."

"Carla," I told her, "*you're doing this to make yourself feel good.*"

"That's stupid!" she immediately exclaimed.

"How do you feel after you cut yourself?" I asked.

"What do you mean?"

"Just that. After you have cut yourself and a few minutes pass, how do you feel?"

"I feel relieved. I feel better."

"Well, think about that answer in the light of what I said about cutting yourself to make yourself feel good. Remember what I told you about how we learned from an early age to make things okay?"

She thought about what I had said for a few minutes. I sat quietly and held her hand. Then she smiled. I could see the realization dawning on her that she was really punishing herself so she could feel good. I then did something that's been magically effective in cases like hers. I said, "Carla, I forgive you for what you did all those years ago."

She was startled. "Can you do that?"

"I not only can," I assured her. "I've just done so." She started to cry, not from pain, but out of relief and joy.

That was not the end of the story. My forgiving Carla for what she had done those many years ago just opened the door for our therapists to help her work through the guilt and remorse she felt. By the time Carla left Passages Addiction Cure Center, she looked different, acted different, and felt free for the first time since her friend had committed suicide. She had not only stopped cutting herself, but she also had stopped being dependent on drugs and alcohol. That was just over two years ago. She's now become quite successful as an actress and she's free from what had been tormenting her for so many years.

Often, the solution isn't that easy, but every once in a while, it is. That's when we all go home feeling very good. The treatment centers that Carla had been in before she came to Passages had been treating her for alcoholism, addiction, and mutilation as if they were the problem, when they were only *symptoms* of the problem. Although it seems like the obvious thing to do, no one had ever thought to explore or uncover the *why* behind her behavior.

## Dependence, Tolerance and Withdrawal

Before we move forward on our healing journey, it's important to establish some basic definitions and understand some basic terminology. First, through prolonged use of certain drugs that have addictive qualities, we can develop a dependency on those drugs. Among these are alcohol, morphine, cocaine, methadone, amphetamines, nicotine, heroin, oxycodone (such as OxyContin, Percodan, and Percocet), hydrocodones (such as Vicodin and Lorcet), barbiturates (such as Nembutal and Seconal), and benzodiazepines (such as Xanax and Valium).

Addiction is defined as the compulsive, physiological need for and use of a habit-forming substance. It is characterized by tolerance and well-defined physiological symptoms upon withdrawal. All addictive drugs produce a reward system in the brain. Using addictive drugs gives us a feeling of well-being and alleviates bad feelings. After using a drug for a period of time, users frequently develop a tolerance to the drug (they need more of the substance to accomplish the same feeling as when they began using the substance). This effect is thought to be related to our body's homeostatic mechanisms. Homeostasis is a relatively stable state of equilibrium (physiological and psychological balance). Homeostasis is our body's optimum state of functioning, and homeostatic mechanisms are the way our bodies achieve this balance. Our bodies maintain this ideal state by neutralizing any source of detriment to it.

For example, when we eat a candy bar, our blood sugar goes up and our pancreas then releases insulin to help us metabolize the carbohydrate and balance out glucose levels. If we exercise and our body heats up, sweat is released to cool it down again. By the same process, if we take a stimulant like an amphetamine, our body will counteract that change by producing sedative-like chemicals to return us to normal. However, as our body gets better and better at counteracting the disruptive effects of a drug, we experience less and less of the drug's effects because our body is essentially learning how to cancel out a great deal of those effects. The problem is, users don't typically say at that point, "Well, the drug isn't doing much for me anymore, so I guess I'll stop." Instead, they take increasingly larger or more frequent doses to produce the same relief from underlying problems.

That process is tragic. When you put a substance into your body that pushes it outside its range of peak functioning, your body learns to counteract that damage, and you must take more and more, which escalates into a terrible race with yourself. If this race continues long enough, your body will commit a desperate act of self-protection. It will get "used to" the drug—that is, it will shift from normal functioning to a new level of tolerance. The moment your body becomes accustomed to life with the drug, the lack of it is going to be felt as a disruption. So now if you don't get the drug, you'll feel symptoms of withdrawal. Once you shift to this new level of tolerance, you will find yourself taking the substance just so you can avoid the withdrawal symptoms.

Different addictive drugs have different withdrawal symptoms. They can include nausea, watery eyes, dizziness, fainting, muscle spasms, seizures, bone aches, muscle aches, headaches, intestinal cramping, runny nose, loss of appetite, insomnia, goose bumps, sweating, hallucinations, irritability, diarrhea, tremors, panic, chills, paranoia, anger, convulsions, heart palpitations, rapid breathing, tachycardia (speeding heart rate), apathy (lack of energy and enthusiasm), delirium, pain, depression, disorientation, fatigue, excessive periods of sleep, and even psychosis (a mental state in which a person loses contact with reality). In some cases, death can occur. The length of time it takes to become dependent to the point of experiencing withdrawal upon abstinence is different for each drug and for each person taking the drug.

A few weeks of abstinence from the drug is usually enough for the withdrawal symptoms to pass, but after the withdrawal symptoms end, we'll experience a return of the symptoms of the underlying condition, which the drug was masking. If those underlying conditions aren't treated, the return of those symptoms may cause us so much discomfort that we'll go back to using addictive drugs or alcohol to obtain relief. That's the primary reason there is such a high rate of relapse among people who have become dependent on alcohol and addictive drugs. It has little to

do with alcohol and addiction themselves and almost everything to
do with the original causes that created the dependency.

## The Killing Effects of Ethanol

Let's unveil the truth about alcohol before we go further. Alcohol
is the drug ethanol. They are one and the same. Alcohol is also
called ethyl alcohol or grain alcohol. It is a chemical compound.
Ethanol is often added to the gasoline we use to run our cars.
The next time you go to a gas station, read the label on the pump
and you'll probably see the words "contains ethanol." Some cars
can run on pure ethanol. Ethanol is also used as a solvent.

In California, when you have eight-hundredths of one percent (.08) of ethanol in your blood, you are considered legally
drunk because your reaction time to an emergency has begun to
slow and you are considered a danger. When you have one-tenth
of one percent (.10) of ethanol in your blood, you start to
become a little unsteady on your feet and your reaction time
slows down even further. When your blood contains fifteen-
hundredths of one percent (.15) of ethanol, your speech
becomes a little slurry and your reaction time has slowed even
more. When you have four-tenths of one percent (.40) of
ethanol in your blood, you are most likely unconscious, and if
you have been able to get a half of one percent (.50) of ethanol in
your blood, you are most likely dead.

It is ethanol that everyone is after when they drink alcoholic
beverages. That is what gives us the euphoric feeling, and that is
what all vendors of alcoholic drinks are selling. Manufacturers
put coloring in their ethanol products to make them look different, additives to make them taste different, scent to make them
smell different, packaging to make them attractive, and different
percentages of ethanol to make them more or less effective in

delivering the euphoric payoff. They advertise their products in such a fashion as to make it seem wonderful to drink their ethanol products. It does not matter if they give their products fancy names like Cabernet Sauvignon or Pinot Noir, or if they put bubbles in an ethanol product and call it champagne—everyone is selling ethanol. And that's what you're after when you drink wine, beer, whiskey, vodka, tequila, or any other alcoholic drink. If you think that's not true, remove the alcohol from a bottle of wine and see if you would pay sixty dollars for a bottle of fermented grape juice.

*Ethanol literally burns and scars your liver.* Cirrhosis, an irreversible hardening of the liver, is caused by scar tissue forming from the burns inflicted on your liver by ethanol. The Mayo Clinic describes cirrhosis as follows: "Cirrhosis is a condition that causes irreversible scarring of the liver. As scar tissue replaces normal tissue, blood flow through your liver is affected, making it increasingly difficult for your liver to carry out functions that are essential for life and health. Among other major tasks, the liver detoxifies harmful substances, purifies your blood and manufactures vital nutrients." Since your liver cannot feel the sensation of burning, you can literally drink yourself to death. It is never a pretty death because you're slowly poisoned by the toxins your liver can no longer filter out. If you could feel the pain of your liver being burned, you would never take a second drink.

## Alcohol Dependency and Psychological Dependence

Alcohol dependency is characterized by craving, loss of control, tolerance, physical and/or psychological dependence, and the production of withdrawal symptoms. Like the tolerance that can develop when we use drugs, developing "tolerance" to alcohol doesn't mean that we can no longer get drunk but that it takes more alcohol to get us drunk than it did when we first began drinking. (Again, although I mention drugs and alcohol separately, they are the same in that alcohol is the drug ethanol.) One of the more insidious—meaning slowly and subtly destructive—aspects of alcohol is that it erodes our "stop mechanisms," or our ability to stop drinking. The process occurs so slowly and subtly that we're unaware that our stop mechanisms are being eroded. This becomes obvious only when we try to stop but can't.

There are many other substances that are addictive and can produce withdrawal symptoms when we try to stop using them. Caffeine, for example, is moderately addictive, and quitting coffee, tea, cola drinks, chocolate, and other products that contain caffeine can create withdrawal symptoms such as headache, irritability, fatigue, and depression. Many people are actually addicted to products such as coffee, tea, and cola drinks because of the caffeine they contain. In North America, 80 to 90 percent of adults report regular use of caffeine.

Caffeine, like all stimulants, flogs the body. It is like beating a tired horse, but it can have many potentially dangerous side effects, such as cardiac dysrhythmias, where the heart is beating irregularly. Left to its own devices, a healthy body produces a steady flow of natural energy that sustains us throughout the day. Using caffeine in the morning forces our brains to produce an unnatural morning high that gives us a boost but robs us of energy we need for later in the day, thereby producing the need for more caffeine. Caffeine is also debilitating to the liver. Practitioners of Traditional Chinese Medicine say caffeine depletes our liver *qi* (or *chi*), meaning its energy or life force. I am not suggesting that you quit caffeine (it's enough for now to end your dependency on other addictive drugs, including alcohol, or your dependency on addictive behavior), but it gives you another example of the effects certain substances have on your body.

In addition to physical dependence, we can develop psychological dependence. "Psychic need" is the perceived need to use a substance to cope with unpleasant feelings such as despondency, heartache, anxiety, stress, or depression. Relief from something unpleasant is a kind of reward called "negative reinforcement." That cycle is worsened by both the physical and psychological discomforts felt during abstinence. When we stop using the addictive drugs or alcohol that we've been using to cope with unpleasant feelings, those feelings return, as does the strong desire to return to the substances that enabled us to cope with them. That's what characterizes psychological dependence.

### How to Tell if You're Dependent

Some people wonder how to tell whether they are dependent. Here's your test: If you can stop using substances or stop your addictive behavior for extended periods of time without craving, you are not dependent. You are dependent only if you can't stop without physical or psychological distress (you have unpleasant physical and/or psychological withdrawal symptoms) or if you stop and then relapse. The easiest way to tell if you've become dependent is to stop your addictive behavior. If you have difficulty remaining free of the substances or behavior, you are dependent upon them.

Some people are able to break free from addictive substances, but they still exhibit the traits of someone who is dependent. You may have heard the term "dry drunk." It means that someone is no longer abusing or using alcohol but is still displaying the characteristics of an alcoholic, such as anger, depression, insomnia, irritability, lying, being emotionally distant and unavailable, having low self-esteem, being in denial about his or her condition, and displaying immaturity, insecurity, anxiety, and other emotional behaviors that are outside the normal range. The same thing can happen with addicts—they may no longer be abusing addictive drugs but are still displaying the characteristics of an addict, most of which are the same as for an alcoholic. Those are the symptoms we see when our clients discontinue using drugs or alcohol but haven't yet gotten to the cause of their dependency.

When you don't treat the real issues behind dependency, you may see another telltale symptom—you may end up trading one addiction for another. We have found that if people use their powers of will to force themselves to abstain from addictive drugs and alcohol without healing the underlying causes and conditions that created their dependency, those underlying causes and conditions will most likely worsen and manifest in some other way. Perhaps they will become workaholics or develop a twitch or an itch or an eating disorder, or they'll switch their addiction to coffee or candy or sex or gambling, or they may become ill or develop some other undesirable tendency. That's because, one way or another, our bodies are always seeking to let us know through our behavior and our feelings that something is wrong and needs to be healed.

## An Epidemic of Prescription Drug Abuse

When we talk about addiction, we're not just talking about alcohol abuse or illicit drug abuse. In a report released in July 2005, the National Center on Addiction and Substance Abuse (CASA) at Columbia University said that prescription drug abuse is skyrocketing. They said, "Our nation is in the throes of an epidemic of controlled prescription drug abuse and addiction."[1] The report admits that the figures they provide (from self-reported data) are probably significantly underestimated and that the real extent of the epidemic is even worse.

Here are some of the disturbing statistics the report reveals:

- From 1992 to 2003, the number of Americans who admit abusing controlled prescription drugs nearly doubled from 7.8 million to 15.1 million.
- The rate of increase among teens has been even faster. From 1992 to 2003, the number of teens aged twelve to seventeen who admit using controlled prescription drugs has more than tripled.
- The total number of people who abuse prescription drugs is more than the number who admit abusing cocaine (5.9 million), hallucinogens (4 million), inhalants (2.1 million), and heroin (.3 million) *combined.*
- Between 1992 and 2003, the abuse of controlled prescription drugs has grown at a rate twice that of marijuana abuse, five times greater than cocaine abuse, and sixty times greater than heroin abuse.[2]

Here are some additional figures about dependency and addictive drug prescriptions that will give you a fuller picture:

- According to the National Association of Chain Drug Stores, the number of prescriptions written in the United States increased from two billion in 1994 to three billion in 1999 and exceeded four billion by the end of 2004. When you consider that the U.S. population is 293 million people, that's about 13.6 prescriptions for each of us per year. Since drug companies have lately begun deluging consumers with advertising in all parts of the media, that huge number will increase dramatically.
- Regarding the tendency of doctors to prescribe inappropriately, of the 21.1 million adults who received any mental health treatment between 2000 and 2001, 79 percent

were given prescription medications to cope with their mental or emotional problems. More disturbing is that 40 percent of those 21.1 million were given prescription medication only, with no adjunct therapy.[3]

- According to the U.S. Department of Health and Human Services Center for Substance Prevention, as of 2003 there were approximately 800,000 websites that would ship prescription addictive drugs with no questions asked.[4] That number has no doubt increased greatly since that time.

- A 2001 National Institute on Drug Abuse (NIDA) report says that 40 percent of doctors reported difficulty discussing the topic of substance abuse with their patients. In contrast, fewer than 20 percent have difficulty discussing depression.[5]

## The Vicious Cycle of Trial and Error, Prescription and Addiction

Almost all dependency on addictive prescription drugs can be laid at the doorstep of doctors. There's a word for it: *iatrogenic*, which means a symptom, condition, or illness that has been brought about inadvertently by a doctor or a medical treatment or procedure. In this case, it means "doctor-induced addiction." The doctor was hoping to alleviate a symptom with a drug, and the patient who took the prescribed addictive drug as directed became addicted to it. Interestingly, studies have shown that medical errors (or iatrogenic causes) are among the top nine causes of death in the United States. According to some statistics, they are possibly even the third leading cause of death, right after heart disease and cancer. And that's just deaths, to say nothing of all the lesser maladies they cause.

I will explain a little more how doctor-induced addiction can happen and how an already complex situation can become a vicious cycle. In medicine, an "ailment" is defined as "a measurable deviation from normal physical functioning." A dislocated shoulder is defined by the fact that its position is different from the normal position of the joint. Streptococcus infection (strep throat) is defined by physically observable abnormalities of the throat (swelling, redness) as well as by the presence of the bacteria that cause it. When you go to the doctor for a medical ailment, he or she will usually determine what is wrong with you by asking questions, examining your body or the part of your body that is bothering you, and running tests such as blood work, cell cultures, x-rays, or scans that measure your physical functioning in an objective way. If you deviate from "normal" in any of those tests, this confirms that you have a certain ailment and will also give the doctor a measurable way to evaluate whether or not a treatment is working once it has begun.

Psychological disorders, on the other hand, are diagnosed using the *Diagnostic and Statistical Manual of Mental Disorders (DSM)*. The *DSM* is a book that includes a series of behavioral checklists for each disorder. For example, if you were to see a psychologist because you were feeling "blue" for a while, he or she would talk with you and watch or listen for behavioral symptoms, such as decreased pleasure in activities or feelings of worthlessness. The doctor would then check these behaviors off on the checklist and eliminate other possible diagnoses until only the most *probable* diagnosis remains, perhaps some form of depression.

Although it's helpful to have a standardized system for identifying psychological disorders, behaviors are not perfect indicators of a disorder. There is no cell culture for depression. You can't see it on a bone scan or an x-ray. Not everyone with depression will show the same behavioral symptoms. Nor could even the best doctor be expected to pick up every behavioral clue provided in a fifty-minute session once a week. Thus, diagnosing psychological disorders is inherently more subjective than medical disorders. Furthermore, because a psychological disorder can't be defined by the measurable way in which a person differs from "normal," there is often no way to verify exactly what disorder he or she has, nor any objective way to tell if a treatment is working other than how the patient is feeling.

It should come as no surprise, then, that the selection of a drug treatment for a psychological ailment relies heavily on trial and error. A patient complains of feeling nervous or fearful. These feelings and behaviors *suggest* that the patient has an anxiety disorder, and the doctor prescribes whatever drug will *most probably* work for an anxiety disorder. However, there's no conclusive way to tell that this patient definitely has an anxiety disorder. Even if the doctor did get the diagnosis correct, there's a great deal of variation regarding which drug class (for example, anti-anxiety drugs versus antidepressants) a particular individual will respond to and which drug within a class (for example, Prozac versus Zoloft) will work best. If the first drug doesn't work, the doctor will try the next one on the list and so on, thus delaying treatment success and complicating the process with the mix-and-match type of treatment. The worst part is that many doctors just prescribe a drug rather than find out what is causing the poor feeling so they can treat it properly.

## Stacking Drugs

When the first medication a doctor prescribes for us fails to work and the doctor prescribes a second and perhaps a third and a fourth one, other problems can arise. These problems stem from the fact that every medication remains in our bodies for a certain length of time that differs for each medication. When we talk about how long a drug's effects last, we talk about it in terms of its "half-life." That's the amount of time it takes for a drug to reach 50 percent of its original concentration. If a drug has a half-life of two days, for example, it takes two days for the drug to wear off to half of its original potency. Valium has one of the longest half-lives of any drug on the market—approximately six days. That means every six days the drug declines by 50 percent of its potency until it has left the body.

Usually seven half-lives are sufficient to rid the body of almost all of the effects of a drug. Thus, if it takes Valium six days to reach its first half-life, and seven half-lives to rid it from our system, Valium remains in our bodies for approximately forty-two days from the time we first ingest it. All the Valium we take in each forty-two day period builds up in our body. At the end of forty-two days, we have quite a load within us of the very addictive Valium.

Consider the following scenario. I go to see a doctor on day one. I complain of anxiety, and he prescribes Valium, ten milligrams, twice a day. As prescribed, I take two tablets, or twenty milligrams, the first day. I take two the second day, two the third day, two the fourth day, two the fifth day, and two the sixth day—"as prescribed." But on the second day, the first day's dosage is still in my body and is still working at more than 90 percent of its original potency. On day three, the dosage I took on days one and two are still in my body at a considerable potency. The same for days three, four, five, and so on. On day six, the dosage I took on day one is still at 50 percent of its original concentration, and it will remain in my body in slowly decreasing amounts for approximately forty-two days. That means that every day for forty-two days, I'm going to be increasing the amount of Valium in my body.

You can see that after three or four weeks on Valium, I may be feeling a little woozy. I may feel as if it's not quite the right drug for me because I don't feel really good taking it. (Can you imagine why?) So I go back to the doctor and tell him that Valium isn't right for me. Does he tell me to wait for forty-two days until the last Valium tablet I took is out of my system? Probably not. Almost every time, the doctor will say, "Okay, try this," and he'll give me another drug. If the new drug doesn't work, he'll give me another drug. (In the case of Valium, keep in mind that you cannot just stop taking the drug without precautions. There are many cases where a patient has had a seizure from stopping Valium, a benzodiazepine, because the doctor didn't provide an anti-seizure medication such as Neurontin.)

I've seen people come to Passages who have been on as many as eighteen different medications. It's called "stacking." Doctors stack the drugs in us, one on top of the other, without waiting for the first drugs to get out of our body—not to mention that some of the drugs do just the opposite of what others are doing, as in the case of stimulants and sedatives.

## Drugs Shut Off Our Built-In Alarm System

One of the key reasons why the use of addictive psychological drugs keeps escalating is that addictive drugs don't cure; they only modify feelings. If the drug is withdrawn, the symptoms that drove the patient to use the drug will surface immediately, showing that the drug has done nothing to heal the real cause of the symptoms. In essence, those kind of drugs shut off your body's alarm system, which is telling you by the poor way you're feeling that something's wrong. Your alarm system is warning you to pay attention because something is out of balance or an illness or malady of some sort is present or pending.

Shutting off that alarm system is an unsatisfactory way to deal with your problems. It may give you a respite from the symptoms, but whatever ailment is causing you to feel depressed or anxious or in pain is still present. The most dangerous part of muffling your natural alarm system is that what's wrong is almost always getting worse. It's as if our house is on fire and we are awakened by the fire alarm, but instead of calling the fire department, we just shut off the alarm and go back to sleep. Your body is, in effect, telling you, "Hey! Wake up! I have a problem!" By using drugs to muffle your body's alarm system, you are replying, "Shut up! Don't bother me!"

The message here is *beware the doctor who prescribes medication without first endeavoring to discover the cause of your malady or imbalance.* He or she has given up the healing practice of medicine and has become a tout for the drug companies.

Unfortunately, drug companies are making it seem okay to use addictive drugs (actually, any kind of drugs) as long as a doctor prescribes them. But many doctors are using us as guinea pigs. They don't know what the drugs do of their own knowledge. They rely on what drug salesmen have told them, on the literature that the drug companies supply with free samples, and the fact that there is approval from the FDA (U.S. Food and Drug Administration). As for the FDA, they do no research on their own but rely on the drug company's clinical trials. Can you imagine anything worse than that?

According to a report by the Pharmaceutical Research and Manufacturers of America, member companies spent $25.3 *billion* dollars on marketing and promotion of their drugs in 2003 alone.[6] While drug companies claim that the high price of drugs is a result of the increasing cost of research and development, a report from Boston University's School of Public Health shows that from 1995 to 2000, brand-name drug companies increased the number of employees in their *marketing divisions* by 59 percent, while their *research staff* declined by 2 percent. [7]

Here's the kind of scenario I'm concerned about: Say a drug salesperson visits a doctor's office and touts the company's latest anti-anxiety drug. The salesperson convinces the doctor that the drug works to ward off anxiety, and the doctor agrees to try it out on some of his patients. The next time you come in complaining of anxiety, the doctor prescribes the new anti-anxiety drug, relying on the drug company's research and on the approval of the FDA. However, the drug is a mood-altering drug that does nothing to eliminate the causes of the patient's anxiety; it merely masks the effects of the anxiety—it shuts off your alarm system rather than discovering the cause of your anxiety.

The drug modifies your mood by blocking receptors within your brain. Because the drug doesn't cure the cause of your anxiety but only blocks its effects, you must keep using it to obtain relief. If you are seeking an artificial calmness on a permanent basis, you will continue to take the drug, often in a dose-escalating pattern. It is not uncommon for people in that situation to seek out other doctors and obtain multiple prescriptions for the same medication; many now buy drugs over the Internet.

After a period of time, you have now become a psychologically addicted person who has become dependent on the mental relief brought about by the drug. That's wonderful for the drug company and bad for you. Because some drugs have physically addicting qualities, the problem will become complicated when you become physically addicted as well. Once that happens, you will experience withdrawal symptoms when you try to quit. That's even better for the drug company and even worse for you.

Often, when a reputable doctor who prescribed a drug realizes that the patient has become addicted, the doctor will refuse to prescribe more. If the patient won't or can't quit, he or she may then either search out another doctor and start the process of diagnosis and prescription over again, or go out "on the street" to obtain the drug illegally. Unfortunately, many doctors will keep supplying the drug even when they realize the patient has become addicted. The doctor, in essence, becomes the patient's drug dealer.

An example of the willingness of our nation's doctors to hand out drugs they know nothing about personally, but rely completely on the drug companies' reports and FDA approval for, is the scandal centering around the drug Vioxx, which was taken by as many as twenty million people. Even after the FDA and Merck, the drug's manufacturer, had received reports from all over the world for several years about the life-threatening qualities of the drug, they did nothing. Merck voluntarily withdrew the product from the market when a study showed that the painkiller could *double* the risk of heart attack or stroke if taken for eighteen months or more. During the five years from 1999 to 2003, it is estimated that doctors wrote 92.8 million prescriptions for Vioxx.

I am in awe of some of the marvelous drugs that pharmaceutical companies have created. Those drugs are a huge benefit to us all. They bring us relief when we're in pain and in some cases bring about a cure. What I'm opposed to is the indiscriminate use of drugs by doctors who are relying on those drugs to take care of every type of mental and physical condition rather than discovering the causes of our ailments and then assisting our own immune systems to cure us.


## Identifying the Real Issues

What is the solution to the vicious cycle of prescription and addiction? What should a competent doctor do under those circumstances? *First, the doctor should run tests to determine the cause of the malady.* All health issues, including the most common ones of anxiety and depression, have biochemical, physiological, or psychological roots in addition to being caused by stressful conditions at home, in the workplace, or from the past. Many illnesses can be traced back to poor diet, poor sleep, poor health habits, lack of exercise, poor lifestyle, and the same four causes that underlie all dependency, which I'll take up in Chapter Five.

For example, anxiety can be caused by a deficiency of vitamin $B_1$ and magnesium or by hormone imbalances. Insomnia is often caused by a need for calcium, magnesium, or potassium, by hypoglycemia, or by thyroid or adrenal problems. Fatigue and low energy can result from chronic viral infections, anemia, weak or low endocrine function, yeast infection, low blood sugar, chemical sensitivity, weak digestion, or poor diet. Headaches and dizziness are often linked to liver toxicity, dehydration, blood sugar problems, low thyroid function, hypertension, or food allergies.

Depression can be due to low endocrine function, nutritional deficiencies, blood sugar problems, food allergies, or systemic yeast infection. Depression can also result from medical illnesses such as stroke, heart attack, cancer, Parkinson's disease, and hormonal disorder. It can also be caused by a serious loss, a difficult relationship, a financial problem, or any stressful, unwelcome life change. It can even be caused by a desired change in life patterns or events. Very often, a combination of genetic, psychological, and environmental factors are involved in the onset of a depressive disorder.

What is called for is an objective assessment of one's functioning before going on the drug (not through a short twenty-minute office visit) and continued observation both on and off the drug. One of the first actions we take at Passages is to ruthlessly scrutinize, always under a doctor's supervision and care, the specific necessity of any mind-altering or mood-altering medications that our clients are taking. As soon as any nonessential drugs are out of their systems, the feelings they were trying to suppress usually emerge. When that happens, we can see what symptoms the client was masking with drugs or alcohol. We can then identify the *real* issues burdening them and we can help them to complete recovery. Every person who has come to Passages and who has gone home cured was *not* cured of alcoholism or addiction, but of the condition that was causing him or her to use alcohol or addictive drugs to make life bearable.

## Seeking Balance

Healing the underlying causes of dependency is all about restoring your mind and body to their natural state of balance. One way or another, our bodies are always seeking to get back into balance. Whenever an imbalance is present in our physical, mental, or emotional bodies, it always manifests itself outwardly on the physical or emotional plane, and usually in an unpleasant or damaging way. That is how our bodies tell us something is wrong. It's how we become aware of imbalances.

Most of us are constantly modifying our moods and physical sensations with substances and behavior patterns. We wake up and feel a little foggy or groggy or slow, and we reach for a coffee. At the end of a meal, if we feel a little unsatisfied, we may have a sweet dessert. If we feel a little stressed or depressed, we may have something to eat. If we feel a bit out of sorts, we might go shopping.

What's the goal of all those behavioral patterns? We're striving to achieve balance. When we have an outburst of anger, we're releasing energy, "blowing off steam," and trying to get back to "normal." The same is true for crying. It releases pent-up emotions and blockages. It's when we use alcohol, addictive drugs, or addictive behavior to modify those feelings, rather than addressing the causes of the imbalance, that we become dependent.

Seeking balance essentially means we are trying to be happy. In the mid-1980s, I learned that everyone is seeking happiness as their primary goal in life. My understanding resulted from a series of workshops I led in Los Angeles to help people who weren't living the life they wanted and who were willing to come and listen to me for a month in the hope of changing that condition.

At the beginning of every workshop, I would ask the twenty-five or thirty people in the room what they hoped to accomplish by attending. Their answers were varied: a home of their own, to get ahead in their field of work, to become more confident, to find their soul mate, to overcome dependencies of every nature, including emotional and financial, to fulfill a dream (one person, an ironworker, wanted to work on the Golden Gate Bridge), to become more capable, and all the other things that we humans seek.

After I had heard from everyone in the room, I would then go around a second time and ask everyone why they wanted whatever it was they had come for. The answer was always the same: "I believe it will make me happy." That was the only response any person ever made. Even those who wanted to make someone else happy were ultimately doing it to make themselves happy.

If you examine your motive for doing anything, you'll soon discover that your reason is that you believe it will make you happy. One of the goals of this book is to show you how to obtain happiness without the use of substances. Blotting out what is making us unhappy by medicating our imbalances with addictive drugs or alcohol comes with terrible consequences. On the other hand, correcting whatever is causing the imbalance in a holistic and healthy manner is a solution that leads to good health, feelings of radiant well-being, and perfect balance.

That's why our program at Passages Addiction Cure Center emphasizes a holistic approach, combining both conventional and natural therapies that aim to bring balance to body, mind, and spirit. You'll read in detail about our three-step approach beginning in Chapter Six, including how to put together your own support team of doctors, therapists, and specialized health practitioners who will help you solve the real problems causing your dependency.

## Blowing the Whistle on Denial

For many years, one of the most widely used buzz phrases has been "being in denial." It means that someone who is greatly in need of help to overcome their dependency is denying their need, saying, "I can quit anytime I want to," or "I'm okay, I don't need to quit." We all have heard those statements many times when we have tried to encourage someone who needs help to get help. Here's the truth: they have *secretly* tried to quit many times and failed. *They know* they need to quit but *cannot*, so they fall back on the above phrases.

Do not be deceived. *They know the truth*. They are also afraid because they have lost control of themselves. Now that you know the truth, you will be able to more effectively help the person in need. *Gently* make a simple statement such as, "I know you'd like to quit, and I know you've tried, but I've found something that will help." Then hand them this book.

If you are the one in denial, know that by reading this book you are no longer in denial. I wish you great good fortune in your new awakening.

Before we move on to explore the causes of addiction and the key steps to recovery that come from the Passages program, I invite you to read the story in the next chapter of my son Pax's battle with addiction, written by Pax himself. It will give you more information about how we evolved our treatment program and what we went through to get to the point where we can now help you. Reading it will also give you a better understanding of dependency—and of what you can look forward to at the other end of the tunnel.

CHAPTER THREE

# TO HELL AND BACK

## By Pax Prentiss

I WAS BORN AT HOME ON MY MOM'S BED IN PACIFIC PALISADES, California, on May 28, 1974. During my birth, my dad stood by with a watch so he would know the exact moment that my head first emerged. It was exactly 7:07:03 p.m. From what my dad and mom tell me, it was a beautiful and natural birth, with no drugs used during the pregnancy or the delivery. Of course, I didn't know it then, but my dad standing by me was going to be a central theme in my life. I didn't have a name for the first month of my life because my dad couldn't think of the right name. My mom told me it was extremely frustrating because she thought it wasn't right for me not to have a name. They called me "baby" or "him." After a month, my dad came up with Pax and I was off and running with a brand-new name. Pax is a Latin word that means "peace."

When I was three, we moved to a little one-bedroom bungalow in Venice. My dad had been working on a film that he was writing, producing, and directing, so I didn't get to see much of him for the first three-and-a-half years of my life, which left my mom as my primary caregiver. After my dad completed the film, the situation changed completely. My mom says that during my first three-and-a-half years, my dad didn't see me much, but after that she never saw me again because I was always with him.

One of my favorite things was going with my dad to the beach at the Venice breakwater to fish. The breakwater is a long expanse of huge rocks and boulders at the ocean's edge. My dad and I would climb up on the rocks and cast our lines out into the ocean and wait for a fish to bite. While we were waiting, I would climb around on the rocks and look for crabs and other small sea animals. When a big wave would come, my dad would grab me and shield me so I was not washed off the rocks. After a day of fishing, we would walk home with our fish and he would cook them for dinner.

My dad has a most unusual philosophy, and he began teaching it to me from my earliest days. I'll tell you a little about it, because it's an important part of what you're going to read both in my story and in the rest of his book.

I was about three-and-a-half when my dad taught me my first life-lesson. He had bought me a new bike, and I loved it so much that it was hard to get me off it. One day, I rode it to the beach when we went fishing. When we came back to where I had left it, someone had stolen it. I was heartbroken and started crying.

"Why are you crying?" my dad asked.

"Because somebody stole my bike!"

"How does it feel?"

"Bad!"

"Where do you feel it?"

"I don't know."

"Well, see if you can feel where you're hurting."

I pointed to my stomach and lower chest area. "Here."

"How do you feel about the people who stole your bike?"

"Bad."

"What would you like to do to them if you found them?"

"Hit them with my bat! And then grab my bike back!"

"Well," he said, "you told me that when you were out with

Mommy yesterday, you saw one you liked better. Remember? The fire-engine red one with the bell on the handlebars?"

"Yeah."

"Well, how about if we go buy you that bike right now?"

So we went off and bought that bike, and then he brought me back to the exact spot where my bike had been stolen. "Now how do you feel about your bike being stolen?" he asked.

"Bad!"

"Why? You have this brand-new one that you like better than your old one."

"So?"

"Well, you couldn't have gotten this bike if the old one hadn't been stolen."

"So?"

"Do you still feel the pain?"

"No . . ."

"How do you feel?"

"Happy."

"And what about the people who stole your bike?"

"I still want to hit them with my bat!"

"Why? If they hadn't taken your old one, you wouldn't have this new one. Which one would you rather have?"

"This one," I said.

Well, you get the point. My dad worked on that conversation with me over the next year or so until I had gotten the point that having my bike stolen was a good thing, and that lamenting having lost it was a waste of time because it only took away from the present moment—the "now," which is all that any of us have.

Over the next few years, he taught me that the events of the past can't hurt us unless we let them. The events are over, but how we treat them and react to them—the power we give them—will determine what they become in our lives. That's only a small part of his philosophy, but it's at the heart of it. My dad is the happiest person I have ever met.

Here's another example of his philosophy. When I was about six, my parents told me that they were separating. My mom found a house in Venice that was eight blocks away from my dad. They decided that it would be best if I lived primarily with her and saw him a couple of times a week and some nights. Of course, my dad took the opportunity to put the spin on it that this was a really good thing because now I would have two houses instead of one. He made the transition for me seem simple, and it was.

I liked my mom's house because it had a big yard, and I got a Labrador Retriever named Sunshine. He was big and beautiful, with a black coat and a white star on his chest. Sunshine and I were best friends, and every day when I came home from school he would be waiting for me to play with him. My dad made the point that it was because of the second house that I was able to have a dog. Seeing it through his eyes, I actually was glad about the move.

Shortly after I moved to my mom's house, she enrolled me in a soccer league. I was a naturally good player, and she would take me to my games on the weekends. During the games, she would run up and down the sidelines yelling and screaming for our team. She was such an enthusiastic and excited spectator that you would almost have thought she was one of the players. I was a member of the soccer league for seven years, and she always made it to my games and practices. My dad always came to the games too, and that made me feel good.

Here is another part of what makes my dad's philosophy so special. He heard about an experimental school on the University of California Los Angeles (UCLA) campus. It was called University Elementary School, but everyone called it UES. Many of the nation's new teaching systems are created at UES. The school has approximately five thousand applicants each year for their kindergarten class, out of which they only take fifty students. When my dad found out about the school, he said, "That's where Pax is going."

He made the application and refused to see any other schools. My mom was furious because she said the chances of my getting into UES were actually only one in a hundred. My dad said that was not so, that they were 100 percent. At the end of the summer, UES called and said I was not accepted. My mom said we had to go look at other schools. My dad refused and said that it would only dilute the energy. He still maintained that even though I didn't get into the kindergarten class, I was going to go to UES in the first grade the following year. My mom said that was ridiculous, that first, one of the kindergarten students would have to drop out, and even if that slim opportunity came to pass, my chances of getting in would go down to one in five thousand.

All year long, that was a bone of contention in my house. As the next summer came, my mom got a little frantic and continued to ask my dad to go and look at other schools for the first-grade session, but he refused, each time saying that I was going to get into UES. And then one day in August, UES called and said that someone had dropped out and I was being accepted. My dad just smiled and thanked them.

My mom found some other kids in our area that were going to UES and she drove my friends and me to school, which was about forty-five minutes from home. In the car, we would play games and laugh. All my friends loved my mom because she was so friendly and happy all the time.

At UES they would split each class in half, and a team of teachers, usually three, would teach half the class a new teaching method. The other three teachers teaching the other half of the class would use a different method. Midway through the year they would switch, and then at the end of the year they would know which method worked the best. Another teaching method was to give us choices. They never would tell us what to do, but they would give us a choice between several options. One year they even gave us a vote on whether or not to get vaccinations. I started at UES in the first grade and graduated from there at the end of sixth grade, which was their highest grade. Some of my fondest memories were created there. Leonardo DiCaprio was one of my schoolmates; he was a cool guy even then.

## THE SKELETON IN THE GARAGE

The years went by, and everything seemed to be fine, but one day, when I was about thirteen, my mom told me that she needed to go into rehab for problems with drugs and alcohol. I knew that she drank, but I didn't realize how much.

I was too young to really understand what the problem was, or how serious it could be. I looked at drug addiction or alcoholism as problems that people could get over if they just put their minds to it. I remember how angry I was with her because she wasn't strong enough to beat her addiction and alcoholism. It was frustrating for me that she was weak and couldn't do it. I couldn't understand why she couldn't just stop on her own, but the cold hard truth was that she had become an alcoholic and an addict and needed help. She had lost her job selling real estate, and she didn't have the money to take care of her house anymore. I remember telling myself that I would never let that happen to me. I would never let myself become addicted to drugs or alcohol, and I would never allow myself to lose control of my life.

So I packed my bags, took my dog, and went to live with my dad. That was the last time that my mom and I would ever live together, and the last time that I would ever set foot in that house.

From the moment my mom went into rehab, our relationship pretty much dissolved. It was as if she just disappeared. She would come out of treatment, but would end up getting strung out again and going right back in. She bounced around, never really getting her life together. I would get the occasional letter or phone call every couple of months, but then she would go missing for months on end, and no one knew where she was. My dad searched for her everywhere. When he would find her, he'd try to help her get assistance, but she always refused.

One day when I was fifteen and she had been missing for several months, one of my friends said he had heard that she was living in a garage nearby. I got on my bicycle and went over to the garage. I yelled, "Mom! Mom!" for a couple of minutes, but nobody came out. Then the side door opened, and my mom walked out and looked at me. She looked terrible. She looked as if she weighed about eighty pounds. I started crying because I could see that she was suffering. Her jeans were dirty and full of holes, she was skin and bones, she didn't have a job or any money, and she was homeless except for that abandoned garage. All she was doing was living in that garage, smoking crack and drinking. Pain flashed through my body as if I had been struck by lightning.

She came closer and looked at me, and I could still see the wonderful woman who used to take me to my soccer games and play with my friends and me. Beneath the layers of filth and the grime, I could still see that loyal, trustworthy person who would do anything for anybody if she could. I could still see the bright inner light that was my mom, but I could also see that drugs and alcohol had taken almost everything she had. Her life energy was dwindling, and there was nothing I could do. The compulsion to drink and use drugs was going to keep taking her and sucking her life until everything that was good in her was gone. She was totally out of control.

She reached out her arms to me and embraced me in a hug, and I started crying even more. All I could feel was a skeleton in her clothing. In the end, it was too painful to stay there looking at her.

"I love you, Mom," I told her. Then I got back on my bike and rode away. I shoved the whole event to the back of my mind like a memory I just didn't want. When I told my dad, he said that it was part of her soul journey and that we would help her all we could, but that what was happening was for her benefit. He told me that we might not be able to see the benefit just then, but that later it would become clear. That's how my dad is, and that's how it turned out.

## It's Party Time

In the next few years, my dad and I traveled when I didn't have school. Sometimes we rented a motor home and drove to Canada, other times to Mexico. We always took one or two of my friends. I was a certified junior diver at ten, and we went to various islands off the coast of North America and in the Caribbean to dive the coral reefs.

During all of our trips, he and I always talked about his philosophy and the Universe. He said that we *are* the Universe, a part of it, and as such we are eternal, just as the Universe is eternal. He talked about cause and effect, and about the part it plays in our lives. I thought that my dad was the grandest person in the whole world, and whenever he praised me for something, it made me feel better than anything else ever did.

Meanwhile, my life went on. I started junior high school in 1987 at Westside Alternative in Venice. That was a shock. It was nothing like UES. I found that the kids were much different from those I had known at UES. For one thing, there were gangs and lots of violence. Some students carried weapons, and a few kept guns in their lockers. For another thing, there were also drugs. Everywhere you looked, drugs were evident. In the Venice public schools, any student could obtain any drug at any moment in time. This was a very different environment from the one I had left.

In ninth grade, I had a couple of friends, Paul and Sonny. One day they asked me if I wanted to drink and smoke pot during the lunch break. You would think that after watching my mom suffer from drugs and alcohol, and after promising myself that I would never try those things, I would have said no, but something inside me was curious. I wanted to know what it felt like to get high. It seemed as if all the cool kids were doing it, so how bad could it be? Besides, I knew enough about it to never let myself get hooked.

So that lunchtime, I decided to go over to Paul's house with Sonny. We smoked pot and drank 80-proof Southern Comfort. It made me feel warm and loose. With each hit and every drink from the bottle, the pain of my problems washed away—the pain hiding deep inside at what was happening to my mom, coping with school, and all the adjustments of being a teenager. I enjoyed being stoned and drunk. The feeling of the alcohol as it went down my throat and into my stomach was amazing. It warmed my system and created a rush of energy that was very pleasing, and the marijuana amplified the feeling.

I knew that I was playing around with something that could potentially be very damaging, but I also knew that I was never going to get hooked. I wouldn't lose control. I just wanted to feel good. I was too smart and too strong to end up like my mom. Little did I know that I had just unleashed a beast that was stronger, smarter, and sneakier than I could ever be. It was the beast of addiction, and it wanted my life, every little piece of it, until I was dead.

After that first time, it took only a few weeks before I was doing marijuana and alcohol every day. But I wasn't hooked; at least I didn't feel hooked. I was doing something that felt good, something that I wanted to do, and I had no intention of quitting because I didn't feel as if I was hurting myself or my life.

On the weekends, several of my friends and I would have big house parties, and all the teenagers in Venice would show up. We didn't do it at my dad's house because he wouldn't have permitted it. There would be a hundred or more of us there running around drinking beer, doing drugs, listening to music, and having the time of our lives. We didn't have a care in the world except to get high and party. We had powerful stereo systems in the houses where we partied. We moved the party around to houses where the parents would be out for the night. My dad knew nothing of what was going on. The music at our parties sounded more like an indoor concert, and we always had at least three kegs of beer, which was enough alcohol to keep everyone drunk all night. We always invited some older kids who would buy the beer and bring the drugs, and they got in for free.

I really enjoyed the high that the marijuana and alcohol gave me, but I was curious to know what the stronger drugs would do for me. I wanted to know if they were better than what I was already doing. If pot made me feel good, then maybe coke would make me feel great, and if coke made me feel great, then maybe Ecstasy would take me to the heavens. I decided that I would try everything.

Within a couple of months, a few of my friends and I, including Paul and Sonny, were doing almost every hard drug around. Cocaine, mushrooms, pot, crack, acid, speed, and Ecstasy were easy to get, and if we wanted something that wasn't around, we always knew somebody who knew how to get it. By the end of the night, the cops would usually show up, but that didn't matter because we always had someone on the roof of the house watching out for them and warning us before they got there. That way, we could hide all the drugs and alcohol and turn down the music before they showed up. We were at the top of our game, and we knew it. The police were nothing to us. We were all smooth-talking con artists who could talk our way out of anything. Not to mention that we were all minors, so even if we got caught, our records would be erased when we turned eighteen anyway.

There were always lots of girls around, and they enjoyed being around us because we seemed dangerous to them. Of course, we weren't, not really, but we lived life on the edge and we knew how to have a good time. We were the bad boys, and being around us was exciting because no one ever knew what we would do next. One minute we could be rocking out at a huge house party on Ecstasy, and the next we would be breaking into a dentist's office to steal a six-foot tank of nitrous oxide so we could fill up balloons and inhale them all night. I guess the girls liked it because it was more fun than hanging out with the guys who were serious about school and stayed at home every night doing homework. It seemed to us that those guys were going to die of boredom long before we died from drugs. Books were for nerds. We didn't care about the future or how successful we were going to be in law school. We were living the lives of rock stars, and we were the most successful kids in town.

When I was sixteen, I started getting hooked on heavier and heavier drugs. I was searching for that euphoria, that feeling of ecstasy, and I found it in methylenedioxymethamphetamine— MDMA, or "X," as it's known on the street. If you could imagine your best sexual experience multiplied by a thousand, you would still only be scratching the surface of what pure MDMA feels like. Lots of people have tried Ecstasy, and it has made them feel good, but not too many have come close to getting pure MDMA, which is a fantastic high. The stuff on the streets isn't pure. It's either fake or, if it is MDMA, it's been cut so many times with other chemicals that it's no longer close to being pure, and the high is only a shadow of what it can be.

But MDMA wasn't my only drug. I also liked the feeling that cocaine gave me. Although X was much better, you couldn't take it every day because your body would build up a tolerance to it so quickly that you would have to wait at least four or five days before taking it again if you wanted a good high. Also, pure X is probably one of the only drugs that's really hard to get. When it does come around, it's only for a few days, and then it's gone and you don't see it again for several months. So, during the down periods we would use coke. A fat line of cocaine has the ability to make you feel amazing, and my friends and I would sit and talk all night until the sun came up, but after the drug wears off, you really start to feel bad. Coming down from coke is terrible, but that didn't stop any of us from doing it. After a night of coke, all you want to do is sleep, and while you're using it, you're never hungry, so we all lost weight quickly.

## THE ULTIMATE HIGH

In the middle of this drug extravaganza, one of our friends was introduced to heroin and how to smoke it. He brought some one night. The heroin he was smoking was a brown tar, but it also comes in a powder form. He would put it on a piece of aluminum foil about six inches square. Then he would hold a match or lighter underneath the foil, which would cause the heroin to heat up and start to smoke. As the smoke went up, you inhaled it through a "tooter," a little tube of tinfoil. This is called "chasing the dragon" because the smoke is supposed to represent the tail of a dragon and you chase the tail trying to inhale it.

I watched him smoke it, and, without any hesitation, I asked for a hit. The first hit that I took was strong. It wasn't like smoking pot. This was much more intense. It had a funny taste at first. I took another hit and held the smoke in and slowly released it from my lungs. At that moment, I finally found what I had been searching for—the perfect high. The feeling ran through every pore and cell in my body. It was as though God himself had scooped me up in his arms and brought me to heaven. It was just too good to describe.

The heroin allowed me to be anyone that I wanted to be. It gave me a feeling of strength and confidence. All my troubles were washed away with the first hit. I felt as if I could do anything that I wanted to. All my fears were dissolved in the euphoria that the heroin provided. It was better than anything I had ever felt. I did it every day for three weeks. At that time, I didn't know about heroin's incredible addictive qualities, or that your body actually builds up a physical dependency on it—or that when you stop, you become violently ill.

Heroin is a very expensive drug, and there was no way that a kid like me with very little money was going to be able to support a heroin habit for long. After doing heroin every day for three weeks, I ran out of money. I also started to feel sick. But this wasn't any kind of "flu" sick. This was much stronger. My bones and muscles started throbbing with pain. I had hot and cold sweats. I was nauseated, and I felt anxious. At times it felt as if my bones were trying to crawl out through my skin. Then I started vomiting violently and I couldn't stop. Everything I put in my stomach kept coming back up. I lay in bed kicking and turning, trying to get my bones to stop crawling under my skin, but no matter what I tried, the bones felt like razors under my skin every time I moved.

I was really scared because I didn't know what was wrong with me. I called up one of my friends who was also using heroin, and I told him I couldn't go out to get drugs because I had no money and I was too sick. "You're not actually sick," he told me.

"You're dope-sick—going through withdrawal. All you have to do is smoke more heroin and you'll get better in a second. I'll come over and bring you some of mine." I was curled up in the corner of my room throwing up on myself, and my hands were shaking so much that I almost kept dropping the phone, so his saying he was coming over sounded great to me.

When he got there, I was still curled up in a ball on the floor, but now I was lying in a puddle of piss because my bones hurt so much that I couldn't get up and go to the bathroom.

"Hurry up!" I begged him. "Put it on the foil so I can smoke it."

He must have thought it was funny, seeing me lying on the floor like that, because he started laughing at me as he put the heroin on the foil. Then he knelt down, careful not to kneel in my piss, and put the tube in my mouth so I could take a hit when it was ready. He then lit the lighter and put it under the foil. Within seconds the foil began to get hot and the heroin began to smoke. Here comes the dragon!

It was like magic. Within seconds, all the sickness and the withdrawal symptoms that had been so intense were gone, as though I had never been sick at all. With heroin, you can go from being so dope-sick that you feel you're going to die, to pure euphoria in a matter of two seconds. After taking a few hits, I sat there and thought for a minute. I looked at myself sitting in my piss, and at the bathroom, with my vomit running down the sides of the toilet and onto the floor, and I realized that I was hooked on heroin. But since I couldn't stop without becoming violently ill, the only way out that I could see was to continue using. But to keep using, I had to figure out a way to get money.

I had just turned eighteen and had been receiving lots of preapproved credit card applications in the mail. I filled them out. I lied about my income and said I was a licensed real estate agent and made $150,000 a year. I ended up getting seven credit cards, each with a $10,000 limit, for a total of $70,000. So there I was—eighteen years old, with $70,000 in credit and a full-blown $300-a-day addiction to the finest tar heroin that money could buy. I stopped doing all the other drugs because they couldn't compare to the high that heroin gave me. It came straight from India and was almost 90 percent pure.

I must have been really good at hiding my highs from my dad, because he never asked me if anything was wrong. I would usually leave during the day and pretend that I was going to work at a photo developing lab, but I didn't have a job. I would meet my friends and smoke heroin all day long. Then I would come home at night and tell him how productive I had been at work. My dad was so busy writing books that he never thought to question it because he never expected that I would lie to him and because I always seemed to have money. My dad writes books on spirituality, and when he is deeply involved in a book he is oblivious to all else. I lived on the credit cards for nine months, until I had maxed all of them out on cash advances and my credit was destroyed.

## A SOBERING CONFESSION

Then, one day, my friend Sam came over. He was a good friend who partied, but he wasn't into drugs the way I was. He asked me to go outside with him so we could talk. We walked out to the sidewalk in front of my house, and the first thing he said was, "You've got to tell your dad that you're strung out on heroin."

I panicked inside. "No way! I can't tell my dad!"

"Listen," he said, raising his voice, "either you tell your dad or I will, because I'm not going to watch you kill yourself."

I was really angry and scared at the same time, so I shook my fists and screamed at him, "You tell my dad, and I'll kick your fucking ass!"—which was funny because I was totally strung out, and there was no way I could have kicked anybody's ass.

We argued back and forth for a long time. I kept yelling and screaming at him and trying to convince him that I really could beat his ass if he told my dad. But really I was terrified at the thought of having to tell my dad that I was a dope fiend who hadn't been doing anything for the last nine months except running up $70,000 in credit-card debt buying heroin. After two hours of arguing and screaming, Sam still held his ground, so I was faced with two options: I either had to let Sam tell my dad, or I would have to tell him myself. I knew that I was going to have to do it. That was the only right way. After cursing the ground for a long time, I mustered all my strength and courage and went inside to tell my dad.

My dad was typing at his computer. He looked over at me, and I immediately started crying.

"What's wrong?" he asked. His voice was gentle.

"I'm on heroin."

He took it amazingly well, which, if I had thought about it, was exactly what I should have expected. What a relief! I guess it was the fear of disappointing him that had made it so difficult to tell him. He then asked me the most important question of my life, but I didn't recognize it at that moment, and I don't think he knew how vastly important it was either.

"Why are you using heroin?" he asked.

I just looked at him helplessly. "Because I can't quit. I'm hooked on it."

He then said those magic words that he's so famous for. "No problem. Don't worry about a thing. We'll fix it in a heartbeat."

He didn't know the first thing about heroin or its devastating potential, but he said he would call our family physician and find out what to do.

I said, "I'm also going to need you to sit by my side, because if someone's not with me when I go through withdrawal, the cravings and symptoms will be so bad that they'll make me walk out the door to score more drugs."

So we called the doctor and he prescribed medications that would help with the withdrawal symptoms—medications to relax my muscles, anti-nausea medications, sleep medications, and pain medications.

If you're not a heroin addict, you may not know drug slang. "Kicking" is the slang word for going through heroin withdrawal because you feel as if your bones are going to crawl out of your skin and the pain makes you kick a lot when you're in bed.

I kicked at home for eighteen days, and my dad was with me every step of the way. He filled hot baths, made my meals, and cleaned my vomit from the floor when I couldn't make it to the bathroom. During the times when I thought I couldn't take any more pain, he would put his hand on my back and talk to me until I was calm again.

My dad has a very soothing voice, and when he speaks to you, he makes you feel as if everything is going to be just fine. He took every day off from work to make sure that I was going to be okay. He was amazing, and if it hadn't been for him, I would never have made it through because those were the days before Subutex and Suboxone, which contain buprenorphine hydrochloride, a drug that lets you stop using heroin without the brutal withdrawal symptoms.

After I finished going through the withdrawal symptoms at home, he smiled at me and told me that it had been a great experience, and he thanked me for it.

"You and I must have needed it to learn something special," he told me. That's how he is.

## Just One More Time

I went back to school, but I had no idea how to stay sober or even what staying clean from drugs was about. When you take away the drug it leaves an empty space inside of you. You may have heard that the Universe won't tolerate a vacuum. Well, it's true in the case of taking away drugs; unless you fill the space with something else, going back to drugs is a near certainty. I never got any counseling or information about drugs and addiction. I was so uninformed that I thought that as long as I stayed off heroin, I could go back to the other drugs. Little did I know that when you stop using one drug and go to another, all you're doing is switching addictions. The life of addiction goes on. So I went back to smoking pot, snorting coke, taking Ecstasy, and using hallucinogens. I still wanted to find one drug, or a combination of drugs, that would give me the feeling of euphoria that I got from heroin. I tried everything, but nothing else gave me the intense rush of heroin.

After about two months of using all those other drugs, the idea came to me that I could use heroin just once and not get hooked on it again. I knew that the mistake I had made in the past was to use every day, so I figured that as long as I didn't use it every day, I wouldn't get strung out again. I was certain that I was stronger than the heroin. I decided that no matter how much I wanted to go on using it, I wouldn't allow myself to use it more than once. I would just have one more hit, and that would be the end of it.

Right after I came up with this insane "solution" that let me convince myself that I could use heroin without getting hooked again, I called the dealer, bought some heroin, smoked it—and immediately reactivated the addiction that was still living so strongly inside me, just waiting for the moment when I would breathe life into it again.

The next morning, my cravings were stronger than ever. I told myself that I could do it just one more time without getting hooked again, and that a second day wouldn't hurt me. That immediately led to days three, four, five, and so forth. The next thing I knew, I was strung out on heroin again. Actually, I had been strung out after the first day, but I just hadn't realized it.

One day, my dad told me that he wanted to get me out of Venice and into a college in Northern California. He didn't know that I was hooked again because I was so good at hiding it, but he probably suspected that something was up. He knew that all my friends who did drugs hung out in Venice, so he probably figured that getting me out of there would be a good idea.

We called the college, but they told him that the registration deadline had passed and that I would have to wait until the following year.

"That's great, Pax," my dad said. "No one else will be registering, so we can go there and we'll be the only ones."

"But registration is closed for the year," I said.

He just winked and smiled and told me to pack. We drove to the college, where he worked his magic and I was admitted.

Four weeks later, I was driving with my dad up the coast of California on my way to college. The drive was long and lonely. I was leaving behind all my friends, and worse, my heroin dealers. I had only a small amount of heroin left, and it was only going to get me through one day. I knew when I woke up the next day I would probably wish that I were dead.

When I arrived at the campus, I went to my apartment and unpacked. Students were running all around the campus having a good time, excited about the new school and the new friends they were meeting. It seemed like a young person's paradise. A lot of them had never been away from home or their parents' supervision. It was as if they were free for the first time. I could hear loud music coming from many of the apartments, and people were on their balconies drinking and smoking pot.

I laughed to myself. It seemed that my dad's vision of that college as a safe, drug-free environment wasn't quite accurate. However, I couldn't join the festivities because foremost in my mind was the knowledge that I had just done my last bag of heroin and that the next morning I would be waking up into my own private hell of heroin withdrawal. After putting my bags away, I lay on my bed and stared at the ceiling. My dad was gone for the day, my friends were gone, and I was in a new world. The only thing I had with me was a full-blown heroin addiction and the terrifying prospect of kicking again.

The next morning I was awakened at the crack of dawn by a pain I hate to think about to this day, a pain that made me think about killing myself rather than suffering through it. Suicide had started to cross my mind more and more. In a way, suicide is like a drug itself in that it provides an escape. Although I knew that I wasn't going to kill myself that day, the idea of suicide was at the back of my mind because it gave me the comfort of knowing that if all else failed, it was a way out.

I managed to drag myself out of bed, get dressed, and drive over to the registration desk, where I was supposed to meet my dad. I parked my car and, trying my best to hide the pain I was in, headed toward where he was waiting. He didn't know that I was strung out again, and the thought of having to tell him again was too much, especially after all he had gone through to get me a fresh start.

Each step I took required all my effort. My feet felt as if they weighed a thousand pounds, and my bones felt like razors in my skin, but eventually I made it over to him. He greeted me with his genuine smile and upbeat attitude and I, with great effort and sheer willpower, managed to give him a small smile. To this day, I can't imagine that he didn't realize I was sick.

Maybe he just couldn't believe that I would have gotten myself strung out on heroin again.

After I registered, we went back to my apartment. I hadn't met my three roommates the night before. I had gone directly to my room, shut the door, and turned off the light because I had been too depressed to be friendly. As my dad was getting ready to leave, I shook hands with him. He gave me some words of encouragement to put a positive spin on the new life I was starting for myself. He has such a wonderful ability to look at things in a positive light. I'm sure I would have responded better if I hadn't been about to vomit on him at any moment.

After he left, I went straight to my room and dropped onto the bed like a ton of bricks. The sickness was getting worse. I could hear students outside running around laughing and shouting. As I lay there, I wished that I wasn't a junkie so that I could have joined in the fun.

I stayed in bed with my door shut for five excruciating days. I was too embarrassed to let anybody see me. I wouldn't let my roommates in, even though they kept knocking on the door and asking if I was all right. I kept telling them that I had the flu and I would come out when I got better. There was vomit on the floor and all over my bed, and I hadn't showered in five days because I didn't want to leave my room. I had urinated on my bed several times because it hurt too much to go the bathroom, so the whole room reeked of old urine. I had not had to defecate because I had barely eaten anything except for a few granola bars and an orange that I had found in my backpack. Eating was pointless because as soon as the food hit my stomach it came right back up.

I kept watching the clock and counting the seconds and wishing that the damn sickness would be over so I could be a normal human being again. Every time the clock ticked over one second, it felt as if I was watching it in slow motion. Seconds felt like hours, hours felt like days, and the days felt like months.

It was much worse because I didn't have any medication to help me get through it. At night I couldn't get even an hour's sleep. I just sat there, awake and staring at the ceiling, kicking and squirming and wishing that something would bring me just one second of relief. At times, the pain got so bad that I got on my knees and asked the Universe to please have mercy on my soul, to give me just one minute of relief. But no relief was ever granted.

On the sixth day, I got a call from Spencer, a guy I knew from back home in Venice. I had never really liked him. My friends and I used to call him "Spencer the Snake" because he was a shady character. He was only out to do what was best for him, and if stabbing you in the back would benefit him in some way, he would do it. He was a heroin junkie too.

He had moved to San Jose, just thirty minutes north of where I was.

"Hey, man," he said. "What're you up to?"

"I'm down here in college, and I'm dope-sick."

Then he said the magic words. "You should come up here to San Jose, 'cause I've got a heroin connection."

Of course, he didn't give a damn that I was sick. The only reason he told me that was because he was out of money and needed someone to hook up for him. Still, it was the best news anyone could have given me. I had been saved. I had a heroin connection again. In less than an hour, I would feel well again. All of sudden, school was going to be manageable. Funny what makes school manageable to some people, isn't it?

## MONEY SCAMS AND SHANTY TOWN

I immediately drove to Spencer's place in San Jose. He came out and greeted me with an evil smile. We drove to an area called "Shanty Town," an old, run-down, mostly Hispanic neighbor-

hood. Spencer told me to walk into that neighborhood and dealers would approach me. This was much different from what I
was used to in Venice, where all I did was pick up the phone,
and my connection would meet me at a designated spot twenty
minutes later. I knew that Spencer wanted to stay behind while
I went into Shanty Town because it was dangerous. He said the
cops were always patrolling and looking to bust people, and the
gangsters and dealers who hung out there couldn't be trusted.
He said junkies were always getting beaten up or jacked for
their cars and money. But I was still in so much pain that I was
willing to do almost anything to stop it, so I got out of the car
and walked into Shanty Town.

Dealers can smell fresh meat a mile off, and in seconds one
came up to me.

He said, "Hey man, you looking for something?"

"Chiva."

I used the Spanish slang word for heroin because if I had said I
was looking for "heroin," he would have thought I was a cop and
not sold it to me. The right terminology is important. So is the right
attitude. You have to let dealers know that you know how things
work. He gave me the dope, and I handed him the money and
walked back to the car. I had sucessfully pulled off my first attempt
to score dope off the streets. But I guess that by growing up in
Venice and being around so much drug activity I was a natural.

We got out of that area as fast as we could and pulled over a
few blocks away. I had tinfoil in the car, so we made up a couple
of rigs—the tinfoil and lighters we used to smoke the heroin. I
took out the heroin and broke off one piece for Spencer and one
piece for me. He grabbed his and got his fire going instantly, like
a starving man seizing food. I put mine on the foil but didn't
light it up right away. My six days of agonizing pain were about
to vanish in a wisp of smoke. Most people who are strung out do
the dope as fast as they can, but I liked to savor the moment for

a while before taking my first hit. I would almost go into a deep trance looking at the heroin on the foil. The knowledge that in seconds the pungent smoke would be traveling into my lungs so it could be pumped into my blood and through every cell in my body was fascinating to me.

After a few minutes, I lifted the lighter up to the foil, lit it, and watched the tail of the dragon begin to emerge from the hot foil. It danced around and I began sucking through the tooter to create a vacuum that would bring the smoke into my lungs. The moment it did, I could feel every muscle in my body relax. A feeling of warmth ran through me, and complete euphoria replaced the pain that had been there just a few moments before.

I was immediately "in my head," where I was free to fantasize, putting myself anywhere in the world and imagining myself any way that I wanted. I could be a star in my own world. We all have dreams that mostly just remain dreams, but when you do heroin, your dreams become a reality. At least that's what it seems like. You can imagine yourself as a strong, courageous hero who always knows the right things to say and do, and the heroin will make that feel real. Heroin always made me feel that I was at the top of my game. It let me look at the world as a playground that I could walk around in, doing anything or being anyone that I wanted.

Spencer was high too. I told him that I wanted to drop him off and go back to school. Now that I was high and knew where to go for more heroin, I didn't need his help anymore. Besides, I wanted to be alone so I could enjoy my own personal heaven alone. He wanted to hang out, but I refused. I drove him back to his place and dropped him off.

From then on, I went back to San Jose every day to get my heroin. It was harder than I anticipated because I had to get money, drive to Shanty Town, do my dope, and then drive home. This routine didn't leave much time for anything else, so my grades were terrible. I was barely passing some classes and was flat-out failing others. When it came down to either getting sick or missing a class to get dope, there was no contest. Dope won every time.

I managed to make it through the whole school year that way. The following summer, I lived on campus with some other people who were staying on, and I took classes to try to get my grades up again. My dad hired a tutor to help me so I could get through the summer and pass my classes, but all I excelled in was doing heroin and coke.

As the new school year started, I ran out of money, so I came up with a little check scam. I would go to the grocery store, write a check for $50 more than the amount of my purchase, and get back $50 in cash. I was quite happy with my newfound wealth. Fifty dollars wasn't much money, but it was enough to keep me from getting sick. Eventually the store owners would catch on and figure out that my checks were no good, at which point I would go to another bank, open up another checking account, and start the whole thing over again. I knew that when the banks began reporting what I was doing, I wouldn't be able to open any new accounts, so I opened six at once in various banks, sometimes using my driver's license and sometimes using my passport. In others I used a phony driver's license. This went on for several months.

One day, after I had committed every possible form of check fraud I could think of and had papered the whole city with bad checks, two men in blue, wearing badges, showed up at my door. I stayed calm, yet I was scared on the inside. I thought for sure I was going to jail.

"Are you Pax Prentiss?" one of them asked.

I looked at them with a stupid "I don't know what's going on" look. "Yes sir, I am."

"It looks as if you've been writing bad checks all over town."

"Of course, officer," I said. "I'm so sorry. My grandmother

just passed away. She was supposed to deposit $20,000 into my account, but before she could—" I paused and looked down at the ground sorrowfully, "she died. So, Mr. Officer, I thought the money was going to be there. I'm sorry, because I really could have used it to help pay for her memorial service."

The cops both gave me sympathetic looks, then they looked at each other, and the one who had been doing all the talking said, "That's all right, son. We're sorry to have bothered you. But please be more careful in the future. You have a lot of people in the community who aren't happy with you."

"I will," I said. "Thank you for being so understanding."

Well, that was easy, I thought, as they left and I closed the door.

I didn't like fooling the policemen because they were obviously fine men, and they had been very nice to me. I believe that the police are generally good people who are doing a tough job, but I had no choice. They had bought my little story, hook, line, and sinker, but I obviously couldn't rely on the check scheme anymore.

So I started applying for student loans and grants. Surprisingly enough, that worked. I had $20,000 in bad checks outstanding, $70,000 in credit card debt, and collection agencies calling me every day, but for whatever reasons, I got two school loans totaling $10,000. I also had my grandmother, who was alive and well, sending me checks and gifts. Of course, my dad was supplying me with an allowance, and I could always get some extra money from him by making up some story about extra books, or an extra class, or karate lessons. That managed to keep things going for a long time, long enough to get me through the school year, the following summer, and the beginning of my junior year in college, but eventually the money ran out and I didn't have enough to support my habit. I began to kick and kick hard. I was as dope-sick as I had ever been and didn't know where to turn to get money for heroin.

## Jacking the Dealers

Now I had only one source of heroin left—the drug dealers themselves. I came up with the totally stupid and extremely dangerous idea of driving to Shanty Town and asking for my usual hundred dollars' worth of heroin and hundred dollars' worth of coke—but this time, when they handed it to me, I would drive away without paying for it. I knew what would happen if they caught me. I had seen people try it, and watching twenty drug-dealing gangsters beating the living daylights out of one strung-out little dope fiend wasn't a pretty sight. I had friends who died trying to jack dealers. They beat one guy I knew until he was unrecognizable, and then they shot him eight times. But in my crazed mind, I thought that this was a really good idea. I reasoned that if I did this, I could never go back to that neighborhood for more drugs because I would be a wanted man.

With this new plan, I had a chance at getting sober, which was what I wanted deep down inside. But even thinking about it made me feel sick. I had no money, but they were used to me driving into their area, and they knew that I always had money for heroin and coke because I had been buying from them consistently for the last year. Every day I would drive to that crazy neighborhood where the gangsters and dealers hung out, and everyone would rush my car because they knew I was a source of ready, easy money, and they all wanted to sell me their dope.

I hopped into my car and began driving to Shanty Town. I could feel my heart pumping faster and faster the closer I got. Sweat started beading up on my forehead when I was within a few blocks. My hands were shaking as I approached the last stop sign before entering the neighborhood. I could feel every cell in my body tingling, my body was full of adrenaline, my heart was racing, and my palms were sweating. As I got closer, I looked at each of the dealers standing on the corners. They all looked as if they had just gotten out of jail, and they were all buffed out with a "Don't mess with me or I'll kill you" attitude. They wore earrings and had tattoos all over. I knew that any one of them could tear me apart in a matter of seconds. I had been doing dope for a year, and at best I weighed 125 pounds.

As I got closer, they all started to rush my car as usual. Everyone saw an easy buck to be made. Little did they know that I was broke, without even a dollar to my name. I stopped the car, but I left it running and in gear with my foot on the clutch. As they approached, I rolled down the window.

One guy looked at me and said in his street tough way, "What do you want, homes?"

My heart was racing at a hundred miles an hour. His arm was only two feet from me, and I knew that if I stalled on the clutch or wasn't fast enough when I drove away, he would reach out and grab me in a second.

I said, as calmly as I could so he wouldn't know anything was up, "Let me have one big day and one big night," which meant a hundred dollars' worth of coke and a hundred dollars' worth of heroin. He reached into his pocket and, without even hesitating, put the drugs in my hand.

I looked at it as I usually did, pretending to inspect it, and as I did, I popped the clutch and shot off like a bullet. Behind me, I could hear the dealers yelling that I was a dead man. I looked over my shoulder and saw them throwing rocks and bottles at my car, but I had made my getaway. I had my dope.

I drove about two miles and pulled over. I couldn't even wait to get home to get high. I needed my fix right away.

After I had it, I started my car and drove off. I had to make a U-turn to get back to school, but the second I did, I saw red and blue lights flashing behind me. I was high, and I had drugs on me. I knew that if I got caught, it was going to be felony charges for sure. I pulled over slowly, stopped the car, and watched the officer get out of his car in my rearview mirror. I was nervous and sweating. My heart was already beating fast from the coke, and now I had this cop right in my face.

I gave him my usual innocent smile, which had worked like a dream for me so many times in the past, and said, "Yes, officer? Did I do something wrong?"

"Did you know that you made an illegal U-turn back there?"

"No, officer. I didn't know it wasn't permitted there. I'm sorry. I'm a student at the local college, and I was thinking about the homework I need to do when I get home. I should've been paying more attention to the street signs."

He hesitated for a minute and then said, "Well, please be more careful next time."

I said, "Thank you, officer. I will."

And that was it. My heart was about to burst from the adrenaline rush, but it only added to my high.

The next morning I woke up dope-sick. Somehow my idea of getting sober by not being able to get drugs because I would be risking getting killed had sounded a lot better to me the day before, when I wasn't going through withdrawal. By about two o'clock, I was so sick that I started vomiting and urinating on myself. I had lost control of my bodily functions. I was curled up in the corner of my bedroom shaking, and next to me were two pots, one to throw up in and another to go to the bathroom in. I had a $200-a-day habit that I was coming off of cold turkey without the proper meds, and I was an absolute mess.

The sickness turned out to be more than I could bear, and I caved in. I no longer wanted to get sober—at least, not that day. Tomorrow seemed like a much better day to try again, but that was the story of my life—always tomorrow and never today to get clean. Today, I had to figure out a way to get more heroin, and fast.

As much as it scared me, I decided to go back to Shanty Town. But this time I would go to a different part of the neighborhood and jack a completely different dealer. I knew that this trick was twice as risky as the day before because I would be running the risk of being caught both by the dealer I was going to jack the drugs from and by the one I had stolen from the day before. I hoped that when I went in, the people from the day before wouldn't see my car. Shanty Town wasn't that big, only about four blocks total, so the probability was pretty high that someone from the day before would see me. If they did, I was a dead man. But the pain was so bad that I was willing to take this chance with my life just to feel better. I promised myself that if I was successful today, I would never go back because there was no way I could jack the dealers three times in such a short time and in so small an area. It would be guaranteed that I would get caught.

I got into my car and drove toward Shanty Town. When I was several blocks away from where the dealers were, I began to get nervous. My heart was pounding even harder and faster than the day before. I couldn't believe that I was doing it again, but even in the midst of total fear, I wanted what they had, and I was prepared to do anything to get it.

When I was a block away, my foot started shaking so violently that I was almost unable to use my clutch. I was terrified that I was going to get caught this time. I could feel my heart drumming in my chest. When I got to within a hundred feet of them, I started to roll down my window. My hands were shaking, so I grabbed the steering wheel to keep them steady. I stopped and one of the thugs approached my car. I left it running and in gear.

"What do you want?" he asked.

I almost couldn't speak, and for a second it felt as if the words weren't going to come out, but then I managed to blurt out, "A hundred of chiva and a hundred of coke."

He looked at me and paused. Something was wrong. And then he said those dreadful words, "Let me see the money."

I wasn't prepared for that question. I had thought for sure that he was going to just hand me the drugs, but I was quick to answer, "I have the money . . . but you don't think I'm going to show it to you without seeing the shit first."

He knew that something was up, but he didn't know what, and he was hesitating. Then, without even thinking, I said, "Why don't you show me a little goddamn respect and give me the shit? People down here know who I am!"

He took a step back in surprise, not expecting a scrawny little junkie to talk so tough. To tell you the truth, I surprised myself, but it made him put the drugs right in my hand because he figured that I was serious. And with that I shot off and was gone, to the sound of yelling and screaming behind me: "We're gonna get you, motherfucker! You're dead!"

Once again I had successfully jacked the dealers at Shanty Town. When I got two blocks away, I started laughing. I was so happy with what I had just done! It's rare that anyone tries to jack a dealer even once, but to do it two days in a row was absolutely unheard of. In the world of junkies, it was a huge accomplishment. Talk about climbing Mt. Everest! I had climbed it twice in two days!

This time I knew it was over. Today was the last day that was I ever going to use heroin and coke again. I had created a situation where it would be impossible to score again, even if I had money. I could never go back to Shanty Town. That was what I wanted, though. I was tired of being a junkie. It was a hard life and I'd had enough. I wanted a life for myself, free from drugs and alcohol, where I could do all the things that normal people do.

## THE DESTROYER

I awoke the next morning to my own personal alarm clock, called heroin withdrawal. I always needed my wake-up dose to get out of bed. This time it wasn't there. It was time to go through the kick and get sober. I lay there on my bed and felt myself getting sicker as the minutes wore on. The depression was starting to set in. My muscles started to ache, my bones started to crawl, and I felt cold yet sweaty. But I didn't move. I was determined to see it through to the end this time.

My mind was racing from thought to thought and then it stopped and focused on how screwed up my life was. I wasn't even going to school at that point. I had completely dropped out, yet I was still living on campus in my apartment. I told my dad that I was in school, but I really wasn't. When you're a junkie, it's hard to think about the future. You're concerned only with "now"—with not getting sick. I knew I couldn't live this lie forever. Eventually everything would come closing in on me. My only chance was to get sober now.

By one o'clock, the withdrawal was unbearable. I tried to block out thoughts of using, but it was too hard. All I could think about was the smell and taste of the heroin smoke and how good it would make me feel. It would be the ultimate release to go from complete sickness to complete euphoria in a matter of two seconds. I kept arguing with myself that it was too dangerous to ever go back to Shanty Town. I kept telling myself that going through the agonizing withdrawal was the only way I could be free of this forever.

The day grew long as I lay there. The seconds on the clock seemed to slow the way only a junkie who is dope-sick could understand. I closed my eyes and thought, "I'll just concentrate on my sickness to help me remember that I've got to do this terrible course of withdrawal."

I looked at the clock. 3:06 p.m. I closed my eyes. I could feel every bone in my body as if they were razors under my skin. I felt the razors cutting me, I felt the nausea, I felt the pee running down my leg. I endured it for what seemed like two hours. I opened my eyes and looked at the clock. It was 3:17 p.m.

Eleven minutes! That frightened me so badly that I lost my breath. That's when I learned that time can stretch, that it's not a fixed moment-by-moment unfolding but something completely subjective. I got up and tried to make myself eat, but I couldn't keep the food down.

The pain was so bad that I wanted to scream. I felt as if I was losing my mind. I could hear myself mumbling, "Please help me . . . please help me." I was saying it without even trying; as if I were a crazy person in a psych ward. The smell of heroin ran through the house as if there was somebody smoking it right next to me, but nobody else was there. My mind was playing tricks on me. I could even taste it in my mouth. I was begging the air to please stop, "Please, I can't take it. It's too much."

Finally, I rolled off my bed by accident and landed on the floor. It was enough to startle me to my senses, and I stood up and tried to walk but fell down. I was shaking too hard to keep my balance. I sat there and started to cry. What was happening to me? How could this be my life? All I could think about was heroin. There was nothing else that could take this pain away, and with that single thought, I decided that getting caught and killed by the drug dealers would be better than sitting there feeling that I was going to die. I decided to go back and try to get more heroin. I looked down at the floor and said to myself, "I can't believe you're going to do this again." I was risking certain death just to get one more hit.

By the way, "chiva" means "the destroyer," and that's exactly what it does.

## THE APE MAN

I cursed myself the whole way as I drove to Shanty Town. I was so sick that I could barely drive. I kept passing out at red lights until people started honking at me and woke me up. As I got close to the neighborhood but was still a few blocks away, I came to a stop sign. I could see the dealers in the distance.

Out of nowhere, an arm reached into the car and grabbed me by the neck. It was the first dealer I had jacked. He was holding a pair of scissors that he was going to shove through my neck. He must have seen my car coming and recognized me.

"Stop!" I yelled. "I have the money! I was coming to pay you!"

He pulled me out of my car through the open window and dragged me by my feet for two blocks into the center of the neighborhood, where everybody rushed me. There must have been twenty guys yelling, "Let's kill him!" and each one of them was holding a different weapon. Some had knives, others had bats, and a few had guns. I thought they were going to kill me right then and there, and I was terrified.

Standing in the midst of the gang was the leader. They called him "The Ape Man." To this day, I've never seen anyone as scary looking as he was. He had piercing yellow eyes and greasy black hair that he kept slicked back, and he was huge. He looked as if he had spent the better part of his life lifting weights in jail just so he could kill scrawny little dope fiends like me. He had a slash of a mustache and long black sideburns. A livid white scar ran from his forehead down through his left eye, and across his mouth. It gave him a perpetual sneer.

Everybody was yelling, "Kill him! Kill him!" but the Ape Man told everybody, "Don't touch him, he's mine!"

My worst nightmare had come true. I was about to die, and die slowly and painfully by being beaten to death.

The Ape Man and one of his goons grabbed me by my feet, dragged me back to my car, and put me in the back seat. He took the wheel. His goon was in the passenger seat. The Ape Man looked at me and said, "You are fucking dead, homes! We're gonna drive you to the desert, you're gonna dig your own grave, then we're gonna beat you until we get tired, then we're going to cut you in the stomach so your guts fall out, and then we're gonna leave you in the grave, buried so only your mouth sticks out."

They started driving me toward the desert in my own car, and after twenty minutes I could see that we were coming to the edge of the city. We came to a dry, dusty road that seemed to go on forever. The Ape Man turned onto it and kept driving. My hands were sweating, my heart was pounding in my chest, and I didn't know what to do. They were going to kill me as an example of what happens to junkies who steal their drugs. They were actually looking forward to it.

"C'n I make the stomach cut?" the goon asked.

"No, dude," the Ape Man said. "You'll make it too fast. I want to watch his face as he feels the knife cutting him open."

My brain was racing at a thousand miles an hour. I knew I had to come up with a plan, but it seemed that there was no way out. I had pushed my luck too far and now it was time to pay. Then it came to me—the realization that drug dealers all want one thing: money. If I could convince him that I had money, maybe he would let me go. But I had to talk fast.

"Ape Man, I have $400, and if you let me go it's all yours." This was a total lie, but it was the first thing that came out of my mouth.

"You're lying," he said.

"No, it's true! I'm getting a two-week paycheck tomorrow and I'll give it to you," I said in desperation. "You can have it all if you'll just let me live."

He stopped the car. "How can I be sure you'll give it to me?" He was obviously interested. I could see that he was thinking it over.

I didn't hesitate for a second. "I'll be back with it tomorrow."

I looked around. There were no houses, no buildings, just a dry, dusty desert where no one would see anything if they killed me. He looked at me and didn't say anything. I was just a sad, worthless, skinny, ghost-white little junkie sitting in the back of my own car begging for my life. My life was in his hands and he knew it. The moment of truth was upon me. He was either going to buy my lie or kill me in the next ten minutes.

His goon friend said, "You're not believing this shit, are you, homes? He's lying, man—"

"No!" I interrupted him. "Please, you've got to believe me! I'll bring you the money tomorrow!"

The Ape Man looked at me again, then turned around and grabbed me by the neck. "Nice try, homie, but today's not your day to live. Today's your day to die."

And with that he dragged me out of the car by my neck and threw me to the ground.

"Please!" I was frantic. Tears were running down my cheeks. "Please, you've got to believe me!"

"Shut up!" he shouted, and smacked me in the face.

As I tried to get up, his goon, who was standing behind me, kicked me in the back and I fell to the ground again. Then they started dragging me off the side of the road. The sticks and stones tore my skin and I cried out in pain, my head bumping along the ground.

"This ain't nothin' homie," said the goon, "Wait 'till you feel the knife tearing across your guts. That's some *real* pain."

They dragged me about hundred yards from the road over to a ditch that had already been partially dug. I realized that this must be a regular event for them because they had a ditch all ready for my body. I was ordered to dig, and I dug, while frantically searching for the words that would save my life. I kept repeating over and over, "I'll have the money tomorrow." The moment I was finished, the goon knocked me to the ground and rolled me into the ditch. He grinned evilly and said, "Now we're gonna hear you scream, homie."

The Ape Man reached into his pants and whipped out a knife about ten inches long. I looked at him and he looked at me, and at that moment I accepted that I was going to die. He reached down and pulled my shirt out of my pants to expose my stomach area. I looked up to the sky and closed my eyes. I took a deep breath and waited to feel the knife slice into my stomach. He laid the cold steel alongside my belly, the point pricking me. There was a moment of calmness that came from the acceptance of death. But what happened next wasn't what I was expecting.

"Boy," the Ape Man said, "if you're lying to me, you're gonna die a slow death."

He grabbed me by the neck, jerked me out of the ditch like I was a rag doll, pulled my wallet out of my back pocket, and took out my driver's license. He started writing down my home address. "You're gonna meet me tomorrow at noon," he said, "and if you don't have all the money, I'll come to your house and cut your throat. I ain't kiddin' either, boy. I promise you—I'll find you and finish what we started today."

Relief washed over me. I knew I was going to live, at least for today.

"I promise you!" I said. "I'll meet you, and you're not going to regret your decision!"

Then they dragged me back to my car and took me back to Shanty Town and let me go.

## A Kick to the Head

I drove home in complete shock. When I got back, I told my roommate what had happened and begged him for $400 so I could go back the next day and pay off the Ape Man. He didn't know whether to believe me or not because I was so heavily into drugs. "You're probably lying to get more money for drugs," he told me, but I pleaded with him until he caved in and gave me the money.

The next day I drove back to Shanty Town to meet the Ape Man and give him his money. I had stashed the $400 in my sock just in case either of the two dealers I had jacked caught me and wanted their money too. I parked at a gas station a block away from Shanty Town and was just getting out of my car when—wouldn't you know it?—the second drug dealer I had jacked pulled up behind me and blocked me in.

He jumped out of his car waving a screwdriver about eighteen inches long. The people in the gas station, apparently too scared to even try to help me, just stood there and watched. I was in a life-and-death situation again. I started talking immediately.

"Wait a second!" I yelled. "I'm here to see the Ape Man!"

The guy kept coming toward me.

"I'm here to meet the Ape Man," I yelled, "and he told me that if I had any problems to say I was meeting him and that everything'd be cool!"

He stopped and looked at me. I thought he was going to believe me, but then, out of nowhere, he sucker punched me in the face and I fell to the ground, almost senseless.

Out of the corner of my eye, I could see him looking around to see whether anybody would see him if he stabbed me with the screwdriver, but all those witnesses were standing around. So he put the screwdriver away and started kicking me in the face with his steel-toed boots. Each kick felt as if the bones in my face were shattering. Each time he kicked, I could feel myself losing consciousness. Blood was streaming from my forehead and into my eyes, which made it hard to see. I pulled myself to my knees to try to cover myself, but it was no use. His kicks were too powerful to fend off.

Eventually, I fell all the way to the ground and landed flat on my back. I couldn't move my arms, but I was still conscious. The kicks kept coming, but I just lay there unable to move. After five or six really good kicks to my face, it was over. He got in his car and left. He must have kicked me in the face close to thirty times. I lay on the ground in a pool of blood, only half conscious.

Everybody was so scared of him that nobody came to help me. After a few minutes, I slowly sat up. There was blood all over me. My eyes were almost swollen shut and I couldn't move my jaw. I tried to stand up but fell down, so I dragged myself to my car on my elbows. I got in and looked at myself in the mirror through the little slits of my eyes, which I could hardly open. Streams of blood were pouring down my face, and all my front teeth were crooked. The left side of my jaw looked as if someone had shoved a baseball into my cheek. I figured that the bones had been broken in half and were trying to come out of my skin. I couldn't move my mouth, so there was no way I could talk.

Then I realized that I still had the money. He hadn't found it. Despite the pain, I knew I had to go and pay off the Ape Man, because if I didn't, he would show up at my house that night.

I got back out of my car. Several people came over to try to help me, but I just pushed them away and started walking. I had a mission to get to the Ape Man, and I couldn't stop now. As best I could, I walked into Shanty Town. It was hard to see because my eyes were swollen shut and the blood was still pouring down my head and face, but I did my best.

When I got to the place where I was supposed to meet the Ape Man, he was there waiting.

When he saw me, he looked shocked. "What happened to you?"

I had to mumble because I couldn't move my jaw. "I got beaten up by one of your friends who I jacked two days ago."

"Didn't you tell him you were coming to meet me?"

"Yes, I told him, but he said he didn't care."

Then he asked me the million-dollar question. "Do you still have the money?"

To which I gave him the million-dollar answer. "No, he took it from me and told me to tell you to fuck off."

"What?!" he screamed.

"It's true," I mumbled. "He took your money."

The Ape Man believed my story because it was obvious that I had been beaten up. Without saying another word, he jumped into his car and drove off after the other dealer and left me sitting there with blood rolling down my face, a severely broken jaw, and $400 in my sock. I stood there in wonderment of the events of the previous two days.

I looked around Shanty Town. It was a quiet afternoon and no one was around except a few dogs. There was an old Mexican restaurant on the corner, and I knew that inside was someone who was always there, sitting at his table from nine in the morning until ten at night—someone who sold some of the finest dope in the neighborhood. I had scored from him many times in the past, and my credit was still good with him because I had never jacked him. His name was Santiago.

I stumbled over to the restaurant and went inside, and there he was at his table. I sat down across from him and didn't say anything. He looked and didn't say anything either. It was just one of those moments when no words needed to be exchanged. He knew what had happened. He was one of the older dealers in the neighborhood, probably in his mid-forties, and there wasn't a lot that he hadn't seen after so many years on the streets. I almost liked the guy, even though he was a dealer and just wanted my money. Still, we had been friendly, and on many occasions he had even encouraged me to get help for my drug addiction.

"Señor Pax," he said after several moments of silence, "when are you gonna get yourself out of this world? This is not for you, man. You're a good kid. Why don't you go to college and make your parents happy?"

"Santiago," I mumbled, "I do what I got to do. This is my life."

He thought about that for a bit and then replied, "Well, Señor Pax, I'm sorry to hear that. I like you. You're a good kid, and you deserve better."

I stopped for a second because I noticed that the blood dripping from my face was forming a small pool on the table. Then I mumbled back, "Santiago, you're a good guy. Why don't you stop selling dope and find some legal employment?"

He laughed at that. He got what I was saying—that it was as unlikely for him to stop what he was doing as it was for me to stop what I was doing. I'm not sure whether it was my comment or the way I had to mumble it that amused him so much.

"Oh, Señor Pax, I cannot do that. This is all I know how to do."

We sat there and shared a moment of silence again, and then I asked, "So, Santiago, what's on the menu today?"

"Well, Señor Pax, I have a new delivery, especially for you. Clean and uncut, just the way you like it." Santiago never used code talk with me because he knew I wasn't a cop.

"Well, Santiago, considering that today is my lucky day, I'll have four hundred worth of coke and heroin."

He spat four balloons out of his mouth into his hand and put them on the table. Two were black, indicating that they were heroin, and two were white, which meant that they were coke. Dealers keep their heroin and cocaine in balloons in their mouth. Each balloon is about the size of a peanut. They also always keep a bottle of water right next to them. That way, if the police ever pull them over, they can swallow the balloons. All the evidence is in their stomach and they don't get busted.

I reached down into my sock and gave him the cash. Then I picked up the balloons. "Good-bye, Santiago."

"Good-bye, Señor Pax," he said as I walked out of the restaurant.

When I got to my car, I drove about a mile and pulled over. It had been another day in the life of a junkie, but I was still alive, and happy because I had my dope. I broke out the tinfoil that I always kept under my seat and made a rig. The first hit was amazing. All the pain in my face went away. Then I did a huge line of coke, which further increased the pleasure of the heroin. After I was good and high, I drove back to school.

When I got home, my roommate looked at me and freaked out. "Oh my God! What happened to you? We've got to get you to the hospital!"

I told him most of what had happened but not that I had kept the money to buy drugs. He thought that I had given it to the dealer.

When I got to the hospital, they x-rayed my jaw. It was broken all the way through the bone in two places and dislocated at the joint. Several of my teeth were crooked. They told me that I needed to get my jaw realigned and that it would have to be wired shut for two months. The procedure would cost $15,000 because they would need an oral surgeon to put everything back together properly.

I knew that I had to call my dad because I obviously didn't have the money. But what was I going to tell him? "Hey, Dad, I've been strung out at school for over a year, not going to classes, plus I owe $20,000 in loans and check debt, and I need $15,000 because my jaw is dislocated and broken in two places because I got beaten up by the drug dealer I stole drugs from."

## CONSEQUENCES DON'T STOP ADDICTS OR ALCOHOLICS

I went home and stared at the phone for an hour trying to muscle up the courage to pick it up. Eventually I did call and tell him everything. Well, not everything, but the part about me getting beaten up.

As you can imagine, it was an extremely painful and hugely embarrassing conversation for me. I love my dad and I hold him in high esteem, and I want him to see me the same way. Imagining him seeing me in such a poor light was my worst nightmare, but you know enough about my dad by now to know what his response was.

"No problem," he said. "I'll call the hospital and make arrangements for you, and I'll be up on the next plane."

I went to the hospital and had my mouth wired shut. They gave me a bottle of liquid codeine for the pain, which was good because the next day I was going to be dope-sick in a big way. I still had two hits of heroin and coke left, and I did them that afternoon. Just as I was doing the second one—wouldn't you know it?—in walked my dad.

He was amazed to see me doing heroin after what I had just been through. He had also seen what I had gone through the first time I had kicked, and he probably couldn't imagine anyone going through it a second time. I guess he figured that I was smart enough not to do drugs again.

We talked then, and I gave him the straight story. He said that what I was going through was just part of my soul journey and that something good was sure to come from it. He is so certain of his philosophy that he would stake his very life upon it. But at that moment, even though I had grown up living with his philosophy, I found it hard to believe that anything good could come from this.

After a while, he asked me the same question that he had asked me the first time he sat with me through detox: "Have you discovered why you're using heroin yet?"

I told him again what I had told him before. "Because I'm hooked on it and can't get off it."

"That's not it," he said. "There's more to it than that. You were off it, you were no longer addicted, the withdrawal symptoms were over, yet you went back to it. There's something driving your addiction."

"It's the greatest feeling in the world," I said. "And I haven't been able to duplicate it in any other way."

"There must be more to it than that."

I again explained about the incredible high, but he just shook his head. "Well, I'm learning a lot about addiction from you. Seeing you smoking heroin with your jaws wired shut totally convinces me that consequences don't stop addicts."

He told me that he had been looking for information about addiction ever since he had learned that I was using heroin. When my dad wants to find out about something, he finds out everything there is to know about it. Finally, he asked me whether I planned on doing it again.

"No," I assured him. "It's over for good and all time. I would never do heroin again." Besides, I thought to myself, I can never go back to Shanty Town again.

The hardest part about having my jaws wired shut was that I couldn't chew. All my food had to be liquefied in a blender. I was already skinny from doing drugs, but this made things even worse because I could get very little food into my system. The huge amounts of codeine I was drinking every day allowed me to get off the heroin, and after about two weeks I was back in school trying to redeem myself.

Everyone knew that I was a junkie, and word about what had happened to me had quickly spread around campus. I hated going to my classes because whenever I had to speak, I could only mumble through my teeth and wires. It was unbelievably embarrassing, having been beaten senseless by a heroin dealer. There's nothing easy about being a junkie, and the longer you do it, the worse things get. At lunch when all the other students were eating in the cafeteria, I had to drink my food through a straw. I could see and hear some of the students laughing and making jokes about me.

After about three weeks, my liquid codeine ran out and I started craving heroin again in a big way. I wanted to use just one last time. I know that you've read this a couple of times already, but I truly believed that I could do it just once and then stop. My dad believed that I had stopped using dope, so this gave me the perfect opportunity to go and score because he wouldn't be expecting it. I know—you would think that after all I had been through, I would have learned my lesson, but I hadn't. The only problem was that I could not go back to Shanty Town again. I needed a new connection.

## Meeting My Connection

I took out the yellow pages and looked up methadone clinics. Methadone is a drug that clinics dispense to heroin addicts to keep them from getting sick so they won't get crazy and rob people or commit other crimes to get money for drugs. Heroin addicts don't get sick when they take methadone because it uses the same receptor sites in the brain that heroin does, but it doesn't produce the same high. It also stays in the system three times longer than heroin. Addicts who take between 40 and 120 milligrams of methadone every day won't get dope-sick.

Many heroin addicts go on "methadone maintenance" programs because they can stay strung out on heroin but never worry about being sick. If they're on methadone and don't have the money to buy more heroin, they don't need to do anything crazy to get it because the withdrawal isn't pushing them to do it to relieve the symptoms.

There is a trade-off, though. When you decide to get off methadone, you're in for the kick of a lifetime. Methadone withdrawal is the mother of all withdrawals—it's twice as bad as heroin and it lasts twice as long. However, I wasn't looking to get hooked up on methadone. I was looking for a connection, and if you want to find a connection, you go to where junkies are: methadone clinics.

I found the address of a nearby methadone clinic and jumped into my car. When I arrived, a bunch of junkies were hanging outside the doors waiting for their morning dose. I hooked up with one of them and told him I would buy him some heroin if he would introduce me to his connection, which he did.

After I got my dope, I drove a few blocks and pulled over. My mouth was still wired shut, so I had to smoke the heroin through my wires and clenched teeth. It was an ugly sight to see. Getting strung out on heroin never has a happy ending, but there I was sucking up the smoke through my wired teeth, chasing the dragon again. I had to have just one more hit. Again I told myself that I wouldn't do it again after that day. I just needed to taste it, feel it, and let it run through my body one more time. But, as you probably know, it wasn't one more time. I had released the animal again, and I started hooking up every day from my new dealer.

Two months later, I got my wires off, but I was strung out and had lost a considerable amount of weight. I'm almost six feet tall, but I weighed only 118 pounds. It seemed that no matter how bad the consequences were, as my dad had said, consequences do not stop addicts. I needed it. It was the only thing I knew how to do really well, and the only thing that made me feel really human. It was my life. I could always rely on it to make me feel good, and it would never let me down.

Then I stopped answering my phone for several days, and my dad began to get suspicious. I believe that the only reason he didn't know I was still using was because he believes in me so much. He jumped on a plane and came to my house and there I was, curled on the couch, drooling on myself because I had nodded out from the heroin.

He didn't even need to ask. It was obvious that I was strung out again. He had wanted to believe that I could do it on my own, which is the denial that most parents have about their kids who are using, but he saw that I couldn't. Most of the time, parents just don't want to believe that their son or daughter is a drug addict, so they push it to the back of their minds and pretend it isn't happening.

But this had gone too far. My dad wasn't going to leave it up to me any longer. He took action. He called a rehab facility in Southern California and made a reservation for me.

I didn't know it then, but my college days had come to an end. I had been there a total of two-and-a-half years, and I had used heroin and coke the whole time. I packed my bags and called the front office to have Larry, the apartment manager, inspect it for damages. When he arrived, my dad and I stood outside while he went through the apartment.

After about ten minutes, Larry came back out. "I found some tinfoil in the bathroom," he told us, "with some pieces of heroin melted onto it."

My mouth dropped open in surprise. I couldn't believe what he had said.

He had found it behind the toilet, which was where I always stashed my drugs, but I had completely forgotten about that stash. And I really wanted that piece right now because I was starting to get sick.

Larry grabbed his walkie-talkie and radioed the campus police department. "C4 to base, C4 to base. I need a police car out here right away. I've found drugs in an apartment."

As soon as my dad heard him say that, he tackled him and grabbed him in a bear hug.

"Help!" Larry screamed. "Help me! I'm being attacked!"

"Get in there and grab that stuff!" my dad yelled to me as he was wrestling Larry. "Flush it down the toilet!"

I ran into the bathroom and grabbed the tinfoil. Then I stopped. I looked at the heroin on the foil. I could feel the sickness in my bones creeping up. Every cell in my body was telling me not to flush it down the toilet.

I stared at it. I wanted it so badly, but I knew that the police were on their way and I didn't know how long my dad could hold on to Larry. I could run into my bedroom, get a lighter, start smoking it, and run the risk of getting caught, or I could try hiding it somewhere else in the apartment. But then I thought that the cops might have dogs with them. I couldn't make up my mind.

Never in my life had I thrown heroin down the toilet! That was an unthinkable act. But I could hear Larry yelling outside, and I knew that my dad was making a supreme effort on my behalf, and some small core of decency that still resided deep inside me caused my hand to release, and I watched the heroin drop into the toilet. I flushed it and watched it swirl away. Then I ran back outside.

By this time, a lot of other students had come out of their apartments to see what was going on. When my dad saw me come out, he let Larry go. I was surprised that he'd been able to hold him because Larry was bigger than my dad and a lot stronger. My dad hurried inside and grabbed some fragments of charcoal from the fireplace. He put these on a piece of foil, hid it behind the toilet, and came back out. Then the police arrived.

Larry told them what he had found and where it was. He also told them that my dad had attacked him. He was holding onto his ribs and was in considerable pain. The cops went into the bathroom and found the foil with the charcoal on it. They inspected it. It was obviously not drugs.

"That's not what I found!" Larry screamed. "And his dad attacked me!"

Then an angel appeared—a young woman who worked at the college. She took Larry aside and told him that the college didn't need that kind of publicity and that he was to leave immediately, go home, and forget all about "black rocks." He looked around helplessly, but she pointed at his car. She apparently carried some weight at the college, because the officers told him to go home too, and then they left as well.

There we stood in a crowd of college kids, some of whom were my friends. They had seen me go through so much craziness over the past two-and-a-half years, yet they just stood there staring back at me.

As my dad came to pick me up, some of the students were watching. They knew that my dad had come to take me to rehab. I gave everybody a half-smile and winked at them as if to say, "Hey, don't worry. Everything's cool." Then I got into the car with my dad and drove away, and that was the last they ever saw of me.

I know that they told stories about me for months. No one had ever seen anyone as crazy as me at that school. I guess it's nothing to be proud about—that I would put my life on the line for a piece of brown tar—but I did. That's the way it goes when you're an addict. We later found out that my dad had cracked two of Larry's ribs, but he never pressed charges.

On the way back to L.A., my dad asked me again whether I had discovered why I was using heroin. I had no idea other than that I was chasing the most sacred moment in my life to that point in time.

"I've been talking with a lot of people," he told me, "and I'm beginning to think that addiction medicine is still stuck in the Dark Ages—like the prison system, which is still punishing people rather than educating them. After all, the number of people who get out of prison and become repeat offenders should be enough to convince anyone with half a brain that punishment isn't the answer."

He said he had talked with the foremost people in the field and that they had all told him the same thing: "Addiction and alcoholism are diseases and they're incurable."

"But that can't possibly be true," he added, "because you're going to be cured."

I was doubtful.


## Running a Marathon

When we got back to L.A., I went into the rehab he had arranged for me. It was a very strict place. We had to get up every morning at 6:30. The first part of the morning consisted of cleaning the facility with all the other patients, which took about an hour. Then I sat in group therapy sessions all day long. That particular clinic took in a hundred and twenty patients at a time, and some of those groups had sixty or more people in them. Talk about boring. It was hard to stay awake.

With that number of addicts under one roof, there were bound to be problems, such as patients having sex with each other and people smuggling drugs into the facility. When those problems arose, the administrators would punish everyone in the whole facility. For example, one punishment was "running a marathon," which meant putting everyone in the dining room in the morning and not allowing any of us to leave until it was time for bed. We weren't allowed to speak or do anything but sit in a hard chair, keep quiet, and do nothing.

This could go on for days. The only breaks we got were for meals and bed. Talk about stupid—that took the cake. They thought that they could punish us out of addiction. Nothing could have been further from the truth. All any of us talked about, me included, was getting out to go use again.

The day I checked in, they just happened to be running a marathon, so I walked into the dining room and sat down. I was kicking heroin cold turkey, so what I really needed was a bed and some medications to help me through the pain. Unfortunately, that wasn't going to happen. Instead, I ended up sitting in the marathon for three days for what turned out to be one of the worst heroin kicks of my life. Usually during a marathon, which lasted three or four days, fifteen or twenty people would just get up and walk out. I guess they preferred living on the streets hooked on heroin or their drugs of choice to going through that kind of punishment and degradation.

As I've already described, time moves unbelievably slowly when you're kicking, but to be in a marathon, where all you have to do is watch the clock and pray for the pain to go away, is unbearable. At night when they let us go to our beds, I would lie there and stare at the ceiling. I didn't sleep for ten days except to pass out every now and then for ten minutes before the pain woke me up again. I could barely see from the lack of sleep. At times, I hallucinated from the pain.

Many of the other patients tried to help me by giving me water and juices, but what I really needed was rest. Instead, I was made to go to groups and get lectured at. It was a very bad experience. Finally, after ten days with no sleep, I passed out. My body had given up. That kick lasted twenty-one days, but it felt like twenty-one years.

At night as I lay in bed, I wondered how I had ended up in rehab. I thought about the promise I had made to myself long ago, that I would never let drugs ruin my life as they had my mom's. Then I thought about her. I felt so bad for her because now I understood why she hadn't been able to stop. It wasn't as easy as I had thought. It took a lot more than just willpower. I thought back to when it was all fun, in my old neighborhood when I was sixteen and doing drugs and partying with all my friends. Then I looked where all that had gotten me. I had always looked down on people who had to go to rehab to get off drugs because I thought they were weak. Yet here I was, in rehab, a heroin addict, a junkie, unable to quit on my own.

The facility didn't permit any type of communication, either in or out, for the first month. After that, I wrote letters to my dad. I was sure that I was going to be sober for the rest of my life, and I thanked him for standing by me. When he wrote back, he asked if I had discovered the reason I was using drugs. I replied that I hadn't, beyond the desire to get high.

While I was in rehab, he went to every meeting there was looking for the answer to his question, "Why are alcoholics and addicts doing it? Why can't they quit?" He believed that there had to be a reason. He talked to all my counselors. He visited psychiatrists, psychologists, drug and alcohol counselors, addiction specialists, and treatment centers. He searched the Internet relentlessly, looking for some kind of treatment program that would be different from the group meeting treatment I was receiving. There were none.

Being in that rehab was an especially nasty experience. Sitting in groups all day long going over the same material that we talked about the day before was boring to the point of tears. Having to get up in the morning and do chores, ugh! Not being able to make or receive phone calls. Being told what to say. Not being able to talk to people of the opposite sex. Being told that we had a disease. Not being allowed to leave the facility. Eating bad food. Sharing bathrooms with fifty people. Sleeping in the same room with four people. Being punished for things that other people did. After three long months, I completed the program. I left, determined never to use again. Never.

## Switching Addictions

My resolve lasted a week—then I was using heroin again. My dad discovered it almost right away that time and put me in a different rehab, but the first week I got out, it was back to chasing the dragon.

After several more rehabs and several more relapses, my dad decided that we had to do it ourselves. We left Venice and went to live in Big Sur, where we had a cabin. He was determined to keep me off drugs.

Big Sur is a beautiful seventy-mile strip of coastline in northern California that offers almost nothing except some of the most unspoiled beauty in the world. From our little cabin, it was a hundred-mile round trip to the supermarket. I guess my dad thought that my being in a place as secluded as that would keep me from getting back into drugs, and he was right—it did. He dropped everything else in his life. He literally gave up everything he was working on, everything he was doing in business, all his relationships—he gave up his life to move to Big Sur with me to help keep me safe.

It was hard for me being there because I was twenty-two years old and needed to be around kids my own age. I spent most of my time working on the property. After a couple of months, I got a job working at one of the local restaurants during the day. I had been living sober in Big Sur for nine months when my dad had to go out of town on business for a few days. It was the first time that I had been alone since we had moved there.

On his first night away, I made a fire in the fireplace and sat down beside it. It was warm and beautiful. During my time in Big Sur, I had learned to enjoy the peace of being alone. But while I was sitting next to the fire, a thought popped into my mind: "Wouldn't it be nice to have a drink while I watch the fire?"

I knew that there was liquor in the house, even though my dad, who never drank much, had stopped drinking completely to help me stay sober. I began to think it over. I had been sober for nine months, and after all that time it felt as if I had gained inner mastery over drugs and alcohol. Now that I was the master, I was sure that I would be able to handle one drink. Besides, alcohol wasn't my drug of choice, so it wouldn't even count as a real relapse.

My thought process convinced me that it was okay, so I went over to the cupboard, poured myself a drink, and sat back down by the fireplace. The fire was big, warm, and bright orange. I sat there and looked at the drink and then slowly raised it to my lips. It felt amazing going down. It had been so long since I had any stimulation from a substance that my system had become very sensitive.

I enjoyed that night of sitting and drinking so much that I went on doing it every night until my dad came home. I didn't tell him what had happened.

Shortly after he returned, a huge storm closed the road to Big Sur. My dad said that was okay because we didn't have to go anywhere, but when the phones went out, he said it was time to go. He needed a phone to do his business. I was happy about that because I was sick of living in Big Sur. I wanted to go home, and that is exactly what we did.

When we returned to Venice, I went to school and got my real estate license. My dad had a broker's license, so we worked together. He also writes books on metaphysics. Generally, our niche was to buy a house, fix it up, and put it back on the market. I enjoyed doing that because I was good at it. I had a natural ability to spot a good deal. During that time, I was still drinking at night after work, but I didn't let my dad know about it. I also managed to stay away from the heroin. My experiences with heroin had truly scared me, and I really had no intention of ever wanting to return to it.

It was good to be back in the old town. I had a lot of good memories, and there was a lot more to do for someone my age. I found out that many of the friends who had partied with me when we were teenagers had suffered similar fates. Many had been to rehab at least once. Some were still using and needed to go to rehab. A few had died from overdoses. That was life in Venice. Out of all my friends, I know of only one, John, who never had a problem with drugs and went on to graduate from a university. John and I, along with two other friends, Bob and Alex, would go out drinking after work and on the weekends. Of the four of us, John was the most conservative. He drank only on weekends, while the rest of us drank almost every night.

Shortly after my dad and I moved back to Venice, he met a woman named Lisa. For a while they just dated, but eventually it became a serious relationship. One day he told me that he was going to move in with her and that I could have his house all to myself. Life was really going well for me during that time. I was working with him and making decent money. I was hanging out with my friends at night, and I had been free of heroin for eighteen months. I was excited about the idea of living on my own. At the age of twenty-three, that's a pretty nice thing.

Most nights after work, Bob, John, Alex, and I would meet at my house and drink. We would sit around and laugh, listen to music, and tell stories about how it used to be back in the days when we were teenagers. Some nights we would go to clubs and dance and drink. Even though I wasn't doing heroin, I was drinking more than I should have, on an almost-every-night basis. Even when my friends couldn't make it over, I would go to the liquor store and get a pint of whiskey to drink alone. But it wasn't so bad that it hurt my daytime life. I was still able to work.

I didn't realize it, but I had switched addictions from heroin to alcohol.

## Chasing the Dragon—Again

My life felt full with the exception of one thing: doing heroin the way I had, I'd had no time for a girlfriend. Bob, John, and Alex all had girlfriends, but not me. I knew that eventually I would meet someone special, so I just remained open to it happening when the time was right.

One beautiful summer afternoon in Marina del Rey, my dad, Bob, and I decided it would be a good day to take Lisa's beautiful 42-foot Chris Craft out fishing. We spent the day having a great time catching yellowtail and getting suntanned. The smell of the salt air and the feel of the sun hitting my face and being out there with my dad and Bob catching fish was truly sublime.

The sun had gone down as we pulled the boat into the main channel where all the boats motor slowly toward their individual slips. The main channel is about a mile of calm protected water, and it takes about ten minutes to get to the slips.

As my dad steered us toward our slip, Bob and I both stood up to prepare to dock. When we were about fifty yards away, I noticed a beautiful sailboat docked right next to our slip, with a group of people standing on the dock. Among these people, one girl stood out to me. She had the most beautiful blonde hair, which she wore up in a bun, and as she moved, it shone in the orange light of the setting sun. I couldn't take my eyes off her. She was beautiful, and she moved with the grace of a dancer, as though she was writing a poem with every step she took. She had a beautiful glow about her, and the closer our boat got, the more beautiful she became.

I nudged Bob, and the words came out of my mouth without my even thinking: "That's my new girlfriend." I didn't know what caused me to say that, and the next moment a hand of fear clutched at my throat. Since childhood I've never been able to talk to pretty girls. The words just freeze up in my throat. Not-so-pretty-girls I can talk to forever, but beautiful girls, not a word. Sometimes not even hello.

Our boat docked right next to hers, and I jumped off. Bob threw me the rope so I could tie off to the cleat. I tried to do this as if I was an experienced sailor, but because I couldn't take my eyes off her, I kept missing the cleat. She started to notice what was going on, probably because it amused her that I was so clumsy. I felt kind of nervous inside, but I managed to say, "Hello."

"Hello," she replied.

And then wonder of wonders—I said, "My name is Pax. What's yours?"

"Ashley."

I stood there as though paralyzed. I couldn't help but notice her big, beautiful blue-green eyes. The next words I wanted to say felt as if they took a million years to form, as though time had slowed and we were the only two people in the world. I hadn't even noticed that I still hadn't gotten the rope around the cleat. My dad yelled down to me from the boat, "What do I need to do to get you to get that rope around the cleat?" and then the funniest thing happened—Ashley's mom yelled back, "Try removing the girl!"

I guess it was obvious that I had been shot by the angel of love. I started to blush. I looked back at Bob to see if he could somehow put the correct words in my mouth so I could finish this conversation. I didn't realize that, while I was looking at Bob, Ashley had taken down her hair and was shaking it out in the sun. Bob's eyes opened wide as he watched her do this. He motioned to me with his eyes in an urgent way that I should keep talking to her.

I turned around and looked at her again, but before I could say a word my dad yelled, "Get the boat tied off!"

I had completely forgotten what I was supposed to be doing. I tried giving the chore at hand my full attention and was finally able to tie off the boat. After completing that Herculean task, which should have been easy, I looked up at Ashley and, although I could hardly believe it, I began to talk. Now the words began flowing like a river, and before I knew it I was having a real conversation with her. I was afraid to stop because I thought if I stopped, the magic would stop and I would be tongue-tied again.

My dad and Bob started washing down the boat, but every now and then I would glance back at Bob for encouragement, which he gave in abundance by hand gestures and facial expressions, as though he was more excited than I was. I continued talking with her, but toward the end of the conversation she told me that she lived about an hour from my house. I knew I should ask her for her telephone number, but my conversational skills suddenly deserted me completely. When her mom told her it was time to go, I just stood there. She looked at me as though she was waiting for me to ask her something, but I didn't. She said, "Good-bye," and she turned and left. I was numb.

Bob rushed over and said, "So, did you get her number?"

"No."

"What do you mean? "No?" That's ridiculous! She's perfect for you!"

I started to think about it, and the more he spoke, the more dreadful I felt. How could I have let such a perfect opportunity slip by? It was starting to get dark when suddenly I saw the faint silhouette of somebody walking toward me in the dim light. It was Ashley. My heart started to race again. It was too good to be true. Could she have felt what I was thinking? Bob got excited as well and exclaimed, "Oh my God, she's coming back!" I resolved not to let this opportunity go by, even if I had to write the question out on paper.

Bob continued urging me on, but I was too fixated on Ashley to hear what Bob was saying. Moving out of the darkness like an angel, she walked right up to me, handed me a slip of paper, and said, "I thought you might like to call me sometime. Here's my number."

I took it, smiled, and just nodded my head like one of those little toy figures people put on their dashboards with the heads that wiggle around. Then she walked off into the darkness again as though she had never been there.

We began dating, and over the next several months, Ashley and I developed a strong love for each other. I told her everything about myself, including my battle with heroin. No one really wants to have a heroin addict as a boyfriend, of course, but she said that as long as it wasn't in our future, she was okay with it. I promised her that she had nothing to fear.

"No matter what happens," I told her, "I'll never do heroin again."

She accepted this, but she also made it clear that if I ever did go back to heroin, she would leave me. I told her that I understood completely.

## What Could One More Hit Do?

Because Ashley lived so far away, we saw each other only on the weekends. During the week I would drink. I also did some coke occasionally because I knew that I could do it without her or my dad catching on. They both knew that I drank, but not how much. My drinking had escalated to the point that I was getting drunk every night on beer and whiskey. If my dad or Ashley called, I could always manage to carry on a conversation and get by without them noticing how intoxicated I was. Then, once a week, I would pick a night when I could do coke and not get caught.

I didn't know it at the time, but the only reason I was still off heroin was because I had replaced it with other drugs.

However, every night that I drank, I got a nagging thought at the back of my head to do heroin. The alcohol was good, but it didn't give me the same feeling that heroin and cocaine did. I kept struggling with the idea of using heroin, even though I hadn't touched it in nearly two years. I knew that I shouldn't be letting myself think about it, but no matter how much I told myself not to, I couldn't help but entertain the thought of doing it one more time. Obviously I had demonstrated that I could stay off it, so what would one more hit possibly do?

I struggled with that idea for several months before one day it finally wore me down. I picked up the phone and called my heroin dealer. Ashley and my dad were both out of town that week, so it was an opportune time for me to get away with getting high. And so, I had a wonderful night of doing cocaine and heroin in the comfort of my own home, and I didn't have to worry about anyone catching me.

Unfortunately, my plan was flawed because I got high the next night, and the next, and by the time my dad and Ashley got back into town, I was fully strung out on heroin again. All I had really done when I stopped doing heroin was to switch the addiction to alcohol, which led to cocaine, which led me back to heroin again. My two-year abstinence from heroin was over.

Of course, when Ashley got back I didn't tell her that I was using heroin again. Instead, I started picking arguments with her so I wouldn't have to visit her on the weekends. I knew that if she saw me, she would know right away that something was wrong. Every time we were about to see each other, I would start another silly argument so I would have an excuse not to go, and she didn't understand what was going on. I turned into a mean boyfriend, and over the next three months, my behavior changed so drastically that we broke up.

My dad started to get suspicious. He was working on another book and I suspect he didn't say anything because he wasn't certain and he didn't want to bring it up if he wasn't sure. I started showing up for work late. I would leave several times during the day to go hook up, and my weight started dropping again. The color left my face, and I made many trips to the bathroom. Everything was pointing to me being back on heroin. There was no way I could keep it secret forever. Deep down, I really didn't want to be a junkie. Every day, I told myself that I would kick my habit tomorrow.

It didn't take long before my money ran out and I was forced to look for other ways of getting cash. I started pawning everything out of my house. I had a beautiful custom stereo system in my car that was worth $3,000. I ripped it out and gave it to my dealer for eighty bucks' worth of heroin and coke. I sold everything of value in the house. I stopped calling my friends. I ruined my relationship with Ashley. Everything was falling apart because my every waking moment was dedicated to either doing dope or figuring a way to get it once I ran out.

Each day my life fell apart more. My room was bare. I had sold all my personal belongings, and because I had stopped talking to all my friends, I was completely alone. I thought about Ashley a lot and wished that she were back with me. My dad was definitely catching on. One day he sat me down and asked me if I was using again. I told him no. I could tell everything inside him wanted to believe it, so he went against his instincts and believed what I said. I knew, though, that my run had to end some time and that I would have to come clean eventually.

I decided that I wanted to get sober again and that the only way to do it was to get out of Venice. I called my friend Alex and asked him if he would come up to Big Sur with me and keep me company while I kicked for two weeks. Alex was indeed a good friend, and he didn't want me to be strung out, so he agreed to go with me.

I took just enough heroin to get me through the drive, and when we arrived I was just finishing the last of it. We unpacked the car and got everything into the cabin. I was back in the same place I had been almost two years ago. It was sad to me. I didn't know how I could be living that dreadful nightmare all over again.

After unpacking, we made a fire in the fireplace and prepared for the kick that would begin the second I awoke the next day. I called my dad and told him that everything was cool and that Alex and I were going to spend two weeks in Big Sur on vacation. I think he was happy to hear this because he believed there was no heroin in Big Sur. What he didn't know was that I was up there to try and get off it. We let the fire burn out and then went to bed. I knew that the next day I would be miserable, but I wanted sobriety badly enough that I was willing to go through the pain.

## MAINLINING

The next morning was horrible. I was sicker than I had ever been in my life. I lasted about three hours before I announced to Alex that we were going to San Jose to get more dope. It was stupid of me to think that I could make it through on my own. It was a joke. I couldn't even make it through one day. My intentions were good, but all the good intentions in the world were not enough to carry me through that horrible kick. What I really needed was a facility where someone would watch over me. Alex tried to persuade me not to go, but it was useless. My mind was made up.

We drove to San Jose, back to Shanty Town, where I was a known man. It had been three years, but I didn't want to take any chances of being seen by someone who might remember me. So I found another junkie on the streets who was looking to hook up, and I told him that I would buy him some drugs if he would buy them for me. He came back with my drugs, and Alex and I drove to the spot where I had smoked after my jaw had been broken.

I put the heroin on the foil but paused before smoking it. I wanted to savor the moment. I looked around and found it amazing that after so many years I was back in the exact spot where I had all but lost my life to drugs. And here I was again, chasing the dragon. It was as though all time had stopped and it was just me and the heroin in the car. The moment was surreal. I lit the lighter and put it under the foil. Within seconds the pain was gone and my mind was in a state of euphoria.

We drove back to the cabin and decided that the only thing to do was to call my dad and have him readmit me to rehab. This time, I didn't have it in me to make the call. It was too hard to tell him that I was hooked on heroin again. Alex made the call for me as I sat by his side. As I heard him speak the words, "Pax is strung out on heroin again," I could feel my body tingling. I wondered what was going through my dad's mind. Alex ended the conversation by saying that he would bring me home the next day. My heroin run was coming to an end again.

When I saw my dad the next day, the first question he asked me was whether I had discovered why I was using heroin again. I said what I had always said—that it was just the high that I was looking for.

"I've been continuing to research all this," he told me, "and I'm convinced that underlying conditions are responsible for addiction. Not just in your case, but for everyone who's addicted. I'm putting together a plan to discover what's behind it."

I was quite lucky that time because I was admitted into detox at a hospital before I went to rehab. The kick was still horrible, but at least it was better than sitting in a marathon with no medication. I was thankful for this but at the same time very depressed. My life was a wreck once again. I had no idea what I was going to do. I had lost almost everything. The only thing I had left was my dad's support.

On my second day in the detox ward, I received a phone call from my mom. I was so happy to hear her voice!

"I've gotten clean," she told me, "and I'm living with my boyfriend." It was another surreal moment for me. My mom was clean and sober and living a healthy life, and I was the one in rehab. I sat there and smiled as I listened to her talk. I went back in my head to the time when I had ridden my bike over to the garage where she was living and had seen her strung out on crack and alcohol. I remembered the promise I had made to myself to never use drugs. It was all so funny to me, and for a second I found humor in my situation. I asked her if she would call Ashley and tell her what had happened to me. I was hoping that Ashley would forgive me and that when I got out of rehab, she might consider taking me back. I also hoped that I could go back to working with my dad. I wanted to put my life back together. But it can be hard to earn back the trust of people once you've deceived them.

After detox, I was transferred to another rehab center for one month. After the month was over, my dad allowed me to come home one more time. I assured him that things would be different this time.

When I got home, I also started to patch things up with Ashley. She was very understanding and supportive, and because she loved me so much, she was willing to give me a second chance. I was very happy about this. Several months went by, and my life was slowly coming back together. I looked healthy again, I had money in the bank from doing real estate with my dad, my relationship with him was solid again, and Ashley and I were happy. It was a dream come true for any heroin addict who has lost everything and then gets it all back again.

Then, after six months of sobriety, one day the craving for heroin hit me like a crushing blow. I fought and I struggled. I wanted to say no, but the thought of being high just one more time was too much for me. I know you may find that hard to believe. I wanted to stay clean, I wanted to be true to my dad and to Ashley and, most of all, to myself. But even after all I had been through—all the pain, the loss, and the terrible consequences I had suffered—I just had to have it one more time.

I caved in. I picked up the phone, dialed the number, and arranged to meet the dealer twenty minutes later.

I drove over to the parking lot of a small store where I would meet my dealer. I was passing the time, listening to Led Zeppelin and tapping on my steering wheel pretending as if I were playing the drums, when I looked out of the corner of my eye and noticed another guy sitting in his car. I knew right away that he was another junkie. There's a unique communication between junkies that allows you recognize them. You just know it.

I got out of my car and went over to greet him. He was about my age. He had tracks running up and down his arms from continuous shooting up. He wasn't a very healthy-looking guy, yet you could tell that at one time he had been a nice young boy like me who had fallen victim to heroin. We started talking, and he asked me how I liked to do my dope.

"Smoking's my preferred way," I told him.

"I used to do that," he said, "but the high's more intense and lasts longer if you shoot up. It's cheaper too, so a little can go a long way."

Because I had been clean for six months, I wasn't low on money, but the idea fascinated me. I had always been curious about what the high must feel like when you shot heroin straight to your heart.

Just then my dealer drove up, so I said good-bye to the junkie and jumped back into my car to follow the dealer. He would always drive about five or six blocks away from where I was waiting just in case someone was watching. He was happy to see me because he knew that it meant another run for me and lots more money for him. He spat out a couple of balloons of heroin and a couple of balloons of coke. I then drove to the nearest restaurant, parked, and headed right for the bathroom. I broke open the balloon with the coke in it and spilled it onto the counter. I pulled out a card and began cutting up a line. It glistened and sparkled in the light, and it had that soft, moist texture that meant it was very pure. I could feel my mouth salivating. After I cut the line, I rolled up a bill, leaned down, and inhaled the coke.

I immediately felt the rush of energy. My teeth started to get numb, another good sign of high-quality coke. As the high increased, I could feel the rush of dopamine hitting my brain and creating that feeling of complete and utter euphoria. I took my finger, wiped up the rest of the coke on the counter, and rubbed it on my gums to increase the high. Then I ripped open a balloon of heroin. The brown, tar-like substance wasn't as pretty as the coke, and the smell of it almost made me puke. I quickly put some on the foil, and just as the coke was reaching its peak, I took a big hit of heroin. The two came together to form a high that mere words could never explain.

I loved the feeling of doing coke and heroin in a restaurant bathroom because it was so sneaky. I had to walk into the restaurant without anyone noticing, do my drugs, and walk out again without getting caught. I loved the risk, the hidden identity that I held, and the secret I was hiding. It made me a feel a little like James Bond.

When I got home that night, I couldn't get the idea of shooting dope out of my head. I knew that the high would be more intense, but I also knew that it was a lot more dangerous. It was easy to overdose and die, or you could get an abscess and have to have one of your limbs amputated. There were many complications that came with shooting dope, and for many years I hadn't been willing to take that risk.

But that night I decided that I wanted to try it.

The next day, I called my dealer and told him I needed a ten-pack of syringes along with my usual supply of dope. He gave me the dope and the syringes and I hurried home. My dad had ended his relationship with Lisa a few months earlier and had moved back into our house, but he wasn't home.

I had seen people shoot up before, so I knew how to do it. I went into the kitchen and got a spoon and then went into the bathroom. I emptied a little coke and a little heroin onto the spoon. This was called a speedball. I knew to use a very small amount because this was my first time and my tolerance to shooting up was low. I also knew that speedballs could kill you if you shot too much. I ripped off a small piece of the filter from a cigarette and put it on the spoon too. The filter was to make sure that no foreign substances got sucked into the syringe. Then I filled the spoon with a little water and mixed it with the coke and the heroin. A moment later, I had a light-brown liquid with the filter floating in it. I then took a syringe, stuck the point into the filter, and pulled back on the plunger until I had sucked up all the liquid. I took off my belt and wrapped it around my arm to get the vein to pop out and make a clear target. Then I took the syringe and slowly poked it into the vein. I slowly pulled back on the plunger to make sure I was into the vein. Blood started to fill the syringe, and I was fully in.

All that was left now was to slowly push the plunger down and release the belt. I paused. I didn't know what to expect. I was scared but at the same time excited. I wanted to be higher than I had ever been, but I didn't want to drop dead on the floor. I pushed the plunger down slowly until it reached the bottom and then I quickly released the belt.

Nothing happened for two seconds, and then all of a sudden I got the taste of cocaine and heroin in my mouth as if I had just eaten it instead of shooting it. Then in the next second it hit me and I fell to my knees. The rush was so intense that I couldn't even stand.

I started breathing heavily and I grabbed onto the toilet to keep from falling all the way to the floor. I sat there for a second and tried to keep focused. The high ran through my body like a tidal wave. I could feel it getting more intense with every beat of my heart until it finally leveled out and I was sailing on a pink cloud. I released my grip on the toilet and let myself lie on the floor. I took a pleasant ride through my mind and lived out all my fantasies without having to take a single step. I was a hero. I was strong. People looked up to me. I relived childhood experiences just the way that I wanted them to have happened. In every experience, I could imagine I was always the hero, or someone super-cool like James Dean. I loved it. I stayed there for thirty minutes before getting up.

## "This Is *Not* How You're Going to Die"

I spent the next six months shooting up all day long. My tolerance began to build, and the more it built, the more I would shoot up. Soon my arms were riddled with track marks and my veins started to collapse from the constant poking of the needle, so I wore long-sleeved shirts to hide them. My health went severely downhill. I would go for days without eating. I was skin and bones. I spent every last penny I had to get more dope.

One night about ten months after I started shooting up, I found myself in a hotel room buying drugs from a dealer who was staying there. I asked him if I could shoot up before I left, and he said I could. I sat down on the bed, filled the syringe, and shot it into my vein. I had been shooting up all day, so my mind wasn't clear, and, without realizing what I was doing, I opened another balloon and filled the syringe again. I didn't even notice that I had shot up just a few minutes earlier!

I inserted the needle into my arm and slowly pushed the plunger all the way down. Suddenly, I felt all the air rush out of my lungs as if someone had kicked me squarely in the chest. I fell to the floor and started hyperventilating. I couldn't keep up with my breathing. I felt as if my chest was violently going up and down without my doing anything. My heart was racing. Then I realized what I had done. I had overdosed and I was having a heart attack from the coke. I started to panic inside. I could see blackness closing in around me, and my vision narrowed to a tunnel of light. As the seconds passed, all I could see was that light.

I fought to stay conscious. I knew that if I could just hold on for another thirty seconds, the high would level out and I would live. But it kept building and I felt myself slipping away. The dealer grabbed me by my feet and started dragging me out of the room. He knew that I was overdosing and he didn't want me to die in his room. I kept focused on the little bit of light that I could still see as he dragged me out into the hallway and left me on the stairs.

I started vomiting as my body tried to get rid of the foreign substance, and I felt my teeth bite into my tongue and almost sever it as I convulsed. Streams of sweat were pouring down my face, and my breathing kept getting more and more violent. I was trying to keep focused and not pass out, but it was hard. I could feel myself leaving my body.

"No!" I told myself. "This is *not* how you're going to die!"

Then, suddenly, as if my commitment to stay alive had worked, I could feel myself starting to level out. The high stopped climbing. Slowly the tunnel started to widen until I could almost see clearly again. In a few minutes, it was all over and I was lying there in a pool of puke. I was still convulsing every now and then, but I grabbed the railing and pulled myself up.

I felt as if I had been run over by a bus. It was about three in the morning, and I felt as if the whole world had seen what had just happened. I was terrified that someone might have called the cops, so I went to my car and lay down in the driver's seat. The cocaine was making me paranoid and I thought that there were cops everywhere. I had been shooting coke all night and let me tell you, when you shoot coke all night the high lasts a lot longer than thirty minutes and the paranoia lasts for hours.

I was still high out of my mind and I was sure that I was surrounded and that cops had their guns drawn. I could even hear them yelling at me to put my hands up. I had my car seat all the way back so they couldn't see me but, convinced that they were moving in to arrest me at any moment, I put my hands up to the window to show them that I was unarmed. After twenty minutes or so, I slowly lowered my hands, but I stayed in that position for three hours until the sun came up. Finally, I gathered the courage to peek my head above the window, only to find that there was nobody there.

After realizing I had been imagining the whole thing, I drove home. I was in no shape to drive, but obviously I wasn't making rational decisions at that point in my life. When I got home, I went to my room. Making certain that I didn't wake my dad, I got into bed and pulled the covers over my head. My heart was still racing, and I could feel beads of sweat rolling down my face.

Then I heard the worst thing I could imagine—my dad's footsteps coming toward my room. My heart began to race even faster and the sweat poured off me like water from a hose. I could hear his footsteps coming closer and closer until he reached my door and opened it. He sat down on my bed and put his hand on my back. I was terrified.

"Are you all right?" he asked.

I kept the covers over my face and muttered, "Yes." There was no way that I was going let him see me in my vomit-covered clothes. "I was up late with some friends." I could hear my voice shaking. "I just need some time to rest."

He got up and left the room, but I think he knew that something was wrong. In fact, I think he knew that I was strung out. It was too obvious for him to ignore—I looked horrible—but he just didn't want to accept it.

I also think that he wished that one day I would be strong enough to kick heroin on my own. Sometimes it seemed as if he was giving me my space. It's hard to say, because I was really good at hiding my high, but after prolonged use, it's hard to hide the effects of drug use on your body.

I finally ran out of money. I never wanted to steal from my dad, but I had sold all my stuff and that only left his. At first I would just take money out of his wallet when he wasn't looking. Sometimes when he wasn't home, I would take things like his camcorder or computer and hock them. When he came home, I would tell him that a friend had borrowed them. I also knew the access numbers for his credit cards, so I would take them when he wasn't looking and withdraw as much money as I could without him noticing.

This went on for months until one day he got hip to what was happening. He had probably known for a while but hadn't wanted to say anything because the last thing a dad would ever want to imagine is that his son is stealing from him. I had been taking his bank statements out of the mail and throwing them away, but one day, after several months of having not received his statements, he called the bank to see what the problem was. He then found out that I had been stealing from him for months. I had stolen many thousands of dollars out of his account, and all of it had gone into a syringe.

That day when I got home, he sat me down.

"Pax," he told me, "I've decided to put you in a sober living house."

"I can stop on my own!"

"No, you can't," he insisted.

"But I can't do that—I've been shooting up! I need a detox center! Sober living houses don't offer that kind of care!"

So we decided that I stay at home and detox with medication for two weeks before I checked into the sober living house.

## "Buy My Shoes for $10"

My dad had to go to work during the day and he needed someone to sit with me. He had taken my car away and I had no money, but he knew that heroin addicts are relentless when they need to score and that I would find a way if I wasn't under constant supervision. He called my mom, who was now a model citizen, and she agreed to sit by my side each day until he got home from work.

She was great. She dropped everything that she was doing in her life and watched me for the next two weeks while my dad went to work. On the first day that she was there, I was already trying to figure out a way to hook up, but I wasn't allowed to use the phone, so that made it much more difficult.

I waited until she went to the bathroom and then I made a quick call to the dealer and told him to meet me at my house. I sat close to the window so I could see him drive by, and when he did I waited until my mom went to get something from the kitchen. Then I ran outside and met him. He didn't like it that I didn't have any money, but I begged him to please front it to me and swore I would pay him back.

He did it that time, but I knew that I would have to come up with the money for the next time. I started to run back inside, but I stopped at the mailbox and got the mail on my way in. My mom was frantic. She had seen that I wasn't in the house and was already on the phone to my dad.

"Mom, wait! I just went out to get the mail!" I said, and showed it to her.

I knew that she was suspicious, so instead of running into the bathroom to do my dope, I went over and sat on the couch. My mom used to be a hardcore addict and it was really hard to fool her, so I sat on that couch for an hour without going to the bathroom. I had hidden the drugs in my sock, and I could feel them rubbing against my leg and yelling at me to hurry up and go to the bathroom. When enough time had passed that I could see that she was starting to relax again, I told her that I needed to use the bathroom because I was going to throw up.

Once I got into the bathroom, my hands were shaking so much from the sickness that I had trouble hitting a vein. But after a few tries I eventually hit one, and I let the plunger push the fluid into my veins and into my heart. I waited a few minutes before going back into the living room because I was totally loaded. Then I went and sat back down on the couch and tried to look normal, but it was hard to hide the intense high. When my mom looked at me, I pretended that I was really sick and that I had been throwing up.

The day went by, and my dad returned to start his shift with me. He is a great dad and he did his best to keep me entertained while I was supposedly detoxing. Actually, I really was starting to get sick again by then because the dealer had fronted me only enough for one speedball. My dad and I spent the evening playing board games, working on puzzles, and watching movies. Afterwards, he gave me ice cream and ran a hot bath for me. He was going to great lengths to make my detox as comfortable as possible, but the only thing on my mind was scoring every chance I got. When it came time to sleep, he made me sleep in the same room with him to make sure I didn't sneak out and hook up while he was sleeping. He was right, I would have. But once I was in bed, he locked the bedroom door and kept the key, so there was no way I was getting out.

The next morning, I was really sick because I had done only the one speedball the day before. My dad went to work and my mom started her shift. She was also doing everything she could to make me feel better by making me lunch and keeping me company. But she did make one fatal mistake. She left her car keys on the table. I noticed them while I was sitting at the table trying to eat what little food my stomach would tolerate. I stared at them for a minute.

They were the keys to my freedom. I waited for her to walk into the other room, and when she did I grabbed them and ran. I heard her screaming, but I didn't care. All I could think about was getting high. I ran outside, jumped into her car, and took off. I saw her running after me in my rearview mirror, but there was no way she could catch up.

After a few miles, I pulled over and got out of the car. My hands were shaking from the detox and I was desperate to score, but I had no money and I knew that the dealer wouldn't front me again. I didn't care what I had to do to get the money, so I started going up to people and asking them if they would buy my shoes for ten dollars. I had left the house in such a frenzy that I had forgotten to even put on a shirt, so it was obvious from my tracks and my very skinny white body that I was a junkie looking for my next hit. That didn't stop me. I kept going up to one person after another begging and pleading with them, "Please buy my shoes!"

Most of the people I approached tried to avoid me, as if I

were a homeless person begging for money, but I kept trying. After a while I found a teenager who agreed to buy my shoes for ten dollars. I took them off and he handed me the money. Then I called my dealer from the nearest pay phone and hooked up.

The minute I had the drugs, I ran into a restaurant that was packed with people and headed straight for the bathroom. I was literally pushing people out of my way. They yelled at me, but no one touched me because they were too afraid of me—a guy covered with tracks, wearing no shirt and no shoes, and looking as if he had just crawled out of the gutter. I knew that the management would probably call the police, but I didn't care. I needed my fix.

I ran into the bathroom, ripped the balloon open as fast as I could, and loaded the syringe. Again my hands were shaking and I had trouble hitting the vein. In a desperate attempt, I shoved the needle right through the vein and out the other side. I pulled the needle out and was about to start stabbing around in my arm again to find another spot when I saw myself in the mirror.

There was blood running down my arm onto the floor. I was pasty-white and weighed 120 pounds. My hair was greasy and I had no shoes or shirt. My teeth were holding a belt around my arm, and in my hand was a syringe with blood all over it, loaded with heroin. The manager was banging on the bathroom door and screaming that he was going to call the police. It was a horrible sight and a horrible situation.

I knew that if I could just hit my vein, I could be out of there before the cops came, so I continued digging in my arm until I finally hit one. I let the plunger drop. A few seconds went by and the pain washed away as the speedball hit my heart. I waited for a minute and indulged in the high. At that point I didn't care what anyone thought of me, so I opened the door to the bathroom with the belt still around my arm and the syringe in my hand and blood rolling down my arm and proceeded to walk

through the restaurant. People started turning around and staring and then screaming, but I didn't care. It was another day in
the life of a junkie. I got into my mom's car and pulled away
before the cops showed up.


## THE DARKEST HOUR
## COMES JUST BEFORE THE DAWN

As I was driving home, the reality of my situation closed in and I
started feeling severely depressed. I knew that when I got home
my dad was going to take me directly to rehab or a sober living
house where I would have to kick with no medication or doctor's
supervision. I had lost everything in my life that was important
except for my parents' support, and I was afraid that would soon
be gone too. I was afraid to return home to face them. I started
thinking about Ashley and about how much I missed her. I felt so
alone that I broke down and started crying. Thoughts of suicide
started racing through my mind. I wanted to die but I was worried about what my parents would do. I didn't want to leave them
with that. If it hadn't been for them, I would have hanged myself.
I was beginning to think that I would forever be a prisoner of
these drugs. The thought of living the rest of my life as a heroin
addict looking to get his next hit frightened me so much that I
decided I wanted to give myself one last chance to get sober.

When I got home, my dad and mom were waiting for me.
There was no use trying to hide what had happened. My dad
wanted to make sure that I didn't have any more drugs on me, so
he frisked me the way a police officer would. It was humiliating,
but I could see the logic in it. He had already packed my bags.

I didn't say anything as he drove me to the sober living
house. It was a sad time in my life. I didn't want to be a bad son.

I didn't want to let my dad down. I felt like such a low-life. I had no idea how this could have happened to me. After having watched my mom go through it, I should have known better.

"Pax," my dad asked me again while we were in the car, "do you know why you use heroin?"

"I don't think I do," I told him, "other than because it makes me feel really good."

"No, there has to be more to it than that," he said. "There has to be something that's driving you to want to use this drug. You should think about this while you're in the sober living house, because if you can find out why you're doing it, you might be able to help yourself heal."

"The only reason I'm using is to get high," I kept insisting.

Finally he said, "I know there's a reason you're using drugs and alcohol. I don't know what it is, but we're going to find out what it is. I've scheduled appointments for you with a number of people who are going to help us look for the answer. There's some deeper reason or problem that has existed in your life from before the time when you started to use drugs that's causing this, and you're going to find it."

At first I refused to accept this concept. I didn't like the idea that there might be more wrong with me than being a heroin addict. I already had enough problems! The last thing I wanted to do was start soul-searching and digging up more problems. But from that moment on, somehow his question about why I was using heroin stayed at the back of my mind in a way that it never had before.

The sober living house had twenty other men living there who were also sober. It wasn't a big house, so the accommodations were crowded. I lived in one bedroom with three other men. There were bunk beds and I had one of the top bunks. I felt very alone and scared. I could feel the sickness starting to creep up in my bones, and I knew that in a matter of hours I would be literally unable to move. I lay on my bunk and stared off into space and wondered why this was happening to me. I had spent ten years of my life doing drugs. I wasn't sure why, but I knew that I now had time to figure it out. I was in the sober living house with no money and no car, and sitting there was my only option. When you're kicking, it can be hard to think about anything other than how sick you're feeling, but I was determined to figure it out.

Why *was* I using heroin? My dad's question kept coming to the forefront of my mind, yet I kept coming up with the same answer—because it made me feel good. Then I started to think about that a little more. What was I feeling so bad about that the heroin was making me feel good about? But I still had no answers.

My dad then made one of the most important decisions of my life. He decided that we would create our own program of healing. He was not going to rely on anyone's opinion but his own. He insisted that there was a reason I was using drugs and we were going to find it.

As soon as the worst of my kick was over, my dad started taking me on a round of appointments and tests. Acupuncture, acupressure, blood analysis, urine analysis, saliva analysis, amino acid analysis, peptides, triglycerides, and hormone analysis. He took me to psychologists, a marriage and family therapist, and hypnotherapists. He also got me a personal trainer, and I began to get strong. I was drug tested at random intervals throughout the weeks that followed. As I began to get healthy and strong again, my mind began to clear. And my dad's question stayed in the forefront of my mind because he kept reminding me, "What we're looking for is the reason why you're doing drugs and alcohol. No one can do this for you. We can help, but you must find the answer yourself."

## Finding the Answer

One night after a particularly hard day of intense therapy, I was lying in a hot bath that I had filled for myself. It was about three in the morning and the whole house was sleeping except for me. As I lay there, I kept thinking about my dad's question, "Why was I using drugs?"

I began asking myself just what my high was all about. What did I do when I was high that I didn't do when I was sober? What was wrong that using heroin fixed?

And then, in a flash, I had it! I knew why I was using heroin. It was as if the pearly gates had just opened and God had walked out and said, "Pax, my son, I'm going to free you from your addiction. I'm going to let you see *why* you've been using heroin and all the other drugs and alcohol for the past ten years."

I absolutely knew *why* with every cell in my body! I practically leaped out of the tub. I knew what lay behind my ten years of addiction.

Every time I used heroin, when I was deep into my high, I always used my imagination to see myself as a powerful, successful person—a person who always knew the right thing to say and the right thing to do. I was the master of every situation. I used to imagine myself as the hero of my dreams. And my dad was part of it, in fact most of it. I had put him on such a pedestal, and we had been so close through all the years of fishing and camping and traveling, and I had seen him do so many wonderful things: he writes books, has written, directed and produced a feature film, conducts seminars, has created several successful companies, is a master negotiator, has tons of friends and people who ask him for advice, owns real estate in different places, he rides horses, is well traveled, completely articulate and holds brilliant conversations that I wish I could participate in but can't because they're over my head.

I felt that there was nothing that he couldn't do, and I despaired of ever being able to measure up in his eyes, which is what I wanted more than anything else. Deep down inside, I secretly believed that he would never see me as I wanted to be seen. But with heroin I could soar, I could fly, I was the conquering hero. I could live out my best dream, do my wildest deed, and all in the perfect safety of my own mind.

I ran down to the telephone. I didn't care that it was three-thirty in the morning—I called him.

"Dad!" I yelled when he picked up the phone.

Can you guess what he said? "You've found the answer, haven't you?"

"Yes!" I shouted. "I've got it!"

He let out a long sigh of relief. "Thank God," he whispered.

The next morning, he and I met for breakfast, and I told him, "In essence, all I've been doing for the last ten years of my life is running away from fears. Drugs were my escape. They allowed me to feel the way I wanted to feel in life but wasn't able to. I knew that I always wanted to be a confident, strong, hand-some, smart, capable person who could do anything, and that was what the drugs did for me. They allowed me to live out the fantasies about all the things I was afraid I wasn't capable of doing in real life. And do you know why I wanted that?"

He just shook his head in wonderment.

"Because I wanted you to think I was as grand as I thought you were."

His eyes filled with tears and he said, "I've never thought anything else, Pax." And then we got up and embraced.

We talked for a long while. He told me when he was my age he didn't know anything either. He said that most of the infor-mation he had acquired came after he was thirty. He told me all he wanted was for me to be happy, to be healthy, and to fulfill the mission that I was on the planet for, whatever that was. He said that my ten years of addiction were going to play a powerful part in what would come later in my life. I had no idea at the time how incredibly prophetic his words were. He told me that at that moment he was as proud of me as it was possible to be.

After he left, I went for a long walk. The realizations were starting to come fast. It hit me that I had a really bad self-image and inner feelings of weakness, as though I didn't have it in me to succeed. It was those feelings that had led me to seek the escape of heroin. Heroin was the coping mechanism that I had used to deal with my underlying fears. They were the real problems; heroin wasn't the culprit, my fears were. This became clearer and clearer to me as the thoughts raced through my mind. And if this was true for me, then perhaps it was true for all the people who were addicted. Maybe it was just as my dad believed; maybe they, too, were medicating their underlying problems. Of course, everybody's problems are different, but the premise is still the same: it's the problems that are causing them to use substances.

My mind drifted back to my three roommates at the sober living house. One was addicted to painkillers because he had hurt his back in a car accident. It was clear that he had started to use drugs to medicate his pain, but the pain was no longer there and I wondered what other pain the meds were helping him with now that the physical pain was gone. He had told me about some of the family problems he'd had, so I thought that the key might lie somewhere in his past.

Then I thought about one of my other roommates. He was bipolar and had severe mood swings between mania and depression. When he was depressed, he said he felt like dying, and the only thing that made him feel better was cocaine. It became so clear to me that if his bipolar disorder received proper treatment, he wouldn't need the coke to feel better.

My third roommate was suffering from one of the most common problems of today, a broken heart. His wife had left him and he hadn't been able to recover from that terrible sorrow. Every night when he got home, he would drink himself to sleep. This process of numbing himself kept him from feeling the pain of his loss. What he needed was a good psychologist to help him process the loss.

I kept going over all the people in the sober living house as if I were a scientist on a research project who had just discovered the missing link to some unsolved problems.

All the rehab programs that I had been in had told me that addiction was a disease, and that it was incurable. Some of them had even said that addiction was something you were born with, and that was why we used. None of the experts ever thought to look for underlying problems as a cause because they didn't believe in that. Their thinking was that if you had the disease, you had it, and you had to learn to live with it.

I had been guided in the wrong direction all those years. Treatment programs all over the world constantly lecture us about this incurable disease that we have. But that concept won't heal anyone's underlying problems because it rules out the possibility of even looking for them! As a consequence, when addicts leave those treatment centers after thirty days, they still have the same problems they checked in with. Nothing has been resolved, nothing has been healed, and relapse is almost certain.

## MEDICATING FEAR AND PAIN

I felt myself start to smile. I knew that my dad had been giving me the missing link from the first. Even though he didn't know exactly what I was running from, he knew there was a cause beyond me looking for a high. Now, for the first time, I could see clearly what he had been saying all those years. There really was a reason for my using drugs and alcohol and, I was beginning to believe, for every other addict's using. I spent the rest of that day and most of the night thinking about all the hundreds of people I had met in rehabs and sober living houses and on the streets. We were all medicating our fears and our pain!

The next morning I called my dad and told him my thoughts. He was excited because he knew that I was on the right track. After that, I continued with my own rehab program. During the day I saw therapists and doctors, and at night I talked with my dad.

As the weeks went on, I noticed that I was getting better much more rapidly than the other people in the sober living house. They still looked sick to me, and they were sad because they had been told that they would always be the way they were due to their unfortunate luck in having being born with a disease. After a while, the other residents started asking me what I was doing to look so good, and why I was so happy.

I told them about my discovery. I started to talk to them about what might be troubling them. I opened their minds to the possibility that they were not addicts or alcoholics, but just guys like me who were medicating their fears. They began to look at drug dependency in a completely different light, one that was promising a successful outcome. I told them about my realizations and said they should get help in finding out what was at the bottom of their dependency.

I was beginning to feel confident about my new strength, but I was also afraid. I had been an addict and an alcoholic for so long that I was distrustful of my new belief, even while I was sure it was correct. I had been working with a therapist almost every day as well as many other healers, including a psychologist, a nutritionist, an internist, a doctor of Chinese medicine, and a shiatsu massage therapist. Even though I was becoming more confident, I didn't want to leave the sober living house until I was sure that all my underlying problems were resolved.

One month later, as I was lying on my bunk smiling and happy that my life was so healthy, I got another idea. If this approach to healing dependency by discovering underlying problems and solving them was working so well for me, maybe it would work as well for other people too.

I ran to the phone, called my dad, and said, "I think we should talk about opening a drug rehab that would focus on healing underlying problems using all the kinds of therapists I'm seeing now!"

Of course, by now you know enough about my dad to imagine his response. "That sounds like a great idea," he replied. "Let's talk about it."

■ ■ ■

That was the start of what has become the world's most successful treatment center. Now that we have used our holistic method to cure hundreds of dependent people, we hold out to every person who comes to Passages that he or she can take a terrible, degenerative addiction and turn it into something wonderful, just as I turned my addiction into a world-class healing center.

My dad had never given up on me, even though I had been doing drugs for ten years. He never gave up on me, no matter how bad things got or how much money I stole from him. Imagine the belief that he had to have had in me to support me in creating Passages when I had continually demonstrated that I couldn't stay sober myself. He knew that I was healed and that I would never do drugs again. To this day, I'm amazed that he decided to help me. He didn't give me just a second chance. It was a fortieth chance, but he embraced it wholeheartedly.

I've now been sober for five years, and my dad and I continue to work at Passages full time. My mom is still sober today and is a wonderful role model for me because she's always so happy.

Ashley found it in her heart to give me another chance, and we're still happily together today. I've never felt better than I do today because I've healed my underlying problems, fears, and weaknesses, so they no longer ruin my life.

I would now like to take this time to thank my dad one more time for believing in me. If it weren't for him, Passages would never have become a reality.

*Dad, you've proven yourself to be a father among fathers. You're the star in my world, and your amazing wisdom lights the way. It has been a true honor to be your son. You're the wisest person I've ever met, and every time I'm around you I feel as though I'm with an ancient sage of unquestionable wisdom. Thank you for teaching me all that you know. Without the valuable lessons you've given me, I would never have become the man I am today.*

Finally, I would like to thank you for reading my story and reaching out for help. You are brave and courageous, and this is the first step toward healing the rest of your life, free from drugs, alcohol, or addictive behavior. It takes a strong person to stand up to his or her fate and overcome the obstacles that stand in the way of freedom and success, but I believe in you. You can do it.

CHAPTER FOUR

# CHANGING THE
# TREATMENT PARADIGM

THE DAY THAT PAX CAME HOME, AT AGE EIGHTEEN, AND told me that he was hooked on heroin, I knew nothing at all about heroin except that it was an illegal street drug and that it was powerfully addictive. I didn't know, for instance, that it was one of the most difficult of the addictions to overcome, that the national relapse rate is 86 percent, and that only about 14 percent of heroin addicts ever fully recover. I didn't know that the withdrawal symptoms are severe.

Pax was crying that day, but not because of the severity of the withdrawal symptoms; he hadn't experienced those yet. He was crying because he wanted more than anything in life to loom large in my eyes. The thought of appearing as an addict was more terrible for him than the imagined withdrawal symptoms. Although his feeling of inferiority was part of what was at the core of Pax's dependency, neither he nor I realized it at the time.

I remained calm. I didn't see what he was making such a fuss about. I thought we would just "get him off the drug" and that would be that. "No problem," I told him. "Don't worry about a thing. We'll fix it in a heartbeat." I didn't know that it was the beginning of a journey into hell.

You've read Pax's story, so I'll keep mine short. I called our family doctor, got prescriptions to deal with sleeplessness, cramping, headache, muscle spasms, pain, and nausea, and sat with Pax for the next eighteen days while he went through detoxification from heroin. The first five days were the worst, with muscle cramps, sleeplessness, nausea, aching bones, and a general feeling that he wanted to die, but I provided lots of videos, conversation, and movies when he felt up to it as well as hot tubs and lots of heartfelt care. After eighteen days, when he was feeling all right again, I sent him back to school. I was glad for the experience and glad that it had been painful and severe, thinking, "He'll never do that again!"

The next six years were a battle for my son's life. I had him clean forty times or more and each time he would relapse. With every setback I would ask, "Do you know why you are doing it?" Deep inside, in that intuitive place we all have, I seemed to know that there was a reason behind his addiction. Yet each time I asked him why he was using, he said he didn't know other than it was the greatest high he had ever experienced. When I asked him what he experienced using heroin, he said it was like "looking into the face of God."

## CURING THE CAUSES, NOT PUNISHING THE PERSON

I took Pax to drug therapists, alcohol therapists, psychologists, psychiatrists, and counselors of every sort. They suggested residential substance abuse treatment programs, twelve-step programs, and more counseling, but not one of them ever sought to discover *why* Pax was using heroin. In addition, most of them wanted to prescribe prescription medications, which we always refused unless Pax was "kicking." In nearly every case, their suggestions were directed to creating an environment that would reduce his chances of using heroin—change his circle of friends, go to twelve-step meetings, don't let him out of the house unescorted, don't let him out of the house at night, pick him up from school, don't reward him with movies, TV, or videos, and have him do housework and yard work. In other words, they were advising me to punish him for his bad behavior and to keep him away from heroin contacts. None of that works. Addictive drugs are everywhere.

The "punishment" approach and "bad consequences" approach to treatment is the kind of thinking that is prevalent in every residential substance abuse treatment center in the United States of which I'm aware. They believe in scrubbing toilets and floors and in general housework. It's part of their rehabilitation process. They believe that treating their clients as if they've been "bad" will discourage them from using addictive drugs or alcohol. Their other big treatment strategy lies in telling their clients, "If you don't stop, you'll lose your health, your credit, your spouse, parents, girlfriends, car, home, money, friends, etc."

However, as you learned in Pax's story, that approach doesn't work, even when someone is at death's door. I've seen alcoholics who kept drinking even when told by their doctors that they would die in six months if they continued to do so. No matter what the threat or danger—divorce, being kicked out of a partnership, being barred from seeing children, losing health, losing jobs, going to prison—alcoholics and addicts continue to use addictive drugs and alcohol. If those kinds of threats don't work, scrubbing floors and toilets and doing housework certainly won't even touch it.

Taking this to an extreme, in 2003 I saw a newspaper article about a successful heroin treatment program in Russia. The treatment center was in Siberia. The method used in the program was to chain the heroin addict to a cot and severely beat him with a belt at intervals throughout the day for thirty days. The center reported a 95 percent success rate. That may be a successful way to treat heroin in Russia, but my guess is that even if it is successful and those addicts stop using heroin, they'll do something else to compensate for the underlying condition that they were using heroin to medicate. That condition will break out in other ways, such as fits of anger, severe depression, nervousness, rash behavior of some kind, perhaps even suicide.

It's the causes, not the dependent person, that must be corrected. That's why I see the United States' "war on drugs" as being fought in an unrealistic manner. This "war" is focused on fighting drug dealers and the use of drugs here and abroad, when the effort should be primarily aimed at treating and curing the causes that compel people to reach for drugs. We wouldn't have much need of a war if people stopped using drugs. It's like taking up a fight against the use of headache remedies; it will never work until the condition causing people's headache pain is healed. Prison programs would also benefit greatly from understanding the importance of treating the underlying causes of behavior. I don't know what the percentage of repeat offenders is, but it's high, and that's proof enough that consequences don't deter them.

## ONE-SIZE-FITS-ALL PROGRAMS DON'T WORK

Treatment for dependency at substance abuse treatment centers must change if alcoholism and addiction are to be overcome in our society. The treatment must fit the malady and *the malady is not alcoholism or addiction, or addictive drugs and alcohol.* Once the correct cause is diagnosed, healing will take place and the hoped-for cure will come about.

Achieving this goal is difficult when treatment programs are not individualized. In almost every treatment center in the world, 96 to 97 percent of their programs consist of group meetings with only one individual session a week. Most centers offer a one-program-fits-all type of service, which is rather like a department store that sells one-size-fits-all clothing. They hope that while clients are sitting in their group meetings, some magic word will drop into their laps that will suddenly make them free of addictive drugs and alcohol.

It doesn't happen like that. Every client is different. The reasons they have become dependent are different. It's like taking ten people to a clinic for treatment, one for a broken bone, one for a cough, one for a cut finger, one for acute diarrhea, another for an eye infection, and others who have different problems, and treating them all by putting a cast on their arms. In the one-treatment-fits-all approach, clients sit in group meetings all day and all evening and listen to each other's stories. At the end of the first week, everyone in the room knows everyone else's story. That goes on for three more weeks, and then most people go home with the same problems they brought with them when they arrived.

Much of the "treatment" consists of those threats I mentioned, threats about the dark consequences that lie ahead, not only for the clients themselves but also for their loved ones, if they continue their substance abuse. Trying to frighten people into sobriety by telling them of dire consequences doesn't stop dependent people. Only discovering and healing the root causes of each individual's dependency puts an end to dependency. One-on-one sessions are key because the individual issues at the core of dependency are just that—completely individual.

Another aspect of the traditional treatment paradigm that contributes to its dismal success rate is that the treatment itself often reinforces a negative self-image. First, think about the stigma that

is attached to the idea that alcoholism is a disease, an incurable illness, and you have it. That's a terrible thing to inflict on someone.
Labeling alcoholism as a disease, a cause unto itself, simply no
longer fits with what we know today about its causes.

Even more potent is the stigma around our image of alcoholics and addicts. When we were kids, we all knew what a
"drunk" was. We saw them scrounging in trash cans, reeking of
urine, and wearing sneakers with holes in them. We saw them
sleeping in alleys and hallways. We heard stories about drunks
who beat their spouses and children. Worse yet, some of us experienced such abuse, and we knew that we didn't want to grow up to
be a drunk. There is a stigma attached to being an alcoholic that is
impossible to erase, even though we're now adults and years may
have intervened. That stigma exists in the minds of everyone. The
same holds true for addicts. We knew about "junkies" and we
knew we never wanted to be one. Yet today, to speak at an AA
meeting, people are asked to introduce themselves as an addict or
an alcoholic or both.

## POWER, NOT POWERLESSNESS

I know that AA and other twelve-step programs have saved many
lives. In 1935, when there were no other programs, the founders of
AA, Bill Wilson and Dr. Robert Smith, stepped up to the plate and
took action to help a crippled population. All credit for the establishment of their wonderful, life-saving group goes to them and to
those who came after them who have continued the tradition.
However, there are hundreds of millions of people who still need
help who are not among the estimated two or three million who
attend twelve-step meetings.

Pax and I handle all the intake calls at Passages, and we talk to
thousands of people. Many of them are dead set against the AA

program. The majority of people we talk to who don't like the AA program tell us that they don't go to AA meetings for the very reason that they don't like calling themselves addicts or alcoholics.

AA purports to be open to anyone, as it is stated in Tradition Three, "The only requirement for AA membership is a desire to stop drinking," but it isn't open to everyone. It's open only to those who are willing to publicly declare themselves to be alcoholics or addicts and who are willing to give up their inherent right of independence by declaring themselves powerless over addictive drugs and alcohol, as stated in Step One, "We admitted we were powerless over alcohol—that our lives had become unmanageable."

To give up our power to change for the better is inherently distasteful to everyone, and to force people to affirm that they are addicts or alcoholics so they can speak in a meeting is shameful and demoralizing. The stigma attached to those labels is so great that most people won't tolerate it. Such declarations ruin a healthy self-image. They convince us that even if we obtain sobriety, we remain broken instead of whole, spoiled instead of fresh and new.

I believe those who are reluctant to affirm that they are still addicts or alcoholics know, even if subconsciously, that the mental programming inherent in proclaiming oneself to be an addict or alcoholic is hugely detrimental. The small benefit attached to that admission—a reminder that the former alcoholic is constantly at risk of relapsing—is far outweighed by the poor self-image it creates. In fact, that poor self-image is what contributes to their relapse. When people who believe themselves to be addicts or alcoholics come under great stress or trauma, they mentally give themselves permission to drink or use drugs as a remedy. After all, aren't they alcoholics and addicts? And what do alcoholics and addicts do? They drink and use addictive drugs.

AA literature proclaims that no one knows what creates alcoholism, that it is a mystery. At one time, people thought that the earth was the center of the universe and that the sun revolved around the earth, but then along came Galileo and Copernicus and changed all that. Today, if people were to spout that kind of nonsense, we would laugh at them. Similarly, the causes of alcoholism are well known today, and you'll read about them in this book. It's time to stop repeating the misinformation that alcoholism is a "mystery" and to instead surge ahead into the future with a new treatment paradigm, one that embraces current knowledge and our innate power, not powerlessness, to heal ourselves completely.

When Pax and I first had the idea to open Passages, an acquaintance of mine recommended that I speak to a lawyer in Beverly Hills who might have some good ideas. Because my acquaintance knew of the reservations I had about twelve-step programs, he warned me, "Be careful. He's a dyed-in-the-wool twelve-stepper."

I called the lawyer and told him about Pax's and my intentions. He asked immediately, "Is your center going to be twelve-step oriented?"

I assured him it was but said I had a few reservations about the twelve-step program. I could hear him bristle over the phone as he asked, "Oh yeah? What are they?"

I said, "Well, Step One—" That was as far as I got.

He exploded, "That's it! You just lost me. I'm outta here!"

"Wait!" I said. "Don't hang up! Tell me what you're so angry about."

"I woke up in the hospital two years ago," he replied. "I had been in a coma for three days from drinking alcohol, and I knew, absolutely knew without a doubt, that I had no power over alcohol. I resolved then and there to do something about it. I called AA, got myself a sponsor, and I call my sponsor five times a day and I go to five meetings a week. What do you think of that?"

"It sounds to me as if your power kicked in," I said. He slammed down the receiver.

How could he have missed seeing what was so evident? He had decided to take control of his drinking habit, and he did. That wasn't being powerless. It was the opposite. Every person in the AA program who's successful is living proof that he or she does have power over addictive drugs and alcohol—the power to stop. When *The Big Book* (the bible of Alcoholics Anonymous) talks about Step One, it says, "We admitted we *were* powerless over alcohol." Note that *were* is past tense, not present tense. It doesn't say that we *are* powerless over alcohol; it says that we *were* powerless over it. That statement can be interpreted in different ways, but it seems to me to imply that, although we were once powerless, we then decided to use our power to do something about our dependency.

## AN OPPORTUNITY OF UNPRECEDENTED MAGNITUDE

Times change and discoveries are made that render earlier techniques and approaches less effective. Change is inevitable. To remain rigid when the whole world is changing and advancing is to invite misfortune. The AA program in particular is challenged with an opportunity of unprecedented magnitude. Failure to meet that challenge will not do justice to the high precedent set by those two courageous men who established AA in the beginning, nor will it see AA surge into the future, blazing a new path for needy people the world over.

I apologize to all the members of every twelve-step group in the world, particularly to the members of Alcoholics Anonymous, for the times in this book when I've written what may seem like uncomplimentary comments about some of the steps and slogans used by AA groups. It is not my intention to offend you. I would love to see the AA program take off and soar, to accommodate many more millions of people. After all, our goal is the same—to help those who abuse alcohol or drugs reach a point where they are fully recovered. Like you, I believe that once recovered, people must never drink or use addictive drugs again. The only difference between us is the path that we advocate to reach and maintain the goal of sobriety.

The days are past when there was no help other than to belong to a fellowship who would lend support to people while they white-knuckled their way to sobriety. There is a more effective way. Bill Wilson and Dr. Robert Smith were visionaries, men who saw a problem and took brave, bold steps to do something about it. In keeping with their great tradition, I wish you the power to change, to slightly overhaul your program and remove the parts that many, if not most, people dislike and don't find helpful.

## RELAPSE IS NOT PART OF RECOVERY

Whenever I have used the word *cure* in speaking about alcoholics or addicts in the presence of people who work in substance abuse treatment, they've cut me off in mid-sentence, as if I had uttered an obscenity. "There's no such thing! Alcoholism and addiction are forever!" I was told again and again. Some therapists actually feel threatened when they hear me speak of a cure, and they become quite aggressive. They constantly hold up that basic precept of Alcoholics Anonymous—"Once an alcoholic, always an alcoholic" and "Once an addict, always an addict"—as proof that they're right that a cure isn't possible.

There is much apparent evidence to substantiate that belief. A government study of more than 1.5 million drug and alcohol users found that more than 25 percent of heroin users had tried five or more treatment centers without success.[1] The national relapse rate for all drugs is nearly 80 percent and even higher (86 percent) for users of alcohol or heroin.[2] Most relapses occur within a few weeks of alcoholics and addicts attempting sobriety, and many occur within a few days. Even people who have been sober for ten, twenty, or thirty years relapse. Most addicts and alcoholics relapse not just once but many times. No matter how desperately they want to quit, they repeatedly return to alcohol or their addictive drugs of choice.

In fact, there is a saying used in twelve-step programs and in most treatment centers that "Relapse is part of recovery." It's another dangerous slogan that is based on a myth, and it only gives people permission to relapse because they think that when they do, they are on the road to recovery. Just because the failure rate of some treatment programs is so enormous does not mean that relapse has to be the norm. *Relapse is not part of recovery.* Relapse is part of failure. Relapse is a return to dependency. *Sobriety* is part of recovery. You may now be starting to understand why the relapse rate is so high—it's because people are just trying to quit without curing the underlying causes, which is like trying to stop scratching while your leg is still itching.

When you look at the worldwide picture of relapse among alcoholics and addicts, it's difficult not to believe the slogan that "Relapse is part of recovery." But the success of the Passages treatment program has proven otherwise. In fact, we have trademarked the term "Easy Sobriety®," which means that staying sober is easy once you have been successful in healing the underlying conditions that were responsible for your dependency in the first place.

Many of our graduates call us with news of their successes in business, life, marriage, relationships, and general living conditions. There is an undeniable air of certainty in their voices, even an air of victory. They are grateful for their cure almost beyond the power of words to describe. And they are free.

We can hear the sound of freedom in their voices when they speak of the goals they have achieved since leaving Passages and the plans they have for the future. There's no sound of uncertainty, no sense that they're fearful that they'll let themselves down in the future as they did in the past. No specter of relapse is hovering over them. They are marrying, having children, beginning new careers, starting new business ventures, carrying on with former business ventures, continuing new interests discovered while in treatment, healing old emotional wounds, renewing broken friendships, and making amends.

## DISCOVERING THE PAIN THAT DRIVES YOU TO USE AND ABUSE

What makes the wonderful recovery of our clients possible? First, they deserve the credit. Each person did it for himself or herself. We helped, but they did it. They participated in our program fully. Even though some of them entered the program reluctantly, within a few days they had fully responded to the atmosphere of healing, to the love, and to the great expertise of our therapists.

They became willing to look deeply into their past, into the recesses of their minds, and into the reasons they were abusing substances or engaging in unwanted behaviors. They became willing to look within for the reasons for their substance abuse or behavior, and they were willing to make changes within themselves to achieve the goal of freedom from dependence. They gave up blaming other people and circumstances for their condition and took responsibility for their actions, both past and present. In many cases, we found physical ailments that were the direct causes of their dependency, and when those areas were healed, their dependence ended, particularly where pain medication was the drug of choice.

An essential key to recovery at Passages is that every staff member regards dependency as no more and no less than someone's effort to cope with life. That's how you should think of it as well. We know that you don't want to be a drunk and you don't want to be hooked on addictive drugs. You do it because you can't cope with your life without some sort of support, even if that support is damaging.

We recognize that you've used substances to try to regain your lost balance, to try to feel the way you did before the need arose to use addictive drugs or alcohol. We know that you use substances to alter your mood, to cover up your sadness, to ease your heartbreak, to lighten your stress load, to blur your painful memories, to escape your hurtful reality, or to make your unbearable days or nights bearable.

Nothing else has worked for you. No doctor, therapist, treatment center, addiction specialist, parent, spouse, sibling, or friend has provided you with a remedy for your problems and your pain, but you've found a remedy, and it works. That's the problem with addictive drugs and alcohol—they work. They may work only temporarily, and they have terrible, killing side effects, but they work.

They provide release from the pain that drives you to use and abuse substances. At Passages, we have never found it to be otherwise—*at the bottom of every person's dependency, there is always pain. Discovering the pain and healing it is an essential step in ending dependency.*

Nancy had been drinking for twenty-five years. She would drink until she passed out, and she had many bruises from her falls. The day Nancy arrived at Passages, a medical doctor took her vital signs—her pulse, blood pressure, and temperature—and said, "My dear, your resting pulse is one hundred and two instead of seventy-two, which is considered normal. Are you drinking to go to sleep at night?"

"Of course," she replied, as if it should have been obvious. He gave her a simple medication that lowered her pulse rate to normal. She finished the program and went home sober. Nancy relapsed twice and came back to Passages each time. The cause of her sleeplessness had been healed, but she was lonesome, having been divorced for several years and it was hard for her to live alone with only a maid for company. She finally came to terms with it all and is now sober more than two years. In a conversation with her about six months ago she said, "I'll never forget you or stop thanking you for saving my life."

So much for alcoholism being a disease—it's not. That poor soul had been knocking herself about for twenty-five years when any competent physician and a few good therapists could have saved her from all those years of abuse.

What people told her was that she was an alcoholic, that she would be one forever, that alcoholism was a disease, that it was incurable, and that she had it. The truth is that insofar as they could help her, alcoholism *was* forever.

What about the twelve-step meetings she had attended where they told her, "Once an alcoholic, always an alcoholic"? Can you see that meetings and centers that don't address the real causes of dependency are almost certain to be of little or no help? They actually can be very damaging.

One of the toughest jobs we have at Passages is to help our clients unlearn what they have learned at other treatment centers. A frequent conversation I have with clients when I first meet them goes like this:

"Hello, I'm Chris. Welcome to Passages."

"Hello. I'm Mary. I'm an alcoholic."

"No, you're not."

"What?"

"You're not an alcoholic."

"Yes, I am."

"No, you're not."

"What am I?"

"You're a sweet, wonderful person, who is hurting inside and who has simply become dependent on alcohol to get through the day."

A short time later, that person invariably comes to me and says, "When you told me that I wasn't an alcoholic, you made my day. It's such a relief . . . you just don't know."


## A BREATH OF FRESH AIR

What you believe is one of the most important aspects of your cure, and of living a happy life. Remember the story I told earlier about Roger Bannister breaking the existing paradigm that it was impossible for a mile to be run in less than four minutes? And how once he had shattered that belief, many other runners did the same thing?

Again, I say: Now it is your turn to end your existing thought paradigm about alcoholism and addiction and you. *You are not an alcoholic or an addict. You are not incurably diseased. You have merely become dependent on substances or addictive behavior to cope with underlying conditions that you are now going to heal, at which time your dependency will cease completely and forever.*

Please take a moment to say aloud: "*I am not an alcoholic*" or "*I am not an addict.*" (If you use alcohol as well as addictive drugs or behaviors, say: "*I am not an alcoholic or an addict.*") Now add: "*I have simply become dependent on alcohol* (or addictive drugs or addictive behavior or all of them) *and I am now breaking that dependency forever.*"

Isn't that a breath of fresh air? You might now be feeling a weight lifting off your shoulders—a weight that might have kept you bowed down for years under the yoke of that falsehood that you have an incurable disease. It will help you to say those positive statements several times a day. It's essential to your complete cure that you believe them.

From the outcome of Pax's story, the information in this chapter, and perhaps even your own experience, you know why the traditional approaches to treatment don't work for most people. Pax and I endured a grueling, horrible six years dealing with his dependency on heroin, cocaine, and alcohol as well as four years before that when he was primarily using marijuana and alcohol. But the end result of that ordeal was worth every second. You can't give up on your children or your loved ones, or on yourself if you're the one seeking the cure. Just remember that *it isn't drugs or alcohol or addictive behaviors that you're battling*, but the causes of dependency, which I'll outline in the next chapter.

You don't need to experience what Pax and I did. You can make it through, I know it. By following the information in this book, you'll soon be completely free of dependency. You can absolutely depend on that.

## CHAPTER FIVE

# THE FOUR CAUSES OF DEPENDENCY

W HAT I WANT FOR YOU IS THAT YOU LIVE YOUR LIFE peacefully, happily, and in good health, being completely free of the need to use addictive substances or behaviors. To accomplish that, you and I are going to go on a journey into the inner recesses of your mind and body, where live the causes of your dependency. There are only four:

**Cause 1:** Chemical imbalance
**Cause 2:** Unresolved events from the past
**Cause 3:** Beliefs you hold that are inconsistent with
what is true
**Cause 4:** Inability to cope with current conditions

Chemical imbalance (Cause 1) is always the main culprit in dependency. Not only can physical problems in our body cause chemical imbalances, but when Causes 2, 3, and 4 are present, they also create a chemical imbalance within us. So even though you could say that all dependency is caused by a chemical imbalance, and you would be correct, you must still uncover the specifics of Causes 2, 3, and 4 that may be at work within you and heal them if you are to be forever free of dependency.

Before reading this, it may have seemed to you that the causes of dependency were actually outside of yourself, but that is not the case. It's easy to see that Cause 1 (Chemical imbalance) and Cause 3 (Beliefs you hold that are inconsistent with what is true) exist within you. In the case of Cause 2 (Unresolved events from the past), those past events live on only in your mind, even though you may be faced with the results of those events every day. In Cause 4 (Inability to cope with current conditions), while the conditions are outside of you, your inability to cope with them lies within you. All the causes are within you, and it is there that we will go to discover and to heal the roots of your dependency.

I do not list alcohol, addictive drugs, or addictive behavior as causes of dependency because they are not causes; they do not even enter into the problem. We can become addicted to certain drugs, such as morphine, because of their addictive qualities, but after a few weeks away from them, the withdrawal symptoms disappear along with the physical dependency. So something else—one of the four causes—has to be at play for us to continue to want to take those drugs. There are many other substances and behaviors to which we can become psychologically addicted because of the high or the rush they give us, but we can easily break those dependencies once we cure whichever of the four causes listed above is underlying the addiction.

I do not list genetic tendencies as a cause of dependency for two reasons. First, they are only tendencies, and while they may predispose you to becoming dependent on alcohol or addictive drugs, you don't necessarily become dependent just because your ancestors were dependent. Some people have a genetic tendency to become fat, but that doesn't mean that they will become fat or that they must become fat. There are many people who are completely sober or who can drink socially, even though their parents and grandparents were dependent on drugs and alcohol.

If you have a genetic tendency to have a poor thyroid condition, it could lead to glandular malfunction, which produces a chemical imbalance. However, rather than dragging genetics into the picture (something you cannot control), it is more accurate to say that you have a glandular malfunction that is creating your chemical imbalance (something you can control because you can seek treatment for that malfunction).

The second reason I do not list genetics as a cause is that even though you may be genetically predisposed to become dependent, one or more of the four causes must be present for you to actually become dependent. The four causes are far more compelling than genetics. Yet I've seen many professionals in the substance abuse treatment industry nod their heads sagely upon hearing that someone had parents or grandparents who were dependent, as if that explained everything.

It's important that you do not assume your family history has fated you to dependency. If you have ancestors who were dependent on drugs or alcohol, and you have learned about the genetic factor, and you *believe* you have a genetic predisposition to become dependent, that will work heavily against you. *Genetics plays a part, but only a small one, and your tendency to become dependent, if you have one, is easily overcome by curing the four causes.*

We have had many clients who told us they had addictive personalities as a result of their parents being addicts, but as often as we looked into the matter, it was always Causes 1 through 4 that were the culprits. Among our successful clients at Passages are many who have claimed they had addictive personalities or who were genetically inclined to be dependent. The biggest chore in helping them achieve a cure was always to convince them otherwise. Additionally, nearly everyone who is dependent has a poor self-image. I don't list that as a cause of dependency because having a poor self-image is a symptom that always has roots in one or more of the four causes.

To help you understand more about each of the four causes of dependency, I will provide some examples of how each one works.

## Cause 1: Chemical Imbalance

Chemical imbalance can come from a variety of sources. The secretions of your body produce chemicals that go to your brain and create feelings such as anxiety, stress, depression, anger, joy, ecstasy, euphoria, and well-being. The foods you eat, the liquids you drink, and the chemicals you ingest also influence the way you feel, which in turn creates more chemicals. In addition, the thoughts you think and the emotions you feel create chemicals within you.

Many people, and perhaps you're one of them, walk around in an unbalanced chemical state feeling terrible almost constantly. Some feel as if they don't have enough energy to get through the day, while others feel as if they can't slow down. Some feel as if they're ill or as if they're nervous, agitated, or even paranoid that something bad is going to happen at any moment. Still others feel as if their thinking is fogged. All those feelings are the result of a chemical imbalance.

Imagine for a moment that you're out to dinner, and after dinner you feel like having a cup of coffee. You don't want caffeinated coffee because you know it'll keep you awake and you have to be up early for an important meeting, so you ask for "decaf." The waiter brings your coffee and it tastes so good that you have two more cups. On the way home, you feel as if you've been given a shot of adrenaline. The waiter obviously made a mistake and served you caffeinated coffee.

You lie awake, tossing and turning, feeling groggy and tense, all the while knowing that you have to get out of bed at six in the morning. You would like to get your hands on the waiter and throttle him. You get up, pace the floor, and drink warm milk, hoping to relax, but at four a.m. you're still wide awake. You feel terrible, as if you've been on a tightrope all night. You're distraught and angry, and you're afraid you'll make a terrible impression at your meeting.

Finally, after only two hours of sleep, you get up feeling as if you've fought World War II. The day goes badly, and by the end of it, you're ready to just crawl into bed, pull the covers over your head, and wait until that terrible time passes. The chemical imbalance caused by the waiter's mistake wasn't your fault. You're not to blame for what happened. However, you had a chemical imbalance and you suffered accordingly.

When you suffer from a chemical imbalance, caused by a malfunction in one of your glands, for example, you may turn to an addictive substance to try and feel better. If you have an excess of adrenaline, you'll be high-strung, nervous, jittery, and unable to relax. That may cause you to use alcohol to depress your nervous system and quiet yourself, or you may turn to a prescription drug such as Valium to slow yourself down. If your body doesn't secrete enough adrenaline, you'll feel sluggish and without enough energy to get through the day, and you may be using cocaine or methamphetamine to give yourself a boost.

In short, you may be a well-intentioned, good person who doesn't have any bad habits and isn't normally a drinker or a drug user, but a chemical imbalance is causing you to feel bad. Not knowing what else to do, you drink or use addictive drugs to modify how you feel. One of the main problems with alcohol and addictive drugs, as I said earlier, is that they work. Unless you identify your core condition and correct it, you'll probably continue to be dependent on substances for relief.

## From Anger to Peace

As I was writing this book, I received the following email from a former client whose chemical imbalance was cured and, along with it, his dependency. I am reluctant to include it because it is highly complimentary to me personally, but it is so representative of mail we receive almost daily from clients whose chemical imbalance we cured that I decided to reprint it here verbatim.

> Dear Chris:
>
> I have wanted to thank you once again—and again—and for the rest of my life—thank you for saving my life!!! You are truly a remarkable person, gifted and blessed you are, but the facts are this: how many people have used the expression "you saved my life"? In jest, we all have said this, but my reason remains. I was barely alive two years ago when I came to Passages, and because of your human compassion to my near death, you showed me the way and gave me the tools in life to be sober and comfortable in my skin.
>
> I will never forget my treatment at Passages, and how you showed me the path and the way it could all be done. I thought you were a very insane man, but my word! All I needed to do was look in a mirror, and well, I was the one who was insane! You are a man that has inspired me to help others as you have done. When I was a little boy, I thought the Wizard of Oz lived in the emerald city; he really never did. I found this out as a grown man. He resides in an upscale seaside community called Malibu, and I know him quite well; his name is Chris Prentiss, the Wizard of Oz, of Malibu, California. I will never ever stop thanking you!!! I have truly the

most wonderful life now—for the first time in my forty-four years—finding peace in my soul, a healing of my body, mind, and soul. Stay in touch forever. I cannot wait until the reunion.

My very best, Joseph

Joseph came to us two years ago, an angry man. There was a restraining order against him preventing him from seeing his children. He had been kicked out of the national company he helped form and he was in the middle of a nasty divorce. He was angry with everyone. He was so intolerable that at the end of his first week with us I asked him to leave Passages because he was being so disruptive to our other clients. Pax came to me and asked me to permit him to stay another few days. I reluctantly agreed.

It was the medical doctor we recommended to Joseph who saved the day. As it turned out, Joseph had an untreated chemical imbalance that had been with him since childhood. The doctor discovered this and put him on a medication that balanced his brain-wave patterns. Within a day, he became the darling of the facility: warm-hearted, generous, kind, helpful, and loving. All of those characteristics were his natural gifts, but for many years he had been at the mercy of a chemical imbalance that created anger within him and for which he was not responsible. Once the imbalance was corrected, Joseph was a treasure of a man and, as you can see from his email, continues to be so two years after graduating.

We've found that those who have a chemical imbalance like Joseph's occasionally require a medication as a temporary healing balm. Only in rare cases do they require ongoing medication. When they do, the chemical imbalance has nearly always been present since birth. In the great majority of cases, however, the cause of the chemical imbalance can be discovered with the right professional help (described in Chapter Seven) and permanently corrected without the need for continued use of medications.

## Cause 2: Unresolved Events from the Past

Carrying around hurts that you've caused others, hurts that others have caused you, or resentment about losses you've sustained—whether financial, spiritual, physical, or emotional, such as the loss of a loved one—all cause disharmony in your present life, creating a chemical imbalance (Cause 1). Childhood events, even those which you do not remember, can be causing you to abuse substances today.

Mary, a woman in her fifties from New York, had been using alcohol to the point where she would pass out nearly every night. She lost weight, couldn't function during the day, and had been hospitalized several times. She was married with two children, and the entire family was suffering. Mary had been in several treatment centers without success and her husband brought her to us without any real hope. Her psychiatrist had recommended Passages, so he decided to try our program as a last resort.

Mary knew the cause of her suffering but was unable to talk about it. She was literally unable to tell us what had happened that was causing her so much pain. She had been so abused and was so ashamed that she couldn't bring herself to talk about the memories that were so shameful and excruciatingly painful. It took two months before we learned the source of her dependency: she had been the victim of incest. Her five brothers and her father had all had sexual intercourse with her over a period of several years beginning when she was still a child. She had suppressed the memories for many years, and when they had finally surfaced she had been unable to deal with them. Alcohol blurred those memories, but she needed enough of it to black out.

At Passages, she was finally able to relate what had happened to her. Once she got it out, her craving for alcohol ended. Although the craving was gone, she was having extremely painful nightmares and she was still terrified. Over the course of her treatment, as she worked with therapists to heal her pain, she became well again. She no longer uses or craves alcohol, and she no longer has the nightmares.

## Cause 3: Beliefs You Hold That Are Inconsistent with What Is True

Beliefs you hold that are inconsistent with what is true will cause you to take actions that do not produce the results you want to bring about. That leads to disappointment, frustration, and disharmony, all of which create chemical imbalance.

Cause 3 is primarily due to the fact that your personal philosophy doesn't support you through difficult times and therefore you experience anguish, stress, and an inability to achieve your goals. If what you believe is contrary to "what is"—what others call "reality" and what I call "Universal law"—you'll butt up against that reality.

For instance, if you believe that the way to win friends is to continually insult new acquaintances, your efforts to turn new acquaintances into friends will be fruitless and you'll soon discover that your belief is inconsistent with the reality of how to win friends. However, if you adjust what you believe so it's in accord with what's true about winning friends and you act in alignment with those beliefs—perhaps by making an extra effort to be friendly, cordial, and helpful—you'll gain friends.

If you believe that the world is filled with people who will cheat you at every opportunity, you will be distrustful and will convey that distrust to everyone you meet. Since no one likes to be thought of as distrustful, making friends and keeping business associates will be difficult for you. If you are an owner of a business and believe your employees will all steal from you every chance they get, you will create working conditions where your employees will not like to work for you. Loyalty from your employees will be difficult to come by. Women who believe that all men are just out to have sexual relations with them find it difficult to achieve true love.

We've all heard people affirm when something seemingly bad happens to them, "That's just my luck," meaning they have bad luck regularly. I've heard many people say, "If it weren't for bad luck, I wouldn't have any luck at all." In actuality, people who believe they have bad luck create bad luck. Then when they experience what appears to be bad luck, they say, "I knew it." On the other hand, those who believe they are very fortunate, that the world is a generous place filled with trustworthy people, live in exactly that kind of world.

Most importantly, if you believe that you live in an unresponsive Universe that is unaware of you and that you are such an insignificant part of the Universe that truly bad things can happen to you, you will live in a state of fear with no confidence in the future. Living in that way produces unhappiness, which in turn produces a chemical imbalance that can cause you to look to drugs or alcohol as a relief. In contrast, when you learn to live in accord with what is true in the Universe, you generate feelings of peace, prosperity, relaxation, happiness, joy, and harmony. These feelings produce a chemical balance in your body, which in turn produces good feelings, which in turn leads to the production of more chemicals that produce good feelings, and so on.

## Changing Our Beliefs Can Change Our Lives

Many people hold beliefs that are not supported by what is true in the Universe, and this can adversely affect everything in their lives. One of our clients, Simone, a thirty-year-old woman from the Bronx, believed she was unattractive. She hung her head much of the time, slouched, and held her shoulders forward to hide her well-developed breasts. She grew her hair long and let it hang down to hide her face, and she had a difficult time mingling with people. Her parents believed she was unattractive and had given her that poor self-image. Her mother used to say, "Simone, you are going to have to learn to please people with your personality because you'll never get along on your looks." When Simone was nine years old, her dad told her, "Simone, don't feel bad because you're not as pretty as the other girls in your class. Daddy still loves you."

I handled the intake with her parents and they told me that their daughter's major problem was that she was unattractive and she knew it. I was surprised when I met Simone because I thought she was quite beautiful.

"I can't help it if I'm unattractive," she lamented during my first meeting with her.

"Simone, you are one of the most beautiful girls I have ever seen," I replied.

"Please don't make fun of me," she said.

"Simone, look at me," I urged. She hesitantly looked at me, but then quickly looked away. "Simone, please look into my eyes and don't look away." It took a few moments, but she finally did it.

"Simone, I swear to you that you are one of the most beautiful girls I have ever seen."

I asked her to stand in front of a mirror with me. She was reluctant, but I insisted. As we stood together in front of the mirror, I asked her to look at herself. She said she didn't want to, and I begged her to do it just that one time, for me. I asked her to stand straight, and then I pulled her hair back from her face and piled it on top of her head. I asked her to smile at herself. The difference was so amazing, even she could see it.

Simone's month at Passages was a tough one, and very embarrassing for her at the start. But she followed the advice of our therapists, kept her hair swept back from her face, learned about makeup, held a broomstick behind her shoulders to straighten her posture, and dressed in a way that added to her already great beauty. When she left Passages, she looked and felt like a radiant woman who had just been reborn. Her parents were so astonished when they came to pick her up that her mother's mouth actually hung open and she put her hand to her cheek and said, "Oh, my God." Today, Simone is a model.

What Simone had believed about herself was not consistent with what was true and it was ruining her life. She was, and is, beautiful. Acting on the false belief that she was homely, she created a miserable, unhappy life for herself. When she adjusted her belief to what was actually true about herself, she brought about the only possible result—a generous, admiring response from everyone she met. During her final week in treatment, we mostly worked on getting her to forgive her parents for the injustice she had suffered at their hands.

## Cause 4: Inability to Cope with Current Conditions

The inability to cope with current conditions in our lives produces anxiety, frustration, stress, and fear, all of which, again, create disharmony and lead to the chemical imbalance in Cause 1.

One of our clients, Harry, had been told repeatedly that he was an alcoholic, that alcoholism was an incurable disease, that he had it, and that he should just "sober up and tough it out." None of those claims were true. He was simply medicating a situation in his life that was unbearable.

At 60, Harry owned a major French winery. He loved working in the wine-tasting room, where he could talk to the patrons. He had been drinking wine moderately since he was a teenager but had become a heavy drinker in the fifteen years before coming to Passages Addiction Cure Center. Harry had been to three other treatment centers in the United States and one in Europe, but each time, he quickly relapsed after being discharged.

All our therapists reported the same thing during the weekly treatment team meetings: they couldn't discover anything wrong other than that Harry was in an unhappy marriage. He was a staunch Catholic with six children, and he believed that divorce was not an option for him. He told our therapists that although he didn't like living with his wife, he was certain that wasn't the reason he was drinking. I had a private session with him and told him that his secrets were safe with us and that if he actually hated living with his wife, he should just say so and we could get on with a remedy.

Finally, he smiled and admitted, "Yes, that's true. She's a constant source of unhappiness for me. I dislike being in the same house with her. She's a nag and a spendthrift, and she doesn't like me at all. In fact, I suspect that she dislikes me as much as I dislike her. I know that's why I drink, but divorce is out of the question."

We asked his wife to come to California and attend his individual treatment sessions with him. We did what we could to create harmony between the two of them, but that failed. It was obvious that his wife was as unhappy with the relationship as he was, but she also felt that divorce was out of the question. Then the treatment team suggested a separation. Harry and his wife acted on that, and he's now as happy as can be and, interestingly enough, so is his wife. They live in the same area, and the children visit them both. Their children are happy because they now have happy parents. When the cause of Harry's stress ended, his dependency on alcohol ended too. No trace of the so-called "disease" remained and now, more than two years later, he is still sober and still works in the wine-tasting room.

■ ■ ■

Whether the underlying cause of your dependency is a chemical imbalance, unresolved events from the past, beliefs you hold that are inconsistent with what is true, an inability to cope with current conditions, or a combination of these four causes, know this: not only are all the causes of dependency within you, but all the solutions are within you as well. You just have to know how to access them. The process starts by diagnosing what imbalances are at work within you. Once you have done that, you can treat those underlying conditions and bring your life back into balance and harmony—and you won't need alcohol, drugs, or addictive behavior ever again.

At Passages Addiction Cure Center, we address the real causes of dependency head-on with a three-step holistic treatment program. The three steps are:

Step 1 Believe that a cure is possible for you
Step 2 Discover and heal the underlying causes with a holistic recovery program
Step 3 Adopt a philosophy based on what is true in the Universe

The remainder of this book is devoted to helping you learn how to discover those hidden areas of your life that have led you to dependency and how to successfully complete the three essential steps to your total recovery.

## CHAPTER SIX

# BELIEVING A CURE IS POSSIBLE FOR YOU

WHAT YOU BELIEVE ABOUT YOURSELF, ABOUT ALCO-
holism and addiction, and about the possibility of a
cure are key factors in determining whether you'll
overcome your dependency on addictive substances and behaviors or remain dependent on them. Some of your beliefs will be
based on what you've experienced and heard about treatment for
substance abuse. Perhaps you don't believe you can be helped
because of what you've heard about some treatment centers. Perhaps you've been to several of them and you've become an un-
believer because of the poor care you received. Perhaps you've
heard that other dependent people relapse frequently, and therefore you've subconsciously given yourself permission to relapse.

Perhaps none of the above applies to you, but you've been
drinking or using addictive drugs or behaviors for so long and
have tried so many times to stop that you believe you can't be
helped. Based on experiences like those, your doubts that a cure
is possible are understandable, but they are neither accurate nor
healthy. I wrote this book to show you that a cure is entirely possible because I've seen it happen over and over again.

Here's a personal example of the power of a belief to influence behavior. When I was young, I received many speeding

tickets and that behavior carried over into my adult life. I live in California, and one day in 1968 I received a notice from the California Department of Motor Vehicles that if I received one more ticket, my license would be suspended for a year. The state suggested that I go to a local DMV office and meet with one of their psychologists. At the meeting, the psychologist commented on the many speeding tickets I had received.

"Everyone gets speeding tickets," I replied defensively.

"That's not true," he informed me. "The average person in California gets only one ticket every four years."

I was amazed. I thought that everyone was like me and got speeding tickets all the time. After that meeting, I stopped getting speeding tickets. I'd had a destructive mindset, and as I believed, so it was for me. As you believe, so it is for you. If you believe that relapse is common, you will subconsciously give yourself permission to relapse, and relapse will indeed be common for you—even though it is not common for people who have received the proper care.

One of the strong beliefs clients have at Passages is that relapse seldom occurs among our clients. *They believe that sobriety is the norm.* Of the people who have graduated from Passages, fewer than 16 percent have relapsed. This incredibly successful rate is the opposite of the national relapse rate, which, as I mentioned before, is estimated to be nearly 80 percent overall for those using any illicit drugs and 86 percent for users of alcohol and heroin.

At Passages, we routinely treat people who have previously been in three, four, or more residential substance abuse treatment centers. Some have been in ten or twelve, and our record-holder had been in eighteen different treatment centers. As I write this, he left Passages about a year ago and has been sober ever since. In contrast, we know of not one client who has successfully graduated from the Passages program who has gone into another residential substance abuse treatment center, except for two former clients who wanted to come back but couldn't wait until we had an opening.

There's a riddle that asks, "Why is the thing you're looking for always in the last place you look?" The answer is "Because once you've found it, you stop looking." The point is, like those graduates of Passages Addiction Cure Center who have stopped the cycle of relapse, you too can be helped if you follow the holistic three-step program outlined in this book. This chapter is focused on Step 1 on your path to total recovery:

**Step 1:** Believe that a cure is possible for you

Step 1 is about the profound impact of beliefs and thoughts and about the power of your mind, as in mind, body, and spirit. I'm not talking about your physical brain, that bundle of nerve tissue in the upper half of your skull, but rather about the part of you commonly known as "the observer," the part of you that thinks. Even though you use the bundle of nerve tissue to think, there is a part of you— a separate part of you—that directs the thinking. That part of you may be outside your brain or inside it, or it may even be that you think with your whole body (more on that later in this chapter).

You've probably been aware of the part of yourself that's a "watcher," that seems to be standing back and looking on while you're engaged in your life. That is the part of you that contains your beliefs—what you believe to be true about the world in which you live, Universal laws, your fellow beings, your role in life, and your values—what I refer to as "your personal philosophy." That part of you plays a key role in your healing.

The human body is an enormous healing machine, wondrous in its complexity and capability. "The body can heal itself," says Dr. Andrew Weil, founder and director of the Program in Integrative Medicine at the University of Arizona in Tucson. "It can do so because it has a healing system," which, he says, is our "best hope for recovery" from illness.[1]

Your healing mechanisms are largely automatic, but they can also be activated or suppressed by the food you eat, the activities in which you engage, the amount of rest you get, and the stress in your life—as well as by what you believe, the thoughts you think, the emotions you express, and the emotions you feel but don't express. Your state of mind is the most important factor in your healing. If you are happy, energetic, and excited about an upcoming event, or generally in a hopeful state of mind, your body's immune system will be powerfully affected and will respond accordingly by keeping you in a state of optimum health. If you are despondent, sad, unhappy, lonely, in pain, or depressed, your immune system will respond powerfully to that as well by mirroring your depressed state. Unexpressed or denied emotions create imbalance, disharmony, and eventually illness.

Not only does our thought/emotion process activate or retard the healing mechanism within us, but it also literally creates us, instant by instant. Research has shown that our thinking influences the moment-by-moment reproduction of cells in our body. What follows is a simplified version of a complicated process.

## Our Incredible Cellular Communication System

In the center of your brain is an amazing gland called the hypothalamus. It is the greatest chemical factory on the planet. Among its other functions, it produces peptides, which are short-chain amino acids, the building blocks of proteins. The type of peptide it produces is primarily determined by what you think and feel. The hypothalamus produces peptides that duplicate every emotion you experience, from anger, hate, sadness, frustration, and depression to joy, enthusiasm, and happiness.

The peptides are channeled to the pituitary gland and then into the bloodstream, where they visit all twenty to thirty trillion cells in your body (about ten thousand average-sized human cells can fit on the head of a pin). Every cell in your body has as many as millions of "receptors" on its face, and each cell has perhaps seventy different types of receptors. A receptor is a single molecule that may be "the most elegant, rare and complicated kind of molecule there is," says Candace Pert, Ph.D., in her wonderful book, *The Molecules of Emotion.*[2]

In the early 1970s, Dr. Pert was the first scientist to prove the existence of these receptors with her discovery of the opiate receptor. She describes a molecule as "the tiniest possible piece of a substance that can still be identified as that substance" and says that the receptor molecules float on the cell's oily outer membrane with roots "snaking back and forth across it several times and reaching deep into the interior of the cell."[3] She goes on to say that "the life of a cell, what it is up to at any moment, is determined by which receptors are on its surface, and whether those receptors are occupied by ligands or not."[4] A ligand is a small molecule that binds itself to a cellular receptor. There are three chemical types of ligands: neurotransmitters, steroids, and the ones we're most interested in right now, the peptides. According to Dr. Pert, as many as 95 percent of all ligands may be peptides.

The peptides dock onto the cells and create minute physiological phenomena that "at the cellular level can translate to large changes in behavior, physical activity, even mood," says Dr. Pert.[5] She further states that these chemicals, the peptides, "play a wide role in regulating practically all life processes."[6] When the peptides dock onto the receptors, they take control of all the cell's activities, including, among other things, commanding whether it will divide or not and the composition of new cells.

It's like the captain of a ship stepping on board and beginning to give orders.

In the breakthrough 2004 film *What the Bleep Do We Know!?*, Dr. Joseph Dispenza explains that when a new cell is produced, it isn't always a clone of the old cell but *a cell that contains more receptors for whatever peptide it had received that caused it to split*. If the cell received peptides produced by emotions of depression, the new cell will have more receptors for depression and fewer receptors to receive feel-good peptides.

There is a constant two-way communication going on between our body and our brain. Do you remember the times when you thought of something dire that gave you a "sinking feeling" in your stomach area?

That's the kind of communication that goes on between brain and body. Recent research has found that not only does your brain communicate with your cells, but your cells communicate with your brain and other parts of your body. In fact, the latest discoveries by scientists are revealing that we think with more than just our brain. We think with our body as well. In fact, it is not inaccurate to look at our entire body as being part of our brain. That may be a new and startling thought, but don't reject it. Many scientists now believe that we're actually a "bodybrain."

The cell's receptors play a key part in our body's incredible communication system. Dr. Pert explains that the "receptors and their ligands have come to be seen as 'information molecules'—the basic units of a language used by cells throughout the organism to communicate across systems such as the endocrine, neurological, gastrointestinal, and even the immune system."[7]

The impact of this information about how our thoughts and feelings create and condition our cells and how our cells communicate is staggering. Think about it . . . what are your cells' receptors communicating to the rest of your body right now?

You rely on cell division for the reproduction, growth, repair, and replacement of damaged, worn-out, or dead cells. An estimated 300 million cell divisions occur *every minute* to replace cells that die. Each day, 2 percent of our blood cells die and are replaced by fresh ones. Every two months, you have an entirely new blood supply. Given what I just wrote about peptides, receptors, and the role of your emotions and thoughts, you can see the chain of events that takes place as new cells are created according to what you think and feel.

If you feel depressed for an hour, you've produced approximately eighteen billion new cells that have more receptors calling out for depressed-type peptides and fewer calling out for feel-good peptides. It's as if trillions and trillions of receptors are all cupping their little hands around their mouths like tiny megaphones shouting, "Send us more depression!"

Thinking gloomy thoughts creates a body that is more able to feel gloominess than joyfulness. It also creates the *need* for more gloomy thoughts. You become addicted to gloominess. You know where that leads because you've been there: dependency.

## Dependency as the Craving for an Emotion

The total number of receptors in your body is beyond imagining. You are, in truth, one vast receptor. What's more, taking the example of depression, you'll actually become addicted to that state because your body is demanding more of what it's been receiving. It has literally developed an appetite for depression. Thus, you can think of addiction as a craving for an emotion. I will repeat that because it is essential that you grasp this concept: *Addiction, any addiction, is a craving for an emotion.*

Whether you're addicted to sex, shoplifting, or any other

compulsive activity, you're engaging in that activity to stimulate a chemical secretion that produces an effect in your brain that brings about the desired sensation, and you're addicted to that sensation. The more you engage in that type of behavior, the greater your desire for it will become. The same is true for anger. We become addicted to it because of the psychological and physiological effect it has upon us. It produces adrenaline, a powerful stimulant. We actually become dependent on the emotion of anger for the stimulation it gives us, so we fight with our spouses, our friends, our fellow workers, and anyone else we can engage in a conflict. The end result is Cause 1, chemical imbalance, because of the overload of adrenaline and other chemicals we create with our anger.

It doesn't matter whether your craving is for emotions such as excitement, anger, depression, or joy, or whether it is for the feelings you get from using addictive drugs or alcohol; the bottom line is that whatever you crave is a result of your bodybrain wanting and demanding it. In the case of addictive drugs and alcohol, when our body doesn't get what we've conditioned it to receive, it puts up quite a fuss in the form of cravings and withdrawal symptoms. Sometimes the "fuss" is so intolerable that we relapse.

The idea that you create yourself by what you think and feel is actually good news. Now that you know how your system functions, you can use your emotions and thoughts to create a body that's more receptive to feel-good states. There's only *one* way to do that—by feeling good. The way to create a body that's more susceptible to happiness and less susceptible to sadness is to be happy. I know that sounds simplistic, but it's true, and you can do it. I'll write more about that in Chapter Eight. (I've also written the book *Zen and the Art of Happiness*, which can help speed you on your way to a happy life.)

## Emotions and Healing

The Greek physician Hippocrates, who lived 2,400 years ago and is considered to be the father of medicine, gave full weight to the emotions. He told his students that negative emotions cause disease and that positive emotions are *a crucial factor in recovery*. Gifted physicians throughout the ages have told their patients that one of the most important aspects of recovery, if not the most important, is the will to live. Remember this: *Your emotional state is one of the most important aspects in curing your dependency*. It could be the *most* important.

About twenty years ago, I heard a recording of a lecture by Norman Cousins. Cousins was a writer and magazine editor who was also named to the faculty of the UCLA Medical School for many years because of his interest in the relationships among the body, mind, and spirit as these affect healing and disease processes. He wasn't a doctor, but he influenced the healing of thousands of patients either through the doctors who followed his practice of healing or by working directly with patients.

In his recording, Cousins told a story about two doctors and their respective cancer patients. One doctor received the lab report for the patient and told him and his assembled family, in effect, "I received the lab report back, and the news is terrible indeed. You have cancer all over your body. Your liver's crapped out, your stomach has crapped out, and so have your lungs. You've got anywhere between three and six months to live." He sent the man home to die.

Cousins was outraged and commented, "The audacity of that man to deliver a death warrant like that! How did he know there wouldn't be a remission? Remissions happen." The patient died within a month.

The other doctor received a similar report from the lab but

told his patient and his family, "I've received the lab report back and it indicates that you have cancer in your liver, stomach, and lungs. But I want you to know that remissions occur. We don't know exactly how they come about, but they do occur and you're going to be one of them! I want you to go home, stop working, go to the beach, laugh a lot—good, deep-down belly laughs—and concentrate on getting well, because you're going to recover!" As I remember the story, that patient recovered and lived for many years.[8]

I want to state this once again: *If you have been told and you believe that you have the incurable disease of either alcoholism or addiction or both, throw that belief overboard now. It is a ball and chain that is weighing you down and interfering with your complete recovery. This is your time to take on the belief that you live in a wonderful world, a magical world, a world where suffering people—not just alcoholics and addicts, but everyone, even those afflicted with the most diverse and difficult diseases—can be healed, and you will be one of them. It is that empowering belief that is foremost in your arsenal of recovery.*

## What Does Your Therapist Believe?

Pay particular attention to what you're about to read, for it will lay the groundwork not only for part of your cure, but also for your continued state of well-being throughout the rest of your life.

If you're not familiar with the term *metaphysics, meta* means "more than" or "beyond," and *physics* has to do with the physical world. So metaphysics is concerned with what's "more than" or "beyond" the physical world. Metaphysics is part of our effort as humans to reach beyond what we see, touch, taste, smell, and hear, to intuit what is beyond nature as we perceive it. Through metaphysics, we discover the true nature of things, their ultimate

essences and reasons for being. For me, metaphysics is a philosophy that incorporates the Universal laws that govern everything in
the physical world as well as the unseen but perceived laws that
regulate and control the world beyond the physical.

Here's a bit of metaphysical law regarding our topic of cure
that relates to one of the basic and most important aspects of
our Universe—cause and effect. Simply stated, the metaphysical
law says: "Every action produces a reaction, and that reaction is
in exact accord with the action." (Do not confuse that metaphysical law with the physical law that states that "for every action
there is an equal and opposite reaction.")

The metaphysical law of cause and effect applies to your
beliefs in the following way. Every belief that you hold manifests
itself in some manner by causing you to take some form of
action, by preventing you from taking action, or by causing you
to feel a certain way. When we apply this metaphysical law to the
cure of addiction, we see that healers and therapists who don't
believe that a cure is possible will not talk about a cure, will not
look for a cure, and will most likely fail to bring about a cure.

Worse than that, they'll poison your mind with the belief
that a cure is impossible and that you're doomed to be an addict
or alcoholic for the rest of your life. That belief results in a self-
defeating attitude that undermines the great gains that are possible. The only time that this poisoning would have any positive
effect would be if you got angry when told that rubbish, refused
to accept that belief, and set out to prove the therapist wrong.

Would you really do your utmost to succeed in the treatment
of any ailment if you believed that you were beyond all hope of
recovery? What caliber of treatment would you expect from a
therapist who believed that? How do you think your body and
mind would respond if you were surrounded by psychologists,
psychiatrists, or drug and alcohol counselors who believed that
"Once an alcoholic or addict, always an alcoholic or addict," that

alcoholism and addiction are incurable diseases, and that your current stay in rehab will be one of many? You would be immediately deprived of hope.

Those misguided "helpers" poison the minds of those who come to them. It's not that they're doing it deliberately; they don't know any better. That is sad, because hope—the hope for a cure, the hope for a bright, clean future free of addictive substances and behavior, and the hope for a return to a normal, healthy life free from the excessive fear of relapse—is the most powerful stimulus for complete recovery.

Compare those misguided healers with healers and therapists who believe that a cure is possible. They will talk about a cure, will look for a cure, and will be more likely to bring about a cure. Most important, they will instill in you the belief that a cure is not only possible, but probable, and that you are definitely going to be among those who will be completely cured. That belief alone results in the self-empowering attitude that sets the stage for your recovery.

## Saying "Yes!" to a Cure

The importance of holding the right belief is based on the fact that a part of your brain can't tell the difference between an imagined experience and an actual one. Some people who imagine hearing a piece of chalk making a screeching sound on a blackboard experience a shiver up their spine. For others, thinking of the taste of a lemon makes them pucker. Dreams are another good example. When the events in a dream frighten you, you feel just as frightened as if the events were happening to you in your waking state.

When researchers from Harvard University tested subjects in a brain scanner, they found that seeing a picture of a tree and imagining a tree activated the same parts of the brain.[9] In the same way, when you imagine that a cure is possible, everything in you—your physical body, your immune system, your mind, everything—responds with healing energy, with a forward, impelling motion that says "Yes!" to a cure.

Your mind is powerful. You may have heard the saying "That which you can conceive, you can achieve." Or, as auto manufacturer Henry Ford said, "Whether you believe you can or you can't, you're right!" If we believe that a goal is possible, we will set out to accomplish it. If we believe that a goal is impossible, we will fail even to begin. In this state of mind, even if help is offered to us, we'll usually reject it because we still believe that the goal is impossible.

Seven years ago, muggers wounded a man of about thirty. They slashed his arm with a knife and cut it to the bone from his shoulder to his elbow. Everything was severed—the veins, ligaments, arteries, muscles, tendons, and nerves. For several years after his wound healed, he continued to experience severe pains in his arm and shoulder. He sought help for the pain and his doctors prescribed Vicodin. It numbed the pain, but the pain returned when it wore off, and he continued the drug.

As a consequence, he became dependent. Because he didn't want to remain hooked on Vicodin, he sought help from many neurosurgeons and psychiatrists. He visited fifteen neurosurgeons in a three-year period without obtaining relief. The last one told him, "Son, you have neuropathy. The nerves in your arm are degenerating, and you'll have pain for the rest of your life. I suggest you go to a pain management clinic." He was devastated by the news, but he refused to believe that he couldn't obtain relief.

About three years ago, he called Passages and I took his call. I told him of our physical rehabilitation program and of our Director of Physical Rehabilitation, Dr. Lyn Hamaguchi, a Japanese woman who was trained in the arts of acupuncture, acupressure, and healing by a doctor of Traditional Chinese

Medicine from mainland China. I encouraged him to come to Passages and I told him of the wonderful cures that Dr. Lyn had helped to facilitate with acupuncture and acupressure. I told him that I would be surprised if she couldn't do the same for him, despite what he had been told by the neurosurgeons.

He believed me and enrolled in our program. In *one* treatment, Dr. Hamaguchi relieved him of approximately 90 percent of his pain, and he then found it easy to overcome his Vicodin addiction. There was, of course, much more to his treatment than just acupuncture. He had to psychologically overcome the pain of the loss he felt at having taken three years to search for a cure and he had to become reconciled to the memory of the attack and the anger he felt toward his assailants.

Can you imagine this man's fate if he had believed what the doctors had told him and had given up? He wouldn't have sought treatment, he might still be fighting his pain, and he might still be hooked on Vicodin or some other pain medication. Today he continues to be completely free of addiction.

## The First Glimmer of Hope

Confucius, who lived 2,500 years ago said, "It is the saddest of all things, when a person gives up." One of the most comforting and important messages we offer those who contact us at Passages for the first time is hope—the hope that they or their loved one will be cured. We can hear the relief in their voices, as if they had been suddenly pardoned from a long prison sentence. The treatment program for that caller or that caller's loved one begins with that first phone call. At graduation ceremonies, graduates frequently refer to that first telephone conversation with Pax or me as the moment they felt their first glimmer of real hope. They also talk about the first fellow client who greeted them when they arrived at Passages.

Meeting someone who is also in the Passages program is an important moment. When clients first arrive and walk through that huge front door and someone who's been in treatment for a week or two or three comes to greet them and tells them that they're in the best place in the world, that they'll be helped, and that they themselves are experiencing a miraculous cure . . . well, it makes all the difference. And because all our clients have had the experience of being welcomed, they're eager to pass along the comfort to another.

Clients and others have also told me of the despair they felt, the same despair Pax and I felt, when they heard for the first time that addiction or alcoholism is a disease, that it is incurable, and that they would be addicts or alcoholics for the rest of their lives. Those statements make us feel as if we've been sentenced to a cold, dark prison cell.

It is essential to your complete recovery that you surround yourself with people who believe that a cure is possible for you. Your therapists should speak quite naturally of a cure and how to achieve it. The people who offer us love and hope when we come in for treatment are supplying us with courage and enthusiastic support at a time when courage and enthusiastic support are crucially needed. It's like being released from that dark prison cell and walking out into a ray of warm sunshine. You may step out of that cell now, because you're being exposed to that ray of healing sunshine in this book.

## CHAPTER SEVEN

# CREATING YOUR HOLISTIC RECOVERY PROGRAM

N EARLIER CHAPTERS, I DESCRIBED HOW CRUCIAL IT IS TO find and heal the real causes of your dependency so you can achieve permanent recovery. I said that the problems underlying dependency always have both physical and psychological components—anything from anemia, hypoglycemia, or a sluggish thyroid to attention deficit disorder, brain-wave pattern imbalances, or deep emotional pain. The "why" may not always be apparent to you because it's hidden by the drugs, the alcohol, and the other symptoms that mask your pain. It takes a carefully selected support team to help you uncover and treat the specific reasons you are depending on addictive substances or behaviors to cope with your life. It takes a personalized approach. That's what Step 2 on your journey to total recovery is all about.

**Step 2:** Discover and heal the underlying causes with a holistic recovery program

This chapter will show you how to put together your own personalized program to achieve total recovery and optimum health by enlisting the help of several key health practitioners. These practitioners will look at your individual situation from different points of view, treating every aspect of you, which is what makes it a holistic approach. *Holistic* means relating to or concerned with wholes or with complete systems rather than the treatment of parts. In this case, it means freeing you of dependency forever by curing all of you—your mind, body, and spirit.

Your team of specialized doctors, therapists, and health practitioners will help you work with your body, your mind, your emotions, and your spirit to stimulate your body's self-healing potential. The right team will guide and protect you as you delve into areas that have been hidden from you but that hold the keys to your freedom. They will assist you to prevent relapse and will support you as you regain your passion for life.

Jane came to Passages to recover from alcohol dependency and, as with all patients at Passages, we took a holistic, integrated approach. Jane was thirty-five and married. She was drinking two to three bottles of wine daily, beginning at sunset and continuing until she passed out for the night. Initial interviews revealed that Jane had been bulimic (an eating disorder). After detoxing from alcohol, she began having panic attacks during the evening sessions, followed by severe nightmares in the middle of the night.

Over the course of treatment, we learned that from ages eight through eleven, Jane had been molested by her stepfather and had never told a soul. The goal of treatment was to resolve the anxiety, guilt, and shame that she had been numbing with alcohol. Her particular treatment program consisted of:

- regular sessions with a medical doctor, who ran a multitude of laboratory tests to diagnose any physiological causes of her bulimia as well as any other maladies that might be present

- treatments from an acupuncturist to improve her vitality and diagnose any areas of imbalance in her organs and other body systems
- sessions with a male psychologist with whom she could discuss the abuse and receive empathy and care instead of further trauma
- sessions with her mother facilitated by the marriage and family therapist to deal with confusing feelings of rage at her mother for not protecting her
- sessions with the hypnotherapist to rebuild a more positive inner sense of self, free of guilt and shame (the hypnotherapist was also helpful in causing the repressed memories to surface)
- training in the techniques of yoga and meditation to facilitate inner calm
- consultation with a nutritionist to facilitate more realistic and healthy attitudes towards food and diet
- weekly physical training to facilitate healthy body awareness and self-care
- weekly sessions with a chemical dependency counselor to learn about the dynamics of alcohol dependency and learn alcohol-free methods for dealing with anxiety and fear
- marital sessions with the psychologist and the marriage and family therapist to build stronger marital communication and to educate her spouse that the issue of childhood trauma was the condition underlying and causing the alcohol dependency
- several group therapy sessions per week, where she could share with others who were nonjudgmental (many of whom had similar experiences), to facilitate her assertion skills and boundary-setting skills and to relieve her guilt and shame about her childhood experiences.

Each one of these therapies and treatments, most of them one-on-one sessions, reinforced Jane's healing in different but mutually supportive ways. They were crucial to her full recovery.

If you are going shopping for a treatment center rather than putting together your own program, always ask the "how many" questions: How many individual sessions will I receive each day, each week, each month? If the answer is forty or less per month, keep looking. At Passages, clients receive about seventy one-on-one sessions per month. Always ask whether the program includes the kinds of effective therapies discussed in this chapter and how many sessions you will receive—how many clinical psychology sessions per week, how many marriage-and-family counseling sessions per week, how many hypnotherapy sessions per week, how many physical fitness sessions per week, how many spiritual counseling sessions per week, etc.

## Knowing Your Body

The state of your body is a key factor in how you feel. When one or more of your body's systems becomes dysfunctional, you can become out of balance. An out-of-balance body can lead you to medicate unpleasant feelings with drugs, alcohol, or addictive behavior, which can then lead to dependency. Once your mind and body are in a state of optimum health, you won't feel the need to alleviate those uncomfortable feelings with addictive substances or behaviors. As you construct your recovery program, it will help you to understand the functions of the various glands and organs that make up your body's systems. Here is a short summary:

> **Glands:** A gland is an organized collection of cells that
> respond to chemical and electrical stimuli and adjust their

secretions in response to these stimuli. There are two kinds of glands, those that have ducts and those without ducts (ductless glands), which pass their secretions directly into the bloodstream. Examples of glands include the pineal, adrenal, hypothalamus, thyroid, pituitary, placenta, pancreas, and parathyroid. Secretions from these glands play a powerful role in obtaining and maintaining your overall balance of health.

**Organs:** Organs are structures that contain at least two different types of tissue that function together for a common purpose. The human body has ten major organ systems:[1]

1. **Muscular system:** The main role of the muscular system is to provide movement. Muscles work in pairs to move limbs and provide the organism with mobility. Muscles also control the movement of materials through some organs, such as the stomach and intestine, and the heart and circulatory system. The main organs are the skeletal muscles and the smooth muscles throughout the body.

2. **Skeletal system:** The main role of the skeletal system is to provide support for the body, to protect delicate internal organs, and to provide attachment sites for the organs. Bones, cartilage, tendons, and ligaments are the main organs.

3. **Circulatory system:** The main role of the circulatory system is to transport nutrients, gases (such as oxygen and carbon dioxide), hormones, and wastes through the body. The circulatory system consists mainly of the heart, the blood vessels, and the blood.

4. **Nervous system:** The main role of the nervous system is to relay electrical signals through the body. The nervous system directs behavior and movement and, along with the endocrine system (glands that produce internal

secretions), controls physiological processes such as
digestion and circulation. Its major organs are the brain,
the spinal cord, and the peripheral nerves.

5. **Respiratory system:** The main role of the respiratory system is to provide gas exchange between the blood and
the environment. Primarily, oxygen is absorbed from the
atmosphere into the body and carbon dioxide is expelled
from the body. Its major organs include the nose, the tra-
chea, and the lungs.

6. **Digestive system:** The main role of the digestive system
is to break down and absorb nutrients necessary for
growth and maintenance and to provide elimination.
The major organs are the mouth, esophagus, stomach,
and small and large intestines.

7. **Excretory system:** The main role of the excretory system
is to filter out cellular wastes, toxins, and excess water or
nutrients from the circulatory system. The major organs
are the kidneys, the ureters (the tubes that carry urine
from each kidney to the bladder), the bladder, and the
urethra (the duct that carries urine from the bladder out
of the body).

8. **Endocrine system:** The main role of the endocrine system is to relay chemical messages through the body.
These chemical messages, in conjunction with the nervous system, help to control physiological processes such
as nutrient absorption and growth. Many glands secrete
endocrine hormones, among them the hypothalamus,
pituitary, thyroid, pancreas, and adrenal glands.

9. **Reproductive system:** The main role of the reproductive
system is to manufacture cells that allow reproduction.
In the male, sperm are created to inseminate egg cells
produced in the female. The major organs are the
ovaries, oviducts, uterus, vagina, and mammary glands

in the female, and the testes, seminal vesicles, and penis in the male.

10. **Lymphatic/immune system:** The main role of the immune system is to destroy and remove invading microbes and viruses from the body. The lymphatic system also removes fats and excess fluids from the blood. Its major organs are lymph, the lymph nodes and vessels, white blood cells, and T- and B-cells.

## Choosing the Right Practitioners for You

The remainder of this chapter will explore the specific kinds of health professionals you can work with to create your own effective treatment program. Each of the therapies and techniques outlined here has helped clients at Passages Addiction Cure Center to achieve success and is key to your recovery program.

In terms of which practitioners to work with in your local area, in each case choose wisely. In Chinese medicine the first priority is always "the intention to heal" because the beliefs of those who are treating you are of supreme importance. Dr. Andrew Weil, who recounts many examples of spontaneous healing and self-regeneration in those who had life-threatening illness and chronic pain, has observed that "successful patients often ally themselves with health professionals who support them in their search for answers. . . . What you want is a professional who believes in you and in your ability to heal yourself." In addition, he says, successful patients "do not take 'no' for an answer."[2]

As I emphasized earlier, you do not want to be treated by someone who believes that a cure is impossible or who believes that addiction and alcoholism are diseases and that you're afflicted with one or both of them. Such people instill a poison in your mind that not only retards your healing process, but also causes illness and despair. Their hopeless words deprive you of two of the main ingredients of healing: hope and enthusiasm.

In addition, the health practitioners you choose for your support team should first and foremost seek to identify your chemical imbalance and discover what is causing it. They should not just prescribe Band-Aids to soothe your symptoms. They must have the intention to get to the core of why you are out of balance and what you are self-medicating with alcohol, drugs, or addictive behavior. All practitioners, especially medical doctors, should be spending 95 percent of their time diagnosing where and why imbalances exist and 5 percent of the time suggesting remedies to correct those imbalances.

Your practitioners should also be communicating with each other. Working together, they can accomplish more than any of them can working alone. Ask your medical doctor to communicate to your psychologist or vice-versa. Have your doctor of Traditional Chinese Medicine (the acupuncturist) contact your medical doctor with his or her findings. It is also helpful to have the psychologist and hypnotherapist communicate with each other. Of course, you can do all the communicating between your therapists yourself, but if you decide to do that, make sure you take notes when talking to your therapists and get copies of test results to pass on. In addition, be sure that each practitioner who is part of your personalized recovery team reads this book. Only then will each one be on the same page as you and the others on your team are.

To give you a balanced perspective on how to go about finding the level of care you need to be cured of your dependency, this chapter has a section on each of the therapies I recommend. Each section includes basic questions and answers. The answers have been provided by therapists and health practitioners who work with dependent people every day at Passages and who are a key part of the success of the Passages program.

You will learn about the role of each practitioner, how the expertise of each one will support you, what you should expect from your doctors and therapists, and how to find qualified professionals who can help you where you live. You may find that we have provided more information than you need, but by reading these pages you will know what to expect. I have started the next part of this chapter with my answers to some of the commonly asked questions about curing dependency with this approach and about putting this program into action.

## SOME FREQUENTLY ASKED QUESTIONS

**Q:**  How long will it take me to cure my addiction?

**A:**  The amount of time it takes to cure an addiction is different for each kind of dependency and each dependent person. First, remember you are not curing yourself of addiction; you are curing yourself of a dependency on either substances or addictive behavior. There is probably a huge difference between this concept and what you may have been taught about your dependency and about yourself. To give you a general answer to how long the program will take, people generally come to Passages for thirty days. Some stay longer, but most stay for thirty days. They receive intense one-on-one treatment. If you set up that kind of intense therapy, you too should be able to cure your addiction in thirty days or less. If you have a less intense program, it may take longer.

For more than seventy years, doctors and therapists of every kind have been trying to learn how to overcome addiction by treating people for addiction. Addiction is *not* the problem and never has been, including addiction to ethanol (alcohol), what they call alcoholism. Treating people for addiction is a fruitless search because addiction to ethanol and other drugs or to addictive behavior is not the problem. Addictions are merely symptoms of underlying conditions. Once you discover what your underlying conditions are and heal them, your addiction will disappear. It will end just as surely as scratching ends when the itching stops and taking aspirin ends when the headache disappears.

In the same way, most of your withdrawal symptoms will end after you have been away from drugs, including alcohol. What cravings remain are due to the underlying cause of your dependency. The cravings hang on if the cause is still present, still causing you annoyance, pain, or discomfort of some kind. Because you have grown used to coping with your discomfort with a substance or with addictive behavior, your learned response is still present. It will cease when the underlying cause or causes are discovered and healed.

Just remember this: there *is* a reason or reasons you are addicted, and it is *not* the addictive quality of the drug or behavior. The addictive quality of the drug will produce withdrawal symptoms, but usually not for very long because our bodies are amazingly adaptive. The underlying cause or causes are one or more of the four causes listed in Chapter Five. When you discover what is really causing your addiction and heal it, your cravings will cease and you will be able to effortlessly stop. We are hearing that report from people all over the United States and from other countries as well. You can do it too.

**Q:** I live in a small town that does not have the kind of therapists you recommend in your book. What can I do?

**A:** Look for practitioners in the big town that is closest to you, even if it is far away. There is no substitute for the therapies I have recommended. It is worthwhile making a temporary move to a larger city or traveling to that city and staying there for a few days out of the week. If you can get several people together who are addicted and need help, you may be able to arrange for therapists to drive to your town on a specific day and treat each person individually, one after the other. Additionally, the therapists could hold a group meeting if the group wants to do that. If there is absolutely no other way, some therapies might be able to be done over the phone, but I have never tried that nor have I ever heard from anyone who has.

**Q:**  I do not have enough money to hire the therapists you recommend in your book. Now what?

**A:**  That's a tough question, but don't let money stand in your way. Try to find the kind of medical doctor, doctor of Traditional Chinese Medicine, or other practitioner described in this book and ask him or her to be part of your team with the idea that once the team is assembled, the doctor would be able to advertise himself or herself as part of a Passages model team. If the doctor or practitioner agrees, you can then assemble the rest of the team on the same basis. That plan will not only bring in new clients for the doctor and therapists, but it will also enable them to offer to their own clients the new and valuable service provided by such a team. They could be at the forefront of the new revolution in addiction treatment. Creating a holistic treatment team is an idea whose time has come, and some medical doctors and therapists are starting to understand that they must embrace the professions of other competent therapists to help their patients.

Working for free is not a new concept. It's called *pro bono* and it has been around for thousands of years. *Pro bono publico* (often shortened to *pro bono*) is a Latin term meaning "for the public good or welfare." It is used to describe professional work that is done for the good of the public without compensation. When you find the doctor you want to help you, give him or her a copy of *The Alcoholism and Addiction Cure*. Once the doctor has read it, he or she may be inspired enough to help you, provided you do the work of finding the other therapists.

Give this book to each practitioner you approach and explain what you are doing. Get them excited about being a part of a wonderful new team approach to healing addiction (or anything else for that matter). Perhaps you could afford to pay for the lab tests, under $1,000, so that the doctor will not have any out-of-pocket expenses. No matter what difficulties you come up against, do not give up. See this through to the end.

**Q:** What if my doctor or other therapists refuse to read the book?

**A:** Look for another doctor or other therapists. It is not healthy for you to work with therapists or doctors who think they know everything and are not open to new information. Pay them to read the book if you must. It is essential that everyone on your team read it so that they will understand your goals and how you want your treatment to be approached. If they do not all read the book, a common goal is unlikely to be achieved.

**Q:** What if someone who needs help won't read *The Alcoholism and Addiction Cure*?

**A:** First, read the section of this book on denial (page 42). I have also recorded *The Alcoholism and Addiction Cure* in an audio version on CD. It is ten hours long. Perhaps the person who needs help would prefer to listen to the audio version of the book rather than read it. If he or she refuses that offer, get someone else to make the attempt. Do not give up. The life of the person you care about is at stake.

Perhaps that person believes that there is no hope or that help is unlikely to be effective. Perhaps that person has tried other books or other treatments without success. Perhaps he or she is disillusioned. Think of other ways to reach the person you care about. Try choosing a particular section of the book you think will appeal to that person and read it to him or her. Then offer the book again. Keep at it and you will eventually be successful. It's a wonderful gift you are offering. It's the gift of freedom—freedom from a life of addiction.

**Q:** What can I do if my doctor will not detox me?

**A:** Go to your local hospital or seek another doctor, one who is knowledgeable about detox. With the medications that are available today, beyond being uncomfortable for a few days, detox should be relatively pain free and safe.

**Q:** If I have been using alcohol or drugs for a long time, is there a danger if I just stop drinking alcohol or using drugs on my own?

**A:** Yes! There is a danger of seizure and other complications when withdrawing from alcohol. Always go to a medical doctor who is knowledgeable about alcohol detox before stopping alcohol intake. The doctor will provide you with anti-seizure medication and anything else he or she deems necessary to protect you while you are detoxing. The same holds true when you are detoxing from barbiturates, benzodiazepines, and opioids; a doctor should also be involved when you are detoxing from those substances. In general, it is best for a physician to assess the risks to your health whenever you plan to detox from any substance.

**Q:** As part of your recovery program, you highly recommend laboratory testing to assess imbalances. Which laboratory do you recommend my doctor use?

**A:**  There are many good laboratories in the United States. As long as your doctor requests the necessary tests, the results should be sufficient. We recommend Genova Diagnostics in Asheville, North Carolina, because they have helped us develop the tests that are most beneficial in discovering potential causes of addiction. Genova's unique testing, such as NutrEval, provides the ability to determine an individual's need for vitamins and minerals, essential fats, amino acids, probiotics, and antioxidants.[3] (The next section explores this topic further.)

## INTEGRATIVE MEDICINE

To reach your goal of optimum health, first enlist the support of a good medical doctor. Search for a doctor who incorporates natural, holistic approaches to wellness, thus integrating mainstream and alternative medicine.

Even if you do not feel that there is anything physically ailing you, be sure to work with a medical doctor. You will be amazed what you will discover about yourself by having a proper diagnostic evaluation made by a competent medical doctor *who also practices alternative medicine.* This is your opportunity to tune up your entire body.

Your physician will help you through detoxification and withdrawal, diagnose minor or major ailments, and evaluate whether your glands and organs are functioning properly. He or she will also check whether you have any allergies and diagnose where you are deficient in key vitamins and minerals, a crucial factor in the health of those who have been alcohol or drug dependent.

Your holistic doctor will probably suggest that you purify the interior of your body with various cleanses, such as a liver cleanse, gallbladder cleanse, colon cleanse, and blood cleanse. These will clear your mind and make your skin glow. Your sense of well-being and vitality will increase greatly within a few weeks of completing the cleanses. If your doctor does not suggest those cleanses, ask for them.

*Before making your appointment, be sure the doctor uses nutritional supplements, vitamins, dietary consultation, diet planning, and changes in lifestyle as a regular part of the treatment regime he or she creates.* When choosing a doctor, you can apply the same "Questions to ask yourself on your first visit" that are included in the section of this chapter on hypnotherapy. Remember, you are creating and are in charge of your plan for a return to optimum health and the doctor is in your employ.

Most doctors who have a holistic approach advertise their specialty. You can look in the yellow pages for a listing. There are also many Internet sources that will help you locate the right doctor. (If you don't have a computer, ask a friend to use his or her computer or visit a place that rents them by the hour.) You can find lists of doctors in every state who practice holistic medicine by going to your favorite search engine and typing in "alternative medicine," "holistic medical practitioners," or "homeopathic medical physicians." The American Association of Naturopathic Physicians also maintains a practitioner's directory on the Internet.

In the following question-and-answer section, Patrick Hanaway, M.D., medical director of Genova Diagnostics in North Carolina, and Gayle Madeleine Randall, M.D., and Litos Mallare, M.D., doctors we recommend to our clients at Passages, provide additional resources to help you find the best doctor for you. They discuss the role a good medical doctor will play in your recovery, what you should expect from your doctor, and why a holistic approach is important.

### Questions and Answers with
### Patrick Hanaway, M.D.

Q:  What is integrative medicine?

**Dr. Patrick Hanaway:** Integrative medicine (also known as holistic medicine, functional medicine, complementary medicine, alternative medicine, or whole medicine) is the modern version of looking at the whole person in the process of regaining health and well-being. Over the past one hundred years, medicine has progressed rapidly in the areas of surgery, emergency care, trauma care, and infectious disease. However, the nature of most health problems is that they recur, as they are the result of poor behavioral choices such as drinking, smoking, overeating, using drugs, not sleeping, not exercising, etc. When our body, mind, and spirit are not in alignment, we consciously or subconsciously medicate with food, alcohol, drugs, sex, television, and other diversions to forget or suppress the symptoms of imbalance.

Many drugs within modern medicine, such as antidepressants and pain pills, have been developed to suppress those symptoms of imbalance. The approach within integrative medicine is to support the individual by listening to the whole story of illness and imbalance within his or her life. The goal is to make sense of what caused the imbalance, understand the triggers that were the "straw that broke the camel's back," and discover the factors that limit the body's ability to return to balance.

Q: Can the integrative medicine approach be used to help someone with addictions?

**Dr. Patrick Hanaway:** Yes! This approach can be used to help treat dependency on alcohol, other substances, or addictive behavior such as food bingeing, smoking, excessive TV watch-ing, excessive Internet surfing, and excessive indulgence in sex, shopping, or working. In fact, treating the whole person—body, mind, and spirit—is critical to success. Healing (a word that comes from the Old English *hælp* and other root words meaning holy, sacred, or to make whole) requires an inquiry into the source of illness and imbalance. At Passages, the goal is to bring many healing modalities together to help each individual dis-cover the source of his or her imbalance and then to support the process of healing. That is true healing. Healing is not simply taking a drug to suppress the feelings of imbalance that are caus-ing the addictive behavior.

Anyone whose body and mind are not in balance will have symptoms like sadness, fear, anger, unworthiness, arrogance, or a feeling of being ill at ease or unwell. A holistic approach to healing requires that we change the way we view these symp-toms. We must recognize these symptoms not as problems but as signposts of imbalance that can start us along the journey to our healing. Ancient medical systems such as Traditional Chi-nese Medicine and Ayurvedic Medicine, which have been in use for 5,000 years, have long recognized symptoms as indicators of imbalance. Western medicine, on the other hand, has focused its energy on suppressing those same symptoms under the mis-taken belief that health is simply the absence of disease.

**Q:** How will a doctor of integrative medicine help me?

**Dr. Patrick Hanaway:** First, a doctor of integrative medicine will lis-ten to your story and inquire about your sources of imbalance—that is, he or she will connect to you and relate to you as a whole person, not merely through some diagnostic label of "addict" or "alcoholic" that he or she has arrived at in a few minutes of conversation.

The results of many studies show that physicians spend only

eight minutes of direct contact time with each patient. The physician, on average, offers only seventeen seconds of listening before interrupting the patient. Usually, that prevents the patient from being able to tell the story he or she came to tell, a story that could reveal the heart of the matter or at least provide clues to the mystery of the imbalance. The integrative medicine physician takes a broader view of healing, allowing more upfront time for discovery and for personalizing treatment, which increases the opportunity for success.

Your physician's role is to evaluate the interconnected systems within you to create individualized treatment that is tailored to your specific issues and needs. The doctor will consider systems of gastrointestinal function, immune function, inflammation, detoxification, energy metabolism, hormonal balance, physical structure, and mental processing.

A multidisciplinary approach like the one used at Passages, where twelve different therapists work with each client, allows the treatment team to more clearly see all of the aspects of an individual, like seeing all of the facets on a diamond. Whereas one therapist may not see the "flaw" in the diamond, many therapists who are all searching for it in different ways are more likely to discover it and set the person on the right path toward healing. Once the "flaw" is discovered, all the therapists are made aware of the discovery and focus their considerable expertise toward restoring the person to perfect balance.

Q: How does nutrition come into play and how are nutritional treatments individualized?

**Dr. Patrick Hanaway:** After acute detoxification, when a person has stopped drinking, smoking, toking, shooting up, snorting, or engaging in other addictive behaviors, the emphasis is on proper diet and nutrition. Functional nutritional evaluation through laboratory testing gives us a unique view into the nutritional needs of an individual. We can measure the metabolic pathways (the series of processes by which food is converted into the energy and the products needed to sustain life) to determine the answer to the question "Does this individual have the right mix of vitamins, minerals, amino acids, essential fats, and sugars to function optimally?" Recommendations are then made regarding the proper mix of vitamins and minerals to achieve optimal health and well-being.

In addition, the doctor will evaluate amino acids (the building blocks of life) to ensure that the diet has a proper mix of protein. Changes can be made in both diet and digestive function to promote and improve the amino acid balance. Amino acids are the necessary building blocks for making neurotransmitters. Neurotransmitters are chemicals that carry messages between different nerve cells or between nerve cells and muscles. Vitamins are also essential factors to help build the neurotransmitters. Thus, poor diet and poor digestion can actually change your mood and change your mind. One of the great truths that comes from the wisdom of the ancient Greek physician Hippocrates, who became known as the founder of medicine and as the greatest physician of his time, is that "we are what we eat."

The lining of our gastrointestinal tract, what we refer to as "the gut," is, in fact, completely regenerated every five days. This lining is critical for managing the selective absorption of macronutrients (fats, sugars, and amino acids) as well as micronutrients (vitamins and minerals). Each individual has different requirements for these macronutrients and micronutrients, depending upon his environment, current state of imbalance, and genetic predispositions.

Nutritional evaluation also looks at food allergies, leaky gut, and the possible presence of heavy metal toxins, such as lead, mercury, arsenic, and cadmium, which can compromise normal enzyme function within the body. When the gut is leaky, the large "foreign" particles overstimulate the immune system. That process of inflammation produces harmful compounds, called free radicals, that damage our living cells and cause our food to spoil. Inflammation distracts the normal healing process of the body and consumes large amounts of our precious antioxidants. Proper intake of Omega-3 fats, found in such foods as fish and fish oil, can decrease this inflammatory process and promote healing.

Other testing (through blood, urine, or saliva) for the ability to respond to stress is particularly important for people who have had problems with addiction. The normal function of our adrenal glands is to respond to acute stress (fight or flight), but in a setting of poor nutrition and chronic stress, these glands lose their ability to respond properly. This imbalance will subsequently lead to depression and chronic fatigue. Many people in our culture have turned to alcohol, nicotine, caffeine, chocolate, and other stimulants to cope with these symptoms. Like covering the emergency oil light on your car's dashboard, this strategy of suppression and cover-up will not work in the long term and will bring a host of its own problems.

**Q:** Do I need to stay on the nutritional changes the doctor might recommend forever?

**Dr. Patrick Hanaway:** No. There is a difference between the nutritional requirements for returning an individual to health and vitality versus those required to maintain balance and harmony. The same principles apply, but the intensity of the application of these nutritional therapies decreases as the whole person is brought back into balance and the body's reserves are replenished. It is essential, however, that you forever nourish yourself properly if you wish to maintain optimal health and vitality.

**Q:** Aren't imbalances and the risk of addiction due to genetics?

**Dr. Patrick Hanaway:** One of the fundamental misunderstandings of modern medicine is to blame imbalance on our genetic structure. Our genomic (gene) variations only play themselves out when the genomic variants are "bathed" in the wrong environment. For example, Joe may have a need for more folic acid than Jean, but this does not imply that Joe has a genetic disease that must be treated. In fact, the genomic variation may never manifest itself as an imbalance if Joe maintains the proper intake of folic acid. Knowledge of these differences can help us determine our unique needs for vitamins, assess our ability to metabolize drugs, and help us refine our understanding of our risk of developing disease. Applying this kind of personalized medicine can help us live happier and healthier lives. (Genova Diagnostics, at 1-800-522-4762, can help with finding a doctor in your area.)

### Questions and Answers with
### Litos Mallare, M.D.

**Q:** What kind of physician should I look for to assist me in curing my addiction?

**Dr. Litos Mallare:** What you are searching for is a doctor who is knowledgeable about treating addiction and who is able to offer effective treatment. It can be difficult to find a medical doctor who is truly knowledgeable about curing addiction. Treating substance addiction is more complicated than treating a simple infection with an antibiotic. Some doctors believe that their years spent in medical school and residency is enough, yet there is a wealth of essential information that medical school and residency do not provide.

Most physicians have experience in addiction medicine through various branches of medicine they practice. The most common specialties where doctors have some training in addiction medicine are family practice, internal medicine, and psychiatry. No matter what the specialty of the doctor you choose, you will want one who can integrate a biological, psychological, and social treatment approach so your cure will be complete. Be wary of doctors who only utilize the biological approach and only offer prescription medicines as treatment. *Those doctors are to be avoided.*

Although medical treatment is an essential component in healing addiction, it is rarely the case that a medical doctor can be the sole healer. There are many factors involved in treating addiction, all having to do with underlying conditions, and only a portion of those factors can be treated by a medical doctor. The physician you choose should be willing to integrate those factors into an individualized treatment plan that should include the other members of your team, as outlined in this book.

It is also helpful to work with a medical doctor who incorporates natural as well as traditional medicine. A good question to ask before you make your appointment is "In addition to Western medicine, does the doctor use alternative approaches to healing, such as vitamin and mineral replacement, supplements, and the use of therapists outside the field of medicine?" Another key question is "Does the doctor take blood samples to send to a laboratory for blood chemistry analysis?" If that is not part of the doctor's usual treatment protocol, make certain that he or she is willing to use the services of a laboratory for blood chemistry analysis. If the doctor is unwilling or reluctant, find another doctor. Blood chemistry analysis is very important and it is an essential part of treatment at Passages.

Q: How will a competent doctor help me?

**Dr. Litos Mallare:** One of your doctor's most important functions is to order laboratory tests, interpret those reports, review the results with you, and provide a plan to correct any deficiencies by enlisting the aid of all members of your team. A competent doctor will also assess the need for detoxification and help you get through acute withdrawal symptoms, if you have any. The doctor will take a medical history and conduct a physical exam to determine if there are any medical issues that need to be addressed while you are in treatment. The doctor may recommend referrals to medical specialists based on findings from your medical history, physical exam, and laboratory tests. The doctor will work with the nonmedical therapists to integrate a multidisciplinary treatment plan that is created specifically for you.

Most often, patients come to an addiction treatment center with a prescription of psychotropic medications, such as antidepressants. The doctor will perform a psychiatric evaluation to assess the need for psychiatric treatment or intervention. *Dual diagnosis* is a term in psychiatry that describes a person who has both a substance addiction problem or a behavior addiction problem plus a psychiatric disorder, such as depression. It is often difficult to distinguish which came first, the addiction or the psychiatric disorder. Did the drug addiction or addictive behavior cause depression or did the depression cause the person to use drugs or some addictive behavior to cope with the unpleasant feelings of depression? A thorough psychiatric history and a period of sobriety can help answer this question.

You or someone you care about can almost always overcome depression with sobriety and therapy without the need for psychotropic medications. The psychotropic medication does nothing more than block the unpleasant feelings while your body does the work of healing itself. The problem with using these medications is that while your feelings are blocked, it is difficult, if not impossible, to discover and heal the underlying cause that is responsible for your unpleasant feelings.

The doctor will follow you through your entire length of treatment and modify or adjust your treatment as needed. He or she will continue to consult with the other practitioners to maximize the effectiveness of your treatment and cure your addiction. The doctor will also make referrals and necessary arrangements for after-care to help you maintain sobriety or freedom from addictive behavior.

**Q:** What is the role of good nutrition in healing dependency and will my doctor recommend specific nutritional supplements?

**Dr. Litos Mallare:** Most people have difficulty maintaining a healthy diet, and that is even more difficult for people who abuse drugs or alcohol or who have other addictive behaviors. Those who are dependent usually neglect healthy eating habits. The side effects of drug and alcohol abuse, such as vomiting and diarrhea, also wreak havoc on diet and good nutrition. People addicted to alcohol are more prone to deficiencies in thiamine ($B_1$), folic acid, other B vitamins, magnesium, and vitamin C. Thiamine deficiency can cause numb feet and hands (neuropathy) and irreversible brain damage, which manifests in memory loss similar to dementia.

Taking multivitamin and mineral supplements within the recommended daily dosages should prevent vitamin deficiencies. Your doctor may suggest other supplements to address deficiencies in absorption of nutrients or to address deficiencies due to dietary choices (such as a vegan diet).

**Q:** Why is diagnostic laboratory testing so important?

**Dr. Litos Mallare:** Laboratory reports are immensely helpful in diagnosing the deficiencies I've mentioned. The role of the laboratory is also critical in assessing your overall physical state of well-being. In addition, it can give deep insight into your emotional state. If, for instance, you have a adrenaline fatigue or a sluggish thyroid, you will be lethargic, less than enthusiastic, and will not feel up to your best game. As a result, you may be doing things to stimulate yourself to increase your dopamine or adrenaline output, such as gambling, risk taking, using cocaine or methamphetamine, smoking cigarettes, or drinking excessive amounts of coffee, caffeinated soft drinks, or "energy drinks."

**Q:** What kind of tests should the doctor order to help diagnose my condition?

**Dr. Litos Mallare:** The doctor will order laboratory tests after he or she has taken your medical history and conducted a physical exam. Drug use and alcohol can do damage to the body and certain lab tests can help us assess this damage. Alcohol, for instance, can cause direct damage to the liver, esophagus, pancreas, and stomach. Certain behaviors related to drug use can cause infections and sexually transmitted diseases. There are also medical conditions that can potentially cause someone to use drugs or alcohol to alleviate their symptoms. One example, as I mentioned before, is hypothyroid, which may cause symptoms similar to depression. A simple blood test can be done to screen for hypothyroid.

Testing for allergies, vitamins, minerals, and heavy metals can also be useful since abnormalities in these areas can alter the way you feel and cause you to use addictive substances or to engage in addictive behaviors for relief. Basic lab tests for things such as electrolytes and complete blood count can also reveal abnormalities that may be altering your mood. Your doctor may order other lab tests or diagnostic procedures, such as x-ray or CT scans (sometimes called CAT scans), if a certain condition is suspected. Again, it is important to do a complete workup in order to assess and treat any medical condition that may be contributing to your substance addiction or addictive behavior.

**Q:** Where can I find a doctor with wide qualifications?

**Dr. Litos Mallare:** It can be difficult to find a medical doctor who is also trained in natural or alternative medicine. If you can't find a medical doctor who practices alternative medicine, the best alternative is to find a medical doctor who is also aware of naturopathic medicine and is willing to at least consult with a naturopath and implement treatment. What is important is the doctor's ability to approach the practice of medicine with an open mind.

Valuable sources for finding the right physician to be part of your treatment team are the American Association of Integrative Medicine (www.aaimedicine.com) and the American Holistic Medical Association (www.holisticmedicine.org). By clicking on the links for a physician referral, you will find a database by city and state.

Referrals from friends, colleagues, family, and institutions are always helpful in finding a qualified doctor. The worldwide web is also a great resource. You can also go online and search for the website for your state's medical board and research a doctor's qualifications. Remember, a qualified doctor does not necessarily mean that the doctor will be right for you. You will have to meet with the doctor, ask questions, and interact with the doctor to determine if he or she is the right physician for you. If you have difficulty, keep looking until you find the right doctor. He or she is essential to your healing.

**Q:** How do I know that I've found the right doctor for me?

**Dr. Litos Mallare:** Sometimes you will not know right away if the doctor you chose is the right one. The establishment of rapport and trust in the beginning of treatment is a good sign that things will work out. Later on in treatment, that rapport or trust may be jeopardized with a disagreement in the course of treatment or progress. It is important in your initial meeting to communicate to the doctor your expectations and concerns about any aspect of your treatment. The right doctor will listen and will also tell you what treatment goals he or she expects from you and for you. Any disagreement later on in treatment can usually be resolved by reviewing what was discussed in the initial meeting.

The doctor should not dictate what you should do but help guide you in finding a cure for your addiction, whether you are dependent on a substance or on addictive behavior. The doctor should provide you with encouragement and hope that a cure is possible. Ideally, the right doctor will make you confident that you will succeed in finding a cure for your addiction.

**Q:** What about methadone maintenance or methadone clinics?

**Dr. Litos Mallare:** Using methadone does not cure one of opiate dependence. In fact, it prolongs it, and coming off of methadone maintenance therapy (MMT) is more difficult than coming off of the original opiates. Methadone stays in the body twice as long and is at least twice as hard to withdraw from.

However, studies have shown that opiate-dependent persons in MMT have lower mortality rates and earn more than twice as much annually than opiate-dependent persons not in MMT. MMT has also been shown to decrease illicit drug use and criminal activity, which are the main reasons the government is behind its use. Criminal activity around newly established methadone clinics always decreases.

There is controversy concerning MMT by leaders in the federal government, medical community, public health officials, and the public at large, many of whom believe that being drug-free is the only valid goal. Passages does not use methadone at all and has an extremely low rate of relapse. The team at Passages believes that individuals can become drug-free and sustain that state, and they regularly prove it. MMT only treats the behaviors associated with opiate dependence and not the addiction.

**Q:** Should my doctor be coordinating with all other practitioners I will be seeing?

**Dr. Litos Mallare:** Your doctor should often consult with and discuss your treatment plan in progress with all practitioners involved in your healing. At Passages, a twelve-person team is assigned to each incoming client. All team members meet at least once a week to discuss treatment and progress, and they sometimes communicate on a daily basis when information relevant to a cure is discovered. Your team should do the same. Sometimes information discovered by one therapist will be vital in guiding your doctor in the development of a more effective treatment plan and helping your doctor bring about a cure.

### Questions and Answers with
### Dr. Gayle Madeleine Randall

**Q:** What is the role of detox in my recovery and how can a doctor of integrative medicine help me through that process?

**Dr. Gayle Madeleine Randall:** Detoxification (detox) is the process of removing harmful substances that have been stored in your body as a result of substance abuse as well as removing toxic products that have been built up in your body from neglect, the environment, and foods that contain harmful ingredients such as pesticides and chemical fertilizers. Everyone abusing substances needs a detoxification process of some kind at the start of recovery.

The goal of a good treatment program is to discover and heal the underlying causes of your dependency on drugs and alcohol (alcohol is just another drug, ethanol). To do that, you must gradually discontinue the use of the drugs you have been using, which may require the temporary use of another, less harmful drug to prevent dangerous problems such as seizures. The treatment team at Passages also supports the taper of pharmaceuticals that mask emotions, such as anxiety-reducing medications, and, in some cases, even drugs such as antidepressants so that the repressed emotions will surface. Then the healing process can be more thorough. The length of detoxification may vary because some drugs are cleared from the body more slowly than others. One of the crucially important goals of detox is to create a clear mental state. Unearthing the root causes of dependency hinges upon having as clear a mind as possible.

It is imperative that a physician be involved with your detox process. Abrupt discontinuation of some substances can be extremely dangerous. Specifically, going "cold turkey" off alcohol, benzodiazepines (Valium, Xanax, Librium, and related medications), barbiturates, and sometimes opioids can cause dangerous or life-threatening events.

During detoxification, the number of receptors in your body is reset. Every psychoactive substance (such as alcohol, benzodiazepines, and opiates) acts on specific sites in the brain and elsewhere called receptors. The substance is like a key; it plugs into the lock, or receptor, that fits it. This key-in-lock action is what causes the nerves to fire and results in the psychoactive, or "high," response that comes from using addictive substances. If a substance is overused, the number of receptors in the brain and elsewhere in the body is reduced because when there is the large amount of psychoactive substance available, the body perceives that it needs less of them. That's why you need more and more of the drug you are taking to achieve the effect you are after. This process results in increased tolerance to the substance; and when more of the drug is taken to overcome the tolerance, nerve damage occurs.

During the process of increasing the number of receptors back to normal in detox, the nervous system is extremely sensitive. Left unmanaged, this process can result in jitters, delirium, and seizures (jerking or shaking movements of body with inability to speak, loss of memory, loss of balance, and sometimes loss of bowel and bladder function). Vomiting with aspiration into the lungs is also possible, which can result in pneumonia or death.

Doctors who do substance detoxification need special education and certification from approved addiction medicine societies and the bureau of narcotics. Physicians with specific training in chemical dependency treatment can be found by contacting the American Society of Addiction Medicine (www.asam.org). In the treatment of opioid dependence, the medication buprenorphine, also known as Suboxone, is frequently used and can be administered by doctors with special training in the treatment of opioid dependence. You can search for a doctor with this training on the Substance Abuse and Mental Health Services Administration (SAMHSA) website (www.samhsa.gov). Methadone taper for detoxification is an older approach to opioid detox and is less popular than it once was because it stays in your body for a very long time. The prolonged half-life of methadone results in difficulty withdrawing from it and drawn-out withdrawal symptoms. However, be assured that if you happened to have ended up on methadone, you can detoxify from it with the right medical guidance.

Regardless of your type of dependency, be sure to tell the doctor that you do not want to be on a maintenance replacement medicine such as buprenorphine instead of opioids, aprazolam instead of alcohol, or methadone in place of heroin. Although it may be necessary to use some of these medicines early in detox, your ultimate goal is to be drug free. Avoid a doctor who wants to treat your substance dependence by replacing it with a pharmaceutical and stopping there. Replacement drugs still leave you addicted, with an open door back to where you came from.

It is ideal throughout your detox and recovery to work with a doctor of integrative medicine, who uses natural, holistic approaches along with traditional medicine. It is comforting to have a knowledgeable physician helping you through the delicate process of detox. Integrative physicians will also suggest holistic therapies to ease and hasten your detox process and recovery. They will recommend holistic measures that are best for your specific situation, as everyone is different and has varied sets of requirements and needs.

It's also important that the physician you choose be a partner in your recovery process. The right doctor will make a plan *with* you. She or he will not just dictate what you should do but help guide you in finding a cure for your addiction. During your visits, a good doctor will spend most of the time speaking with you and listening to your needs. Research has proven that patient outcome is improved when practitioners listen, communicate effectively with patients, and are compassionate.[4]

**Q:** How will a doctor use laboratory testing to help me recover?

**Dr. Gayle Madeleine Randall:** Most people are likely to have a number of physical ailments that contribute to their chemical abuse issues and that may, in fact, be part of the cause of their dependency. Often, the abuse of the chemicals can result in additional physical problems or make existing problems worse. You need a doctor who can sort out the factors underlying your specific situation. Your doctor should use laboratory testing for blood chemistry and endocrine analysis. Examination and testing play a role in discovering significant physiological as well as psychological factors that can undermine your recovery and sabotage your healing.

Two other areas of laboratory testing that are of immeasurable value are tests for neurotransmitter levels and nutritional deficiencies. Neurotransmitters are almost always imbalanced with drug dependence. Neurotransmitters are the chemical messengers that transmit impulses throughout every system in your body. They are the juices that are responsible for the function of all your organs, your brain, your thoughts, your muscles—everything. I have observed that when neurotransmitter imbalances in patients with dependencies are appropriately addressed with supportive therapies, recovery is greatly enhanced and cravings are reduced or eliminated.

Nutritional deficiencies are also common with substance dependence because of neglect as well as the direct toxic effects of the substance abused. Laboratory testing can pinpoint your deficiencies so that your doctor can make specific recommendations to help you improve your health. Maintaining a healthy diet and lifestyle are the keys to wellness. All people, whether or not they are chemically dependent, can benefit from exercise, good nutrition, and vitamin and mineral therapies. Those in the grips of a progressive addiction have often let their health slide. If you use drugs or alcohol, health maintenance has likely not been a priority, which is an even more pressing reason to focus on it during your healing process. In my private practice, the words I use are "your health deserves optimal attention." The perfect doctor for you understands this principle, is holistic in her or his approach, and will be attuned to and assist the natural healing processes of your body as well as your mind and your emotional-spiritual self.

You may not be able to find a doctor that manages detox and also has an integrative holistic approach. In this case, find a doctor to help you get off the substance you are dependent upon, and then find a practitioner to address your chemical and nutritional imbalances.

**Q:** How are advances in mind-body medicine changing the course of addiction treatment?

**Dr. Gayle Madeleine Randall:** The science behind mind-body medicine focuses on interactions between the brain, mind, body, and behavior. Mind-body medicine recognizes the powerful ways in which emotional, mental, social, spiritual, and behavioral factors can directly affect health. Ned Kalin, M.D., director of psychiatry at HealthEmotions Institute in Madison, Wisconsin, summed it up when he said, "What is happening in the field of Mind-Body is equivalent to the advent of quantum theory in physics."

Prior to the development of recent technology, mind-body medicine was often dismissed by doctors of traditional Western medicine as unproven or "woo-woo" medicine. Even though great pioneers such as Herbert Benson, M.D., offered fantastic research as early as the 1970s, the field of mind-body was still rebuffed until the last decade. Dr. Benson coined the term "relaxation response" and had a best-seller describing his findings. He showed that meditation that induces the relaxation response results in decreased heart rate and rate of breathing and slower brain waves. This is the opposite of the "flight or fight response," which is experienced frequently by patients with dependencies who self-medicate and those undergoing detox. Meditation and the right kind of slow breathing causes changes in the autonomic nervous system and hypothalamus and increased brain activity correlated with positive emotions, changes in states of consciousness, and improvement in the immune system.[5] Mindfulness breathing is routinely included as part of recovery at Passages.

The work put forth by Dr. Candace Pert has also been a cornerstone in bringing us to where we are today in understanding the mind-body connection and how that interplays with the treatment of dependencies. Dr. Pert was a graduate student when she discovered the opiate receptor in 1972. Just as importantly, she discovered that receptors can be found outside the brain in many parts of the body. This led to the realization that neurochemical processes, even thinking and emotional processes, are not all brain driven. We actually "think" with our whole body. This key finding has, once and for all, dislodged the brain-only centered view of emotion and is another piece of the puzzle for the mind-body connection.[6]

Dr. Pert teaches that "your body is your subconscious mind." What affects the mind affects the body, and what affects the body affects the mind. For instance, when you experience body symptoms from drug dependence, it affects your emotions; and when you experience emotional distress from your addiction, it has ill effects on your body. Everything is connected! This is why you need to address the healing of your whole body and mind when you are recovering from addiction. Those who detox without getting to the root psychological causes driving their dependency almost always relapse. When dealing with substance abuse, attending to emotional healing without also addressing the body's imbalances often results in relapse because of body cravings and discomfort.

**Q:** Are there other advances in science that are creating changes in the way we approach addiction treatment?

**Dr. Gayle Madeleine Randall:** Another body of work that impacts the dynamics of dependency has been chronicled by neuroscientists, Western psychologists, philosophers, and Buddhist scholars in Daniel Goleman's book *Destructive Emotions: How Can We*

*Overcome Them? A Scientific Dialogue with the Dalai Lama.*[7] Destructive emotions are those that cause harm to ourselves or others. Dr. Richard Davidson of the University of Madison, a pioneer in the field of affective neuroscience, pinpointed the brain circuitry involved in a range of destructive emotions, from the craving of addicts to the paralyzing fears of a phobic (someone with an intense, unrealistic fear that can interfere with the ability to socialize, work, or go about everyday life).

His data holds great promise for addiction treatment. It shows that meditation with mindfulness breathing can result in beneficial neurochemical changes, strengthening the brain sites that inhibit negative thinking and destructive behavior. When these sites are strengthened, disturbing feelings can be replaced with those of equanimity and joy.[8] By simply breathing in a mindful way and learning to meditate, you can help reduce your cravings and the negative thinking leading to alcohol and drug abuse. In addition, the brain sites responsible for inhibiting negative thinking can be beneficially modulated through balancing neurotransmitter levels, particularly in the left prefrontal lobe.

**Q:** Can you tell us more about neurotransmitters?

**Dr. Gayle Madeleine Randall:** Addiction and substance dependence profoundly affect the processes of the brain by altering the level of neurotransmitters and the number of receptors for them. These kinds of changes inevitably result in changes in behavior. At Passages, clients' recovery is helped immensely by studying their neurochemical levels and treating their imbalances.

Most people diagnosed with depression and anxiety disorders suffer from chemical and neurotransmitter imbalances. Some people call this "neurotransmitter disorder," a term I do not like because it implies a disease, when, in fact, this is an *imbalance* resulting from stress, addiction, or other factors. Neurotransmitter imbalances can also result from bulimia, anorexia, fibro-myalgia, chronic fatigue, insomnia, chronic pain, menopause, or any condition that induces serious stress on the system.

One way the imbalance in neurotransmitters has been treated medically is through selective serotonin reuptake inhibitors (SSRIs) and selective norepinephrine reuptake inhibitors (SNRIs), two kinds of antidepressants. Since the inception of these medications in the late 70s and early 80s, their prescription usage has soared. Evidence-based medicine has produced studies and reviews revealing a number of clinical implications for SSRI and SNRI usage, including the treatment of depression, insomnia, anxiety, menopause, addiction, and other conditions. The explosive use of SSRIs and SNRIs has shown that the medical world has discovered and recognizes the clinical impact that neurotransmitter levels have on health.

Unfortunately, even though neurotransmitter levels have a tremendous effect on health, the effectiveness of SSRIs and SNRIs has recently been brought into question. I said earlier that neurotransmitters are essential chemical messengers that regulate brain, muscle, nerve, and organ function. The most common neurotransmitters are serotonin, GABA, dopamine, norepinephrine, epinephrine, glutamate, and acetylcholine. Low levels of these important chemicals are extremely common in people with poor lifestyle and diet, which is often the case in drug-dependent individuals. Conventional treatment uses SSRI drugs such as Zoloft, Prozac, etc., which may offer some patients symptomatic relief. They work by redistributing serotonin from inside the nerve cell into the synapse (space between communicating nerves), where it transmits its chemical message. This artificial redistribution allows for chemical messages to be sent even though the total body neurotransmitter levels are low.

The problem with this approach is that these drugs do *not* replenish deficient serotonin or other imbalanced neurotransmitter levels. In fact, they may further deplete neurotransmission by increasing activity of enzymes called monoamine oxidases (MAO), which break down neurotransmitters. It is common for people to experience only temporary improvement due to this effect. As a result, anitdepressants are often changed to a different type or increased to higher and higher doses to accommodate this decreased effectiveness. This is one way people become addicted to antidepressants.

It's worth repeating that the problem with SSRIs and SNRIs is that they only fool your body into thinking it has more neurotransmitters than it really has by selectively blocking the reuptake from the synaptic space between nerve endings. That means that the neurotransmitter lingers in between communicating nerve cells that use it. Within the literature on this topic there is a description of "Prozac poop out." This happens when no matter how much SSRI you take, you cannot get a beneficial effect. The reason for this is that the SSRI antidepressants do not replenish your serotonin pool; they only fool your body into thinking you have more serotonin than you really do by collecting it and holding it in the synaptic space.

*Harvard Magazine* reported that a 1995 study by Maurizio Fava, professor of psychiatry at Harvard Medical School, found that the beneficial Prozac effect wears off within a year for about one-third of those who take it. In 2000, Joseph Glenmullen, M.D., clinical instructor in psychiatry at Harvard Medical School and University Health Services physician, wrote a book called *Prozac Backlash*, pointing out the negative and underreported effects of antidepressants. In their review of this book, *Harvard Magazine* wrote, "*Prozac Backlash* documents not only tolerance, withdrawal syndromes, and drug dependency, but a panoply of dangers linked to 'Prozac-like drugs'—selective serotonin reuptake inhibitors (SSRIs). 'We now have unequivocal evidence from a wide range of side effects that Prozac-type drugs impair the normal functioning of the brain,' Glenmullen says."9

In addition to these issues with SSRI antidepressants, there is another issue that has surfaced that further complicates the issue. Very recent reports have revealed that the effectiveness of antidepressant medications may be less than what has been presumed from published studies. The study that has called attention to this issue was led by Erick Turner, M.D., assistant professor of psychiatry, physiology, and pharmacology at Oregon Health & Science University and medical director of the Portland Veterans Affairs Medical Center's Mood Disorders Program. The study by Turner and his colleagues, published in the January 17, 2008 issue of *The New England Journal of Medicine*, suggested that selective publication in reporting the results of antidepressant trials exaggerates the effectiveness of the drugs. They studied reviews from the Food and Drug Administration (FDA) for trials of twelve widely prescribed antidepressant drugs approved between 1981 and 2004 involving 12,564 patients. They ran literature searches to determine whether results of studies submitted to the FDA had been published in medical journals. They also compared results of published trials to the FDA version of the results.

It was clear that whether studies were published or not depended on how they turned out. Turner and his team found that, according to the published literature, nearly all of the studies conducted (94 percent) had positive treatment results. In contrast, FDA data showed that only about half (51 percent) of the studies were positive. Turner's study was careful to point out that the results do not mean that particular drugs are ineffective but that selective publication in medical literature "can lead doctors and patients to believe drugs are more effective than they really are, which can influence prescribing decisions."10 The finding that medical literature may be exaggerating the effectiveness of antidepressants by not publishing studies with negative results means that doctors may, in fact, be overprescribing antidepressants based on what they have felt was reliable information from their peer-reviewed journals.

Q: How can the research on neurotransmitters help me in the treatment of alcoholism, drug addiction, or other addictions?

**Dr. Gayle Madeleine Randall:** New research and technological progress that allows us to measure neurotransmitter levels is a major new advance that shows promise for dependency treatment. As with all technology, medical applications are destined to grow, and this is certainly true of the clinical applications associated with neurotransmitters. Clinical medicine experienced an evolutionary shift when neurotransmitter testing moved from the research arena into the clinical setting within the last five years.

This new technological advancement has seen fantastic growth over the past few years and has now evolved into new therapeutic applications that can help with addiction treatment. There are a couple of companies that have the technology to measure levels of neurotransmitters and they have developed supplements to treat imbalances.[11] Technology also exists that allows us to more accurately assess adrenal function.

The main neurotransmitters that are active in our bodies are divided into two types—those that inhibit or calm and those that excite or stimulate. The main inhibitory neurotransmitters that we can measure are serotonin and GABA, and the main excitatory neurotransmitters are dopamine, norepinephrine, epinephrine (or adrenaline), and glutamate. Not surprisingly, these are gravely affected with substance abuse and also with toxicity and prolonged stress, which is always associated with substance dependence.

Most importantly, the data strongly suggests that depending

on the substance(s), the duration of use, and the length of time since last use, neurotransmitters can be rebalanced with targeted amino acid and vitamin therapies. This balancing can result in improved recovery, manifesting as improved sleep, increased feeling of well-being, improved energy, and decreased anxiety and cravings, to name a few of the observed results. Amino acids are obtained from dietary protein, but not in adequate levels to correct even a moderate neurotransmitter deficiency. Targeted amino acid and essential neuro-factor supplementation can replenish low neurotransmitter levels naturally.

This process should be monitored by a knowledgeable practitioner because there is a specific order and time over which these chemicals need to be restored, depending on the pattern and causes of the imbalances. If neurotransmitter levels are restored without taking the pattern and causes into account, unpleasant side effects and undesirable mood changes can result. Patients who have had dependencies may take longer for complete restoration of levels and nerve healing.

My recommendation for patients with dependencies is to have their neurotransmitter levels evaluated and receive appropriate therapy from a practitioner who understands this field. This is an incredibly helpful tool for healing dependencies. When you are given selective amino acids and other herbal and vitamin building-block precursors specific to serotonin, you can replenish your pool and feel better naturally without impairment of normal brain functioning. This same technology and principle can also be applied to other neurotransmitters that are depleted as well as to your adrenals.

Healing is all about reestablishing balance. Based on the findings of the Passages team within the addiction model, Passages has designed a system of nutritional supplements that can help your body recover from addiction naturally by providing you with the building blocks for the neurotransmitters you may be missing. You can find out more about the supplements at www.TheAddictionCure.com. These supplements in no way replace the care of your practitioners and doctor. Remember, a doctor should always be consulted before discontinuing substances and for detoxification, especially from alcohol and benzodiazepines. In addition to proper medical care, these supplements can greatly help your recovery naturally.

Every "body" has its own innate ability to balance itself with the right nurturing, love, and support. Your immunity, neurochemistry, and metabolism have self-righting mechanisms that are encoded within your genetics. Despite the tremendous deleterious effects on your body's systems from the chemicals and the lifestyle you may have chosen up to this point, your body can and will heal. With detoxification, the crucial help of the various therapists described in this book, and a program of natural vitamin, mineral, and neuro-support therapies, you can also heal your deep emotional wounds and achieve what we all want for you—balance of the mind, body, and spirit that results in lasting well-being and physical vigor.

## TRADITIONAL CHINESE MEDICINE

Your next step in creating your holistic healing program is to find a doctor of Traditional Chinese Medicine. That means that he or she is licensed to practice acupuncture and herbology. The approach of Traditional Chinese Medicine is very different from Western medicine. It aims, above all, to bring balance to the body. A doctor of Traditional Chinese Medicine will most likely give you a program of acupuncture, acupressure, and herbal teas. The teas sometimes have a bitter taste, but I have grown to like them; they taste like the earth. If you do not like to drink the tea, capsules can be made to swallow with water.

Herbal teas strengthen and rejuvenate as well as detoxify and cleanse your body. Acupuncture and acupressure stimulate the *tsubos* (pressure points) along the body's meridians (nerve pathways or channels through which the body's energy flows) to improve circulation to the organs, balance *qi* (energy), relieve tension, release stored toxins from the cells, and improve all bodily functions.

At Passages, a great many cases of dependency are cured as a direct result of Eastern medicine techniques. Many of our clients who have been addicted to pain pills such as Vicodin, OxyContin, and methadone, and to other opiates such as heroin, have responded well to acupuncture and acupressure. These techniques can release endorphins, the body's natural "feel good" chemicals, which have become suppressed through drug and alcohol abuse.

"Acupuncture seems to calm precisely the part of the brain that controls the emotional response to pain," says Dr. Kathleen K. S. Hui, a neuroscientist at the Martinos Center for Biomedical Imaging at Massachusetts General Hospital. We have also found that food allergies, stress, depression, anxiety, anorexia, bulimia, chronic fatigue, organ malfunction, gland malfunction, and other imbalances of the body respond particularly well to Eastern medicine techniques.

You can find a doctor of Traditional Chinese Medicine in your area by going to the website of the National Certification Commission for Acupuncture and Oriental Medicine (NCCAOM). Tell the doctor honestly and exactly why you are seeing him or her and what your condition is. After the doctor has examined you, ask what he or she believes is the condition of your system. Ask what the doctor's treatment plan is and what period of time is needed for the treatment. Be sure to have your doctor of Traditional

Chinese Medicine communicate with your medical doctor.

Dr. Ji Zhang, L.Ac., O.M.D., is a doctor of Traditional Chinese Medicine from mainland China. He was trained in China first as a medical doctor, then as an acupuncturist/acupressurist, and then as an herbologist. He has written what some critics say is the most comprehensive encyclopedia of herbs ever published. It lists over ten thousand different herbs. Unfortunately, it is only available in Chinese. He says that blending Eastern and Western medicine is of great value; each has its own virtues and the two together can accomplish more than either one can alone. The following insights provided by Dr. Ji Zhang will help you understand why Traditional Chinese Medicine is essential to facilitating a cure for alcoholism or addiction.

## Questions and Answers with
## Dr. Ji Zhang

Q: What is unique about Traditional Chinese Medicine (TCM)?

**Dr. Ji Zhang:** A holistic approach and individualization are the two unique characteristics of Traditional Chinese Medicine (TCM). Chinese medical theory involves looking at physical, emotional, and spiritual health rather than addressing only physical symptoms. It recognizes that people are individuals with different constitutions and relationships to the environment, and therefore treatments are tailored to each person's special requirements.

Perhaps the strongest feature of TCM is its ability to treat chronic conditions or difficult cases for which conventional medicine has no answers. Currently TCM is rapidly growing in acceptance in the West because it is effective and produces a lasting cure. It primarily focuses on diagnosis to correct the underlying cause of the disease.

**Q:** What does Traditional Chinese Medicine include?

**Dr. Ji Zhang:** Chinese medicine is a 4,000-year-old healing method. The ultimate goal of TCM treatment is to balance the body's yin and yang energies by promoting the natural flow of qi (vital energy) in the body. Treatment can involve a variety of techniques, including acupuncture, bodywork, herbal medicine, exercise, dietary therapy, and meditation. In the fifteenth century, Jesuit missionaries in China created the term *acupuncture* from the Latin words *acus*, meaning needle, and *puncture*, meaning puncture.

Over the centuries, the use of acupuncture has spread worldwide. Today, more and more medical physicians and scientists agree these treatments do work. According to Dr. David Brestler, Director of UCLA's Pain Center, "More people have been treated by acupuncture than by all other systems of medicine combined." Thousands of documents published in the last decade have proven the scientific basis of acupuncture and have successfully demonstrated its effectiveness through the use of many different research methods.

Acupuncture is increasingly being seen as an effective treatment and a valuable medicine, and we are seeing the integration of modern medical science and Chinese medicine. In March of 1996, the U.S. Food and Drug Administration (FDA) approved acupuncture as a medical treatment method. Due to the great demand from the public for TCM along with the extensive scientific research, the FDA incorporated acupuncture into mainstream medicine in April of 1997. In July of 1997, Senate Bill 212 was signed into law, expanding the definition of "physician" to include acupuncturists for the treatment of injured employees entitled to worker's compensation medical benefits. In November of 1997, the American Health Counsel identified acupuncture to be useful for the treatment of pain, nausea, asthma, and arthritis. In China, doctors even use acupuncture as a main method of anesthesia for performing many different surgeries, especially when the patient is allergic to anesthesia medication, the body constitution is too weak, or receiving anesthesia medication will put the patient at severe risk.

**Q:** How does acupuncture work?

**Dr. Ji Zhang:** Acupuncture encourages the body to promote natural healing and improve functioning. This is done by the insertion of very fine needles and the application of heat or electrical stimulation to precise acupuncture points of the body. In ancient China, doctors discovered that there are fourteen major acupuncture channels in the body, involving over seven hundred different points distributed on the surface of the skin, which individually connect different organs and other tissues. The qi (vital energy) is flowing and circulating in these channels and collaterals to produce the functions of various organs and to irrigate and nourish the tissues.

In Chinese medical theory, disturbances and dysfunctions in yin (negative, shade, female, cold, inner, and upper, etc.), yang (positive, bright, male, heat, outer, and lower, etc.), qi, and blood create all disease. Through various manipulative stimulation methods, such as invigoration (used for deficiency and asthenia) and elimination (to disperse excess and clear away pathogens), acupuncture works to adjust, correct, and balance disturbances and dysfunctions to cure illness.

Recent research has found evidence that acupuncture points are strategic conductors of electromagnetic signals. Stimulating the points along these pathways through acupuncture enables electromagnetic signals to be relayed at a greater rate than under normal conditions. These signals may start the flow of pain-killing biochemicals, such as endorphins, and of immune system cells to specific sites in the body that are injured or vulnerable to disease.

**Q:** What does acupuncture feel like?

**Dr. Ji Zhang:** People experience acupuncture needles differently. Typically most patients feel no pain whatsoever when the needles are inserted; some may experience minimal pain or discomfort. Acupuncture needles are very thin and solid and are made of stainless steel. Because the point of the needles is smooth, their insertion through the skin does not feel the same as the insertion of needles that are used for injections or blood sampling. Once the needles are in place, most patients describe feelings such as "heaviness," "numbness," "tingling," or a "funny sensation." These are good reactions to the stimulation of points. Acupuncture is safe because no drugs or hazardous equipment, such as x-rays, are used. No irreversible procedures, such as surgical operations, are performed. Only disposable needles are used.

**Q:** How does Chinese herbal medicine work?

**Dr. Ji Zhang:** Chinese herbal medicine, a primary component of Traditional Chinese Medicine, is itself a powerful method of healing. Herbs are all natural and come from living matter, including plants, minerals, and animal products. Over 10,000 herbs have been identified in China and about 400 of these are commonly used in the U.S. today. Using the power of medicinal plants for healing is a worldwide tradition. The people of ancient China have used herbs for thousands of years. Herb usage is increasing throughout the world for a variety of health enhancements as consumers become increasingly aware of the beneficial effects of herbs.

Our body is composed of trillions of cells and each cell needs special nutrients to function properly. Most of the nutrients we give our cells come directly from the food we eat. An "improper" diet or an illness can impair our ability to adequately supply our cells with nutrients. Herbal dietary supplements combined with a proper diet can help correct nutrient deficiencies and help restore the proper balance to the cells. Since herbs are natural substances, they are absorbed easily by our bodies and rarely have any adverse effects. Each herb has a unique combination of constituents that interact directly with the body's chemistry. These specific chemical interactions influence entire organs or tissues.

Chinese herbs are most often given in combinations and formulas designed for each individual person. Combining herbs does more than simply add to the effects of each individual herb. An herbal formula can have a synergistic or a buffering effect, depending on how the herbs are combined and depending on the body's requirements. A good formula will maximize the effect of each herb and nutritionally support various systems in the human body.

Traditional drugs often control symptoms but do not alter the disease process. For example, antibiotics eliminate bacteria but do not improve a person's resistance to infection; diuretics eliminate bacteria but do not improve kidney function.

Chinese herbs in proper combination may enhance the body's healing process by providing a balanced, holistic ingredient. They replicate the teamwork naturally found in the body's immune system and enhance the ability of white blood cells as well as some serum proteins to work together to defend the body's health. Chinese herbs thereby treat the underlying condition, not just the symptoms. Herbs rarely cause unwanted side effects.

**Q:** What is Chinese therapeutic massage like?

**Dr. Ji Zhang:** Chinese therapeutic massage, or Tuina, is a technique based on the same principles as acupuncture. Instead of needles to stimulate the qi flow in the channels (meridians) of the body, it uses the pressure of fingers, hands, elbows, etc. It is applied on specific acupuncture points along a meridian or to a whole area of the body in order to help the body regain balance.

Tuina massage is a deep and vigorous means of encouraging circulation and rejuvenation and of preventing disease. The long-term results are usually less profound than acupuncture, but the immediate release of stress and tension makes Tuina an extremely valuable medical technique. Tuina also helps with disorders such as insomnia, indigestion, body aches, joint problems, back pain, and neck stiffness.

**Q:** Why is Traditional Chinese Medicine essential to finding a cure for alcoholism or addiction?

**Dr. Ji Zhang:** In China, Traditional Chinese Medicine has been used to treat alcoholism for over a thousand years. Two hundred years ago, Chinese medical doctors began to search for a therapeutic method as well as detoxifying herbs to treat opium addiction. In most addiction treatment centers in China today, a combination of Western medications and Eastern medicine, including acupuncture and herbs, are used to treat patients.

When Western medications are used as the main therapy during the detoxification process, many patients have various symptoms, such as fatigue, stubborn insomnia, anxiety, depression, irritability, restlessness, agitation, muscle spasms, quivering and cold limbs, constipation, lack of appetite, alternating chills and fever, and tingling, stabbing, and aching sensations all over the body. Even after detox, some patients still have these symptoms, known as abstinence syndrome. This is an important factor leading to relapse. When acupuncture and herbal prescriptions are added to the program, both the physical and mental situation greatly improve. Acupuncture can balance and correct the central nervous system by invigorating the brain to generate more endorphins, which can relieve physical pain and moderate emotions.

When a patient has a long history of addiction, the endorphin generation system in the brain has been damaged by the overuse of an external chemical drug that is similar to the endorphin in chemical structure. In such cases, feedback signals to the brain decrease internal endorphin generation. Acupuncture stimulates and invigorates endorphin generation and is thereby able to calm the central nervous system, relieve the stress, moderate anxiety and depression, and give the patient a greater sense of well-being. This assists in relieving the mind of the psychological craving for drugs and alcohol and works with Western medications to treat psychiatric illnesses.

When those who have been addicted continue a course of acupuncture treatment, their very weak generation of endorphins is gradually restored to a normal level. After recovery, the endorphin generation system will remain strong enough to prevent relapse because it is now normal; in other words, the patient no longer has the physical craving for the drug.

Currently, the mechanism of relapse, which is related to the disturbance of various parts of the nervous system, is not very clear. Therefore, it is difficult to correct it by a single Western medication. Traditional Chinese Medicine, as a holistic diagnostic and therapeutic medical system, follows multiple approaches to figure out the problem. That is why Chinese herbal medicine is also used to help alcoholics and drug addicts.

**Q:** How will Chinese herbal medicine help me achieve recovery?

**Dr. Ji Zhang:** Chinese herbs work to relieve the body of any remaining toxins and clean the body through these different approaches:

- Promoting urination to drive out the toxins.
- Clearing away toxic heat and damp heat. This method is especially useful in treating alcoholics. (In Chinese medicine, "heat" may manifest as a red complexion, irritability, anger, difficulty falling asleep, loose stool and foul-smelling diarrhea, a red tongue with a yellow and greasy coating, or a rapid pulse.)
- Unblocking the bowels to drive out toxins, especially when the patient has constipation.
- Promoting blood circulation and qi circulation to remove toxins from the organs and other tissues. Recent research indicates that in addicted patients, Chinese herbal medicine effectively promotes and regulates microcirculation and helps to drive out toxins.

Chinese herbal medicine can also:

- Calm the spirit, reduce the sensitivity of the nervous system, improve the patient's mental condition, and prevent a drug and alcohol relapse.
- Tonify deficiencies, strengthen the constitution, and restore the internal generation of endorphins.
- Relax mental tension, moderate anxiety, and relieve depression.

**Q:** How does Traditional Chinese Medicine work in conjunction with Western medicine? How and why do the two together accomplish more than either one can alone?

**Dr. Ji Zhang:** Western medications for treating alcoholic and addicted patients are usually very strong chemicals and generally achieve an immediate result. The addiction stops easily. The downside to this is that some of these medications have severe side effects or can easily cause a new addiction. In some cases, patients have to take a substitute medication for the rest of their lives. On the other hand, Traditional Chinese Medicine is a natural therapy with fewer side effects. It can invigorate, regulate, and balance rather than injure the body. TCM focuses on the factors and sources of the problem, not only on the symptoms.

In Chinese medical theory, addictive drugs damage the body, leading to various kinds of deficiency involving yin deficiency, yang deficiency, qi deficiency, and blood deficiency. These kinds of deficiencies cannot disappear immediately after detox and will linger for a long time. Therefore, it is optimal to first use Western medication as a main detoxifying method and then use Chinese medicine to assist in improving the symptoms. After detoxification, the Western drug dosage can be gradually decreased and the patient can use the Chinese treatment to support the body's constitution, to prevent the reappearance of symptoms, to maintain health, and to finally and permanently quit the addiction and the use of all substitute medications.

**Q:** What qualifications should I look for in a doctor of Traditional Chinese Medicine?

**Dr. Ji Zhang:** The doctor should have a strong background in both Chinese and Western medicine. Ideally, the doctor should have graduated from a prominent school of Traditional Chinese Medicine and been practicing for at least five to ten years. If you cannot find a doctor of TCM who also has a background in Western medicine, make sure your Chinese medical doctor regularly consults with and communicates with your medical doctor.

The doctor should have specialized experience in the field of treating addiction and alcoholism. It is even better to find a doctor of Traditional Chinese Medicine who is working with an addiction center.

**Q:** How should I prepare for a visit to a doctor of Traditional Chinese Medicine?

**Dr. Ji Zhang:** Tell the doctor of TCM your entire medical history, especially relating to addiction and alcohol use. Get a copy of all your medical tests from your M.D. and bring them to your appointment.

Describe to the doctor your current symptoms and your chief complaint. Fully inform the doctor, as well as each practitioner with whom you are working, of all the other medications and treatments you are receiving so that the practitioners and their treatments support each other and do not work against one other. For example, some herbs might not be advisable to take if you are currently on other medications.

Before visiting the doctor, do not eat or drink anything and do not do any exercise, as these can affect the tongue and pulse, which are very important for correct Chinese diagnosis.

**Q:** How quickly can I expect to see results from Traditional Chinese Medicine?

**Dr. Ji Zhang:** For pain, one can sometimes feel the improvement immediately from acupuncture. For mental disturbances, you may feel relaxation during the treatment, even while the needles are still in the body. Normally, you will see faster results with acupuncture than with Chinese herbs since herbs usually work more gradually.

When using herbs for some chronic symptoms, you can

expect to see results after one week. While herbs are more effective in treating the source of the problem, acupuncture is more effective in treating the symptoms. It is generally best to combine acupuncture and herbs.

**Q:** Can you give an example from your practice illustrating how Traditional Chinese Medicine or acupuncture helped someone make the leap to recovery?

**Dr. Ji Zhang:** Eric, age forty-one, was suffering from addiction to marijuana for twenty-five years and he also smoked regular cigarettes. He came to me to treat his muscle tingling, aching, and spasms as well as his anxiety, irritability, and stubborn insomnia. I told him, "If you want to cure the source of your problem, you had better quit smoking and taking drugs." He agreed.

I used ear acupuncture first and put five herbal seeds on the ear acupuncture points on the surface of the ear, covered them with a small part of a bandage, and told Eric to press these points several times each day. I treated him with body acupuncture once, inserting about ten needles into his body, and gave him herbal medicine, instructing him to drink the herbal tea twice a day. After only one week, he was able to smoothly and totally quit smoking both marijuana and cigarettes.

■ ■ ■

In addition to Dr. Ji Zhang's story, here are a few other examples of the effectiveness of Traditional Chinese Medicine in treating our clients at Passages. Two years ago, a doctor came to Passages to be treated for addiction to pain medications. His shoulder had been crushed in an automobile accident several years earlier, and the pain was continual and severe. He had undergone surgery three times in an effort to relieve the pain, but without success. In his first acupressure session, our therapist removed 80 percent of the pain by opening the meridians that provide energy to that area of the shoulder. After that, it was an easy task to cure his addiction to his pain medications because the pain was gone.

At Passages, we have also had great success in relieving headaches by using acupuncture and acupressure to open the meridians that supply energy to the shoulders, neck, skull, and scalp, which is where the pain is being generated. Headache pain is not generated by the brain itself (although it feels as if it is) because your brain tissue can't feel pain. The bones of the skull and the brain's tissues lack pain-sensitive nerves. Headache pain originates from the nerves in our scalp, from the muscles in our neck and heads, and from blood vessels at the base of the skull.

Perhaps two dozen people have come to Passages whose main complaint was that they suffered from migraine headaches. In some cases, the migraines were "knock you to your knees" headaches, the kind that had sent them to the nearest emergency room for medication. In every case, the client was using pain medication to deal with the headaches and had become addicted to it. Every one of those people left Passages with most of their headache symptoms gone and their dependency cured.

Even clients who don't have migraine headaches but have chronic headaches report that these have disappeared after a few treatments with acupuncture, acupressure, herbs, and deep-tissue massage. They have also found yoga, psychology, physical training, and nutritional counseling to be effective in helping alleviate these symptoms.

About thirty million of us experience chronic headaches, and most of us experience them occasionally. If you've become addicted to pain medication, don't go on trying to mask the pain with drugs. Instead, get help to identify its cause and to treat that.

## CLINICAL PSYCHOLOGY

A clinical psychologist can be of great benefit in your life by helping you understand and resolve the underlying pain you have been running from or drowning out with drugs, alcohol, or addictive behavior. Make certain the psychologist knows you are *not* hiring him or her to treat your substance abuse or addictive behavior. Since alcoholism and addiction are not the problems but are just symptoms of the problems, you are hiring the psychologist to help you discover and deal with underlying psychological issues that have led to your dependence. If the clinical psychologist you choose is unaware of the difference, find another one immediately. You are not there to educate him or her.

You can find a clinical psychologist by using your telephone directory or searching on the Internet. The websites www.PsychologyToday.com or 1-800-Schedule.com will provide you with a list of clinical psychologists in your area. You can also go to your search engine and type in "clinical psychologist search."

In your first visit to a clinical psychologist, you will be evaluating how you feel about working with that person. Be frank with him or her.

Say that you are having a dependency problem, that you are following a program to discover underlying issues that might have caused you to become dependent on substances or behaviors, and that you are pursuing other healing modalities as well.

I suggest that at first you arrange to see the psychologist three times a week. If you are only consulting with your psychologist once a week, treatment can take much longer. Three sessions a week will not only be more effective, but they will also produce results far more quickly. Working with a psychologist is not a long-term arrangement. You are there to get to the bottom of what's causing your dependence and then to get on with your life.

"Dependency comes from a desire to escape pain," says Keith McMullen, Ph.D., Clinical Director at Passages Addiction Cure Center. "Continuing sobriety requires understanding the sources of pain and addressing them rather than finding a quick way to mask the pain." In the section below, Dr. McMullen explains why working with a clinical psychologist can help you to heal your pain, how to choose the psychologist who is best for you, and what to expect from your therapy.

### Questions and Answers with
### Dr. Keith McMullen

**Q:** What is a clinical psychologist?

**Dr. Keith McMullen:** A clinical psychologist is a therapist who has received a Ph.D. in clinical psychology to gain expertise in the evaluation, diagnosis, and treatment of mental disorders. A clinical psychologist has several years of academic training, has one or more years of practice as an intern, an additional 3,000 hours of supervised experience, and has passed state licensure examinations. In addition, a psychologist has written a dissertation showing specialization in some area of the field of psychology.

**Q:** Why is working with a clinical psychologist essential to my recovery?

**Dr. Keith McMullen:** Chemical dependency is symptomatic of underlying issues, and clinical psychologists are trained to assess and treat underlying psychological issues. In most states, psychologists are required to have special training in chemical dependency and are knowledgeable about the particular needs of those suffering from chemical dependency as well as the underlying psychological issues that patients avoid by using drugs and alcohol. The stringent internship and practicum requirements give the psychologist in-depth training in assessment and treatment.

**Q:** How will a clinical psychologist help me?

**Dr. Keith McMullen:** A clinical psychologist helps by beginning with a full assessment of a client's symptoms. In the initial interviews, a psychologist listens to the specifics that the client presents as problems and interviews the client to get a full psychological history. If the issues and diagnosis are complex and confusing, a clinical psychologist is trained to administer a full psychological test battery for diagnostic clarification. After assessing the nature of the underlying issues, the psychologist collaborates with the client to develop a treatment plan with mutually agreed-upon interventions, short-term goals, and long-term goals. The methods of intervention vary according to the theoretical orientation of the psychologist, but they are characterized by self-disclosure by the client and empathic support and guidance from the psychologist.

**Q:** What should I expect when I go to a clinical psychologist?

**Dr. Keith McMullen:** When you are interviewing therapists to find the right one for you, you should expect full disclosure of all business aspects of the professional relationship, including fees, schedule, missed appointment policy, insurance, after hours accessibility, and related issues. The psychologist should openly describe the theory and methods he or she offers and what they expect from you. The goals of the therapy should be determined with your full participation. The psychologist should answer your questions clearly, openly, and nondefensively. You should always feel safe and heard. Never continue in therapy without a feeling of safety and respect. After the work commences, it is possible that interpersonal conflicts may need to be processed as a valuable part of healing, but at the outset a client should feel a strong sense of safety and trust. Interview several therapists to find someone you feel safe with and confident in.

**Q:** How should I prepare for a visit to a clinical psychologist?

**Dr. Keith McMullen:** Prepare a clear statement of exactly what you need and expect. Be ready to offer a clear description of your problems or symptoms as well as your goals. In addition, prepare a list of questions for the therapist. What do you need to know about the psychologist to assist you in deciding whether or not you have found the right person? As much as possible, have a clear idea of what you need and ask questions to find out if you've come to the right place. Be ready to offer a detailed history of your life experiences. Having one written in advance can help facilitate the assessment of underlying issues.

**Q:** What results will I see?

**Dr. Keith McMullen:** Initially, you may experience an increase in pain as you delve into your underlying issues. Dependency results from a desire to escape pain, and sobriety begins with learning how to tolerate feeling that pain. As the causes of pain are discovered, you will develop a deeper understanding of the learned patterns that perpetuate the pain and you will develop new ways of coping. The goal is to eliminate the self-destructive patterns, relieve the constant pain, and learn ways of adapting when pain recurs. Pain is a sign that something needs to be healed. Continuing sobriety requires understanding the sources of pain and addressing them rather than finding a quick way to mask the pain.

**Q:** What are some of the common psychological issues that cause people to self-medicate?

**Dr. Keith McMullen:** At a very young age, we learn patterns for survival. The environment into which we are born conditions these patterns. These patterns "work" in our family of origin, but they usually don't work so well when we take them into life outside of our families.

Dependency can result from a feeling of powerlessness when our patterns do not work. There are many issues that cause people to self-medicate, and one of the primary is an inability to adapt to our current circumstances. We get stuck in conditioned patterns and are unsuccessful at adapting. This creates low self-esteem, depression, mood swings, anxiety, eating disorders, obsessions, identity disturbances, lack of purpose, and many others conditions. Any of these issues can underlie chemical dependency as a way of coping.

**Q:** Does everyone who is addicted to a substance need to see a psychologist?

**Dr. Keith McMullen:** Everyone who has become dependent on drugs or alcohol can benefit from professional therapy. Some people can drink alcohol without it taking control of their lives and leading them into repetitive self-destructive behavior; others cannot. If you have lost control of your life, you have done so for reasons much deeper than the enjoyment of feeling high. If getting high is more important than one's health, loving one's family and friends, or having a meaningful life and career, there are issues underlying such behavior that must be addressed.

Q: Can you give some examples of how working with a psychologist can make a big difference in breaking free from alcoholism or addiction?

**Dr. Keith McMullen:** One client at Passages, Fred, had been smoking marijuana daily since age fourteen and drinking heavily since age sixteen. His father was a prominent attorney, and he and his older brother were partners in his firm. At twenty-five, Fred had become increasingly unreliable, was not completing his casework and was showing up later and later for work. His highly successful brother had become more and more angry at having to pick up the slack. His father had threatened to fire Fred from the firm more than once, but he never held to it. Instead, he always made sure Fred had a place to live and paid all of his expenses.

After detoxing from marijuana and alcohol, Fred seemed excited about treatment and participated actively in all modalities. He spent the evening playing his guitar and singing for the clients and frequently requested passes to attend local music events. It became apparent that Fred was not on earth to be an attorney but was a musician at heart. He came to see that he had been using marijuana and alcohol to deal with the stress and dissatisfaction of being in a career which he had no interest in whatsoever.

Treatment consisted of validating Fred's true calling and building his confidence in clarifying and attaining the long-term goal of becoming a professional musician. Fred also took part in family therapy to help him learn to assert himself to his father and brother and to facilitate their acceptance of Fred's true identity. Fred's father agreed to pay for Fred's musical education as long as he remained sober, with the understanding that beyond the educational expenses, there would no further financial support. Once Fred was able to live in accord with his true passion in life, he no longer needed pot and alcohol to bring him a sense of well-being.

Another client, Sophie, the daughter of a royal family, also broke free from addiction when she learned to be honest about her real desires, which were at odds with her family's expectations. Over the course of treatment, she revealed that while the prestige of being royalty had its benefits, beneath her exalted façade she was more interested in the simple things in life. As a young girl, she would sneak away to the servants' quarters to play with the servants and their children, taking them gifts and ensuring their comfort and well-being. As a child, she also kept her pain hidden, always maintaining a controlled, polished exterior.

She carried these patterns into adulthood, living the life of an actress and model, hiding her desire for a simpler life, and keeping her pain and her needs under wraps. She dealt with her hidden self by medicating the pain. Through treatment, Sophie was able to come out from behind the protective persona, to talk about her pain in individual and group sessions, and to experience being loved and accepted for her true self. She was able to admit her needs and learn ways of communicating them. Rather than always being the one doing the giving, she also allowed others to give to her.

At treatment's end, Sophie had plans to combine the two sides of herself in projects where she could help those in need while exercising her valuable talents as an actress and performer. By being expressive of her pain and not hiding it, she was able to find support and relief from friends and family rather than from cocaine.

## MARRIAGE AND FAMILY THERAPY

Marriage and family therapy focuses on family and relationship dynamics. "Hurts and injuries that occur in the context of our family can lead to substance abuse," says Noah A. Rothschild, one of the marriage and family therapists at Passages. "A marriage and family therapist can help someone suffering from dependency discover the origin of their dependency and resolve its cause." Seeing a marriage and family therapist can also help you "uncover the layers blocking your core self from being fully realized and expressed," he says. In the section below, Noah explains in more detail how this process unfolds. He also describes how marriage and family therapy can help both you and your family resolve issues around your dependency and become more authentic and communicative with each other.

### Questions and Answers with
### Noah Rothschild

**Q:** Why is it important for me to work with a marriage and family therapist (MFT)?

**Noah Rothschild:** A marriage and family therapist creates a safe environment to help you discover the origin and underlying causes of your dependency. Dependency starts as some form of past pain, which usually originated in our early family dynamic. In essence, we all come into this world with a core self that is who we really are. That part of us knows that we are perfect, whole, and complete just as we are. Depending on how our primary caretakers respond to our needs, that core self is either encouraged or discouraged. Early childhood is very important in determining how we will cope with relationships and life's challenges and whether we will form a negative dependency later in life.

Many addicts suffer from either an early scenario of abandonment/loss or an early scenario of inundation/not being allowed to have a separate self from their parents. Some examples of an abandonment scenario would be having an addicted parent, an absent parent, an early loss of a parent, or simply not being heard in the way we needed to be heard in our family. Examples of a scenario of inundation would be having parents who used us to fulfill their need for companionship, parents who were addicted (which forced us as a child to parent them), or parents who were simply too smothering. Both kinds of scenarios would lead a child to hide their core sense of self.

As a child, in order to protect yourself from being hurt by losing someone or from being smothered and losing yourself, you did the only other thing you knew—you learned to bury yourself and your pain. Over time, you had to construct more layers and defenses to protect yourself. As a child, you did what you needed to do to survive, but if you had been able to express and resolve that pain, you probably would not have become addicted.

Dependency is just another defense against experiencing pain. If you are someone who had an early abandonment/loss scenario, you may have been highly sensitive or felt too much, and therefore you wanted to numb your feelings and pain through dependency. If you had a scenario of inundation or not being allowed a separate sense of self, you might have learned to deaden yourself from the overwhelming needs and demands of your parents. Later on, in order to feel something, you sought aliveness through substances and became dependent.

These are only a few of the many scenarios that might be applicable to you. Regardless of what your scenario is, underneath dependency is usually a core negative belief about the self, such as *I am unlovable. I am bad. I am not good enough. If people really knew me, they would leave me.* A marriage and family therapist can help you uncover the layers blocking your core self from being fully realized and expressed. Your therapist will provide you with insight into how your early family scenario continues to play out in your present. With this newfound awareness, you will be able to uncover the past pain that led to your dependency and heal it.

**Q:** Why is it important to work with other members of my family or my significant other when seeking a cure?

**Noah Rothschild:** It is important to work with other members of your family for several reasons. For one, they hold vital information about who you are, your behavior, and how your dependency has affected them. In addition, in order for you to want to give up your dependency, you need to understand how your dependency has affected those closest to you. Without our family's feedback, we are often unaware of how we are behaving and how our dependency is destroying our life and relationships. With the information your family provides, you can begin to take responsibility for your dependency and its effects. This will empower you to recognize that you are responsible for your change.

Part of your change and giving up your dependency will involve making amends for your behavior. With your family present, you will have the opportunity to release pent-up emotion, shame, and guilt. You will also be able to ask for forgiveness from your family in a therapeutic environment, where your therapist will assist you. Having a therapist present is more beneficial than attempting to converse about difficult material with family members on your own. Additionally, this process will help you and your family to become authentic and fully communicate with each other. Your family relationships and communication have probably been distant or cut off for some time because of your dependency, so this is your chance to reconnect.

You and your family's ability to communicate will go a long way to helping you maintain your sobriety.

Having family therapy also helps prevent your dependency from being passed on to your children. Believe it or not, your dependency has impacted your children. They deserve the opportunity to learn from your experiences and share with you how your dependency has affected them. Without this treatment opportunity, your children are more likely to become dependent.

Finally, by being in therapy and resolving your dependency, you will change and it is important for your family to change with you by being part of therapy. Family roles are highly defined, and family members may unconsciously put pressure on you to return to your old role unless they change along with you, making it difficult for you to maintain sobriety. For treatment to be successful, it is best to have family members involved.

**Q:** Does my whole family have to be involved?

**Noah Rothschild:** Once a relationship has been established between you and your therapist, it is imperative that all age-appropriate members of your immediate family be involved in regular family therapy sessions with you. These sessions can either be done with your therapist or with another therapist. If another therapist is working with the entire family, have your individual therapist communicate with the family therapist as to the goals and progress of therapy.

Ideally, both your spouse and your children should be in their own individual therapy to explore and resolve their issues around your dependency. If your children are open to the idea, it is especially important for them to be in their own therapy so that the dependency is not passed on to them. As family members have their own therapy, they will be able to bring more of themselves to the family therapy sessions, which will bring more unresolved issues to the surface and thereby improve the overall functioning of your family.

Q: What results will I see from family therapy?

**Noah Rothschild:** By uncovering the layers that are blocking you from fully realizing and expressing your core self, you will become more self-aware and feel more alive in your everyday life—without substances.

You will find yourself making new choices and living in a way that is most in harmony with your true self, not some false self that was created in the past. You will be able to live your life with a sense of purpose and be fully present in your relationships. As you become more of who you truly are, you will experience improved relationships with others and you will have the courage to release toxic relationships. Moreover, you will learn new ways of coping with life without negative dependency.

Q: How will being treated and cured change my family's relationships?

**Noah Rothschild:** Therapy will improve your family relationships in the long run. You can expect to experience better communication in your family relationships. However, be aware that often, as an addicted person gets better, someone else in the family may initially get worse or start having problems. This may, in part, be due to the resentment and pain this person repressed in the face of your dependency, which is now coming to the surface to be healed. When the family is involved in therapy, these issues can be worked through and fully expressed in a safe setting.

Q: What if a family member refuses to be involved in family therapy with me?

**Noah Rothschild:** If family members refuse to be involved in therapy, you should express to them how important it is to your sobriety and treatment to have them involved. If they still refuse, ask them what it would take for them to become involved. Many times, family members have difficulty trusting that you are really committed to change and they have been burned in the past by your dependency. Perhaps showing them how seriously you take your sobriety by demonstrating that you can maintain sobriety for a certain period of time would be enough to convince them to attend family therapy.

See if they would be open to any involvement. For example, if they were not open to meeting in person with the therapist, they might be open to phone sessions. If they still refuse any involvement, encourage them to at least begin individual psychotherapy. Hopefully, after some time in individual therapy, they will choose to become involved in family therapy.

It is important, however, to respect a family member's decision. You can choose to see this as an excellent opportunity for you to lead by example. By seeing you change, a family member may be inspired to make a change.

**Q:** What should I expect when I go to a marriage and family therapist?

**Noah Rothschild:** You should expect to enter into a relationship that has the potential to transform your life. You should expect to see your therapist individually once a week at a minimum. Twice a week would be most beneficial. Expect a marriage and family therapist to be warm and provide a sense of safety for you to explore yourself and your dependency. Ideally, your therapist would be someone who views you as a person suffering from a dependency and doesn't simply label you as an addict. You should expect your therapist to take a thorough history of your life, including your early family scenario, current family/relationship status, recent stressors, and drug and alcohol use.

A marriage and family therapist will likely ask you to commit to the therapeutic process for several months in an outpatient setting. In a residential program, it would be ideal for you to commit to stay in a program for at least one month (two would be better) and then be part of outpatient therapy. You should know that things might feel worse before they feel better, but if you are committed to the process, you will feel better, look better, and your life will be better. Your therapist will often be supportive and understanding, but expect to be challenged as well.

We all have a natural tendency to resist change and maintain the status quo. A good therapist will point out your resistance and challenge you to grow. As a result, during some sessions you may really like your therapist and at other times you may become angry at your therapist for pointing out parts of yourself that are difficult to confront. Know that this is all part of the therapeutic process and continue to acknowledge and work through resistance as it arises. You should also realize that most therapy takes place outside of the session. When issues are talked about in therapy, you will become more aware of problems and issues in your life and relationships. Keep the perspective that problems that arise are opportunities for you to grow and become more of who you really are. Your therapist will be your anchor and will be there with you every step of the way.

**Q:** How should I prepare for the visit to a marriage and family therapist?

**Noah Rothschild:** You should prepare for the visit by coming to the session sober. It is very difficult, if not impossible, to do therapy when someone is intoxicated. You should come to the session with an open and honest attitude. Therapy is not the place to hide information or to be deceptive or manipulative. You will get the most out of each session if you are truthful and candid with your therapist.

Hopefully, you are already well aware of the negative impact your dependency has had on your life and you are ready to change. You would be surprised, but this is often not the case, and many times clients will come to therapy because their spouse or family pressured them to. Anyone entering therapy should at the minimum have some willingness to overcome their dependency and improve their life.

**Q:** Do I need to see a marriage and family counselor if I'm already seeing a clinical psychologist?

**Noah Rothschild:** If your clinical psychologist specializes in dependency and family therapy, it would probably be unnecessary to see an MFT. If you can afford the cost and the time, however, it is best to see both, as they will come at the subject from two different vantage points. What distinguishes a clinical psychologist from an MFT is that psychologists often perform psychological testing. Many psychologists are better trained at research, psychological testing, and working with the chronically mentally ill. Most marriage and family therapists have had training and expertise that specifically focuses on family and relationship dynamics. Again, it is in the context of one's family that a predisposition to dependency is formed, so someone who has extensive training and experience in this area would be most appropriate.

**Q:** Can you give an example of how marriage and family therapy can be a key to recovery?

**Noah Rothschild:** Jeff, a young man in his mid-twenties, came to therapy complaining of week-long cocaine binges and illicit sex with prostitutes. After acting out his dependency, he would go through brief periods of wanting to commit suicide. He came to therapy at the urging of a friend to whom he had disclosed his suicidal thoughts. At the time of his first session, Jeff hadn't used cocaine for a week, felt extremely depressed, and was thinking of suicide because he felt hopeless about overcoming his dependency. He agreed to contract with me to not harm himself, and we agreed to meet twice a week. He also agreed not to use any drugs and to call me if he was going to use.

Jeff revealed that his mother had had several miscarriages before giving birth to him and that he was an only child. Even though Jeff said he didn't remember feeling much of anything as a child, he did say it seemed as if his parents were afraid of losing him. He remembered being told that he was not allowed to play certain contact sports or other activities that frightened his parents. After high school, he left home for college for one semester, but got suspended for drug use in his dormitory. He returned home and shortly after began working for his father. He was still living at home with his parents in their guest house and worked in his father's business.

After a few sessions, it became clear that Jeff had never been allowed to separate from his parents. It was obvious that this pattern was continuing to play itself out in the present, but he was not ready to acknowledge that. For several weeks in his therapy sessions, Jeff maintained that he liked living at home because he could save money by not paying rent and eating his mother's food.

Around our sixth session, a breakthrough came when I challenged him to really look within at why he was so unhappy with his life that he had to use cocaine and have sex with prostitutes to feel good. At this point, he really saw that his relationship with his parents was crippling his life. He admitted that he hated working for his dad and hated that his dad could never stand up to his mother. He claimed that his dad was a different person when just the two of them were together.

Jeff admitted that most of the time he felt numb inside, not knowing what he wanted out of life. He was ashamed that he had never had a long-term girlfriend and said that when he had sex with prostitutes, he just wanted to feel something. He said the only time he did feel something was when he was high or when he came down and thought of suicide. Then he would quickly avoid depression by using cocaine again. I empathized with Jeff's anger and told him that "any little boy that had a mother and father that wouldn't allow him to be himself would be very angry and learn to hide."

In our next session, Jeff really identified his feelings. He said he felt that it had never been okay for him to be himself and that no one would love him if he was himself. I pointed out that he had learned this early in life and held a basic faulty belief that "It's not okay for me to be myself, and I am unlovable if I am myself." Admitting that at his core he felt unlovable, he cried and released much sadness. Jeff also came to realize that as a young child, he had disconnected from himself and his emotions to cope with his fearful parents. He had spent almost twenty-five years abandoning himself.

Slowly, he started to reclaim himself. Jeff had already stopped using drugs and given up prostitutes and now he was starting to feel again. There were sessions where he expressed sadness and anger, but he acknowledged that he was happy to feel. He began to learn to love himself and was proud of himself for not needing drugs to feel alive. He even enrolled in an acting class, which is something he had always wanted to do.

Jeff then took the initiative to get his parents involved in therapy and he began to share his feelings with them. At first, his parents were guarded, but eventually they were able to hear their role in their son's pain, which had led to his becoming addicted. Jeff also learned about his parents' childhood and began to see them as they really are. After all, once they, too, were children who didn't get their needs met, and now they were doing the best they could with what they knew.

We soon developed a plan for Jeff to move out of his parents' house and live on his own, and he continued to do well. He stopped working for his father after finding work he enjoyed more. He has now been sober for almost two years and makes appointments with me every few months.

## HYPNOTHERAPY

In some cases of dependency, especially if you are not able to discover the underlying cause of your dependency in any other way with any other therapist, hypnotherapy can hold the key. If you feel you need the help of a hypnotherapist, be sure to spend enough time finding the right one for you. I was given permission to reprint this excellent guide to choosing a hypnotherapist by Paul Gustafson R.N., B.S.N., C.H., who runs Healthy Hypnosis in Burlington, Massachusetts (website: http://www.myhypno .com). You can also use these guidelines in choosing any health practitioner.

How to Select a Hypnotherapist<br>By Paul Gustafson

"Reputation, recommendations and the yellow pages are frequent first steps in choosing professional help of any type.

Don't be too impressed with anyone's reputation. Although good credentials and lofty achievements are both admirable qualities, what's most important is how they will match with your specific needs and your personality. So shop around. A good rule of thumb is to spend as much time seeking out a good therapist as you would a new car. The success of a friend or relative may be a good indicator but you should make an informed decision and find who is best suited to you.

"Questions to ask yourself on your first visit:

- Does he/she make me feel welcome?
- Does he/she treat me with respect?
- Does he/she ask a lot about me?
- Does he/she seem interested in my issues?
- Is he/she punctual?
- Is he/she a good listener?
- Does he/she make me feel comfortable?
- Does his/her office seem like a haven?

"Questions to ask a hypnotherapist:

- How long have you been in practice?
- Can you give me references?
- What are your qualifications?
- What can you do to help me with my specific issues?
- What do you charge?
- Do you teach self-hypnosis?
- What makes you better than other hypnotherapists?
- Do you tape the session?
- Do I receive a copy of the tape?
- Do you use hypnosis yourself?

"Competent hypnotherapists treat you with respect. Their priority as professionals should be your well-being and success. They will immediately begin to form a positive rapport with you. They are your ally. Their interest is to teach and guide you to achieving your healthy goals. They will teach you self-hypnosis. They should also have a system of gathering helpful information about you and your area of concern. It's important for them to have a profile about you, your fears, likes, dislikes and certainly any health issues. Informed therapists use that information to organize and create hypnotherapy sessions that are custom tailored to your specific concerns as well as to you as a person.

"Fees for hypnotherapy services vary. How you decide on a therapist should not be fee based, but rather on the above information you gather. Your path to health and happiness should be based on professional quality care. By asking the right questions you will get a sense of who you feel comfortable with, his or her approach and treatment suggestions, and an idea of how many sessions may be involved and the cost.

"A good hypnotherapist may give you an estimate of the number of sessions required to effectively bring about the desired results. Ask about the hypnosis process.

"*The hypnotherapist is merely the facilitator or tour guide leading you to your own inner space where lie the answers and the solutions to all ailments.* You do all the real work. Nearly everyone who embraces the soothing, relaxed and focused state of hypnosis, and who has the desire to make changes in their lives is successful. A good therapist will help put you at ease and lead you to your goals. You will supply the desire and open acceptances of positive suggestions that can help you make enriching changes in your life."

■ ■ ■

In the following section, MaryLou Kenworthy, one of the hypnotherapists at Passages, explains how hypnosis can help us get in touch with the hidden causes of dependency, often associated with childhood memories. "As children, we have only a few ways of coping, and quite often, burying hurt feelings is all we are capable of doing," she says. "This helps us survive trauma and pain. However, it does not serve us as an adult, for what is buried in our subconscious mind to some extent drives our behavior and runs our life. One way to free ourselves to live the life we deserve is through hypnosis."

### Questions and Answers with
### MaryLou Kenworthy

**Q:** How can hypnotherapy help me find the hidden causes of my dependency?

**MaryLou Kenworthy:** Here is an example of how hypnosis can help disclose the hidden roots of our pain so that we can learn to deal with them. Michael was a thirty-year-old successful overachiever, always on the go, unable to commit and settle down. His pattern would be to sabotage himself when things were running too smoothly in his life. Bingeing with alcohol and cocaine was one way he would do this. Did he feel unworthy? He didn't think so because he felt confident. He talked of being angry quite often and sometimes fearful, but he was unaware of why he had these feelings. He claimed his childhood was typical and normal.

In hypnosis, I had him tap into his feelings of anger and fear, which enabled him to think back to the first time he had had those emotions. What he uncovered was far from a normal childhood. This man had been repeatedly abused by his dad and humiliated in front of his friends. His feelings of anger and fear brought him back to a time when he was only six years old and had been told he could only play outside if he stayed in the front yard. When his dad found him playing on the sidewalk (only inches from the edge of the yard), he was belittled, kicked in the ribs, and pulled indoors by his hair. All of this was done in the presence of the neighborhood kids, adding embarrassment and humiliation to his wounds. The physical and emotional abuse continued until his mid-teens.

His fear of his dad and the world grew along with his anger. He became an overachiever at a young age, trying to be "good" for his dad. Then suddenly he would get angry and sabotage himself with an "I'll show you" attitude. The family moved several times while he was growing up, creating even more insecure feelings within him. He started daydreaming about hurting his dad or wishing his mom would divorce his dad. When she finally did, he felt guilty.

Building a tough exterior was the way he coped and protected himself. As an adult, he found that whenever he felt comfortable, he would begin sabotaging himself. Now that he had a highly successful business and a new wife, he was drinking more and using cocaine. Deep down inside, he still felt like that "bad little boy" and not worthy of having good things in life. He was expecting to be punished, so he punished himself.

By going back to the source of his anger, fears, and insecurities, he was able to feel the emotions, express in our sessions what he needed to say as a child to his dad, and release these feelings. He was able to understand that he was a good boy, he survived, and he was worthy of having a good life. This process released the pattern of sabotage. Since alcohol and drugs were a means of sabotage, the need for them was also released. Michael began to feel respect for himself.

At times, repressing memories and the feelings associated with them helps us deal with pain. In a child's world, this is often the only way to protect oneself. However, as an adult this does not serve us because feelings buried alive never die. They become poison to us and will manifest in our lives as diseases of some sort.

**Q:** How can hypnosis help us break old patterns that we're not aware of?

**MaryLou Kenworthy:** I once worked with a client who was an angry, defiant young woman in her mid-20s. She had abused cocaine, but denied she had a drug problem and blamed everyone else for her problems. This young woman minimized and stuffed her feelings. She would laugh to cover up deep hurt and had done this for so long that she didn't recognize it. She had difficulty trusting and had very low self-esteem. Over the last ten years, this young woman had developed a deeply set pattern of running from her feelings. She would seek approval and love from her father, and when he didn't have the time for her, she would lash out and hurt him.

As therapy progressed, she revealed that her world had started to fall apart when her parents divorced. This happened when she was in her early teens (a sensitive age) and she felt abandoned. She had been close to her father up to that time and suddenly he wasn't around. Mom and dad were wrapped up in their own lives and she felt invisible. She remembered feeling a deeper pain concerning her dad, almost as if he had personally rejected her. She began searching for love wherever she could find it, becoming promiscuous, and using drugs to cover her pain.

Treatment was a roller coaster ride for this young woman, depending on whether her father was paying attention to her that week or not—until she had a breakthrough. We worked on all the times (past and present) that she felt abandoned and hurt by her father. She appeared not to really care about her mother, dismissing her as unimportant.

Then in therapy I took her back to the *very first time* she had felt unloved. This had to do with her mother's response to her when she was an infant. Her mother had avoided holding her in her arms and never cuddled her. She had never felt safe, secure, wanted, or loved from the time she was in the crib. As a young girl, she searched out her father because of this initial rejection from her mother. When her parents divorced and her dad left home, the feelings of being unwanted and unloved resurfaced. She felt vulnerable, insecure, and completely alone.

By going back to the initial event of being rejected by mom, this young woman was able to look at the incident and feel it all over again in a safe environment. In hypnosis, she was able to confront her mother "as the child" and express her pain and anger. This process finally allowed her to release, understand, and forgive. She broke the pattern that was causing her so much pain, resulting in the release of her need to numb her feelings with cocaine.

**Q:** Can hypnotherapy help me get in touch with my feelings?

**MaryLou Kenworthy:** Getting in touch with our feelings is a key part of healing dependency. In the following case history of Amy, you can see how events from childhood can cause us to suppress our feelings, leading to escalating substance abuse.

Amy was dependent on alcohol and marijuana, with a past history of using cocaine, LSD, and ecstasy. She was twenty-eight years old and highly intelligent, but she had trust issues, fears (of pain and failure), resentments, and feelings of pressure from herself and parents. She said she had always been a fearful and very sad child, and she did not understand why fear appeared to be the emotion that was running her life. About a week into our sessions, I had her feel the fear and sadness and sense where these feelings were being held in her body. This process brought her back to ages three and five, the very first times she had experienced fear. Amy had been in a car accident at age three and reliving it in session brought up details that were meaningful and revealing.

She had been thrown into the windshield, and as she was being carried into the hospital in her father's arms, she could hear him yelling, scaring her even more. Then she saw the fear on her mother's face, which brought up tears as she sat in our session. She was left with the doctors and was not able to see her parents for a while, which left her feeling alone, more fearful, and even angry. As Amy looked back, she realized the most significant thing about this event was the look of fear on her mother's face. Being so young, that fear was imprinted in her subconscious mind.

Under hypnosis, the next event she recalled was a surgery at age five. She was afraid, in pain, and again experienced feelings of abandonment. At this age and even older, a child doesn't understand why they cannot be at home with mom and dad. It is traumatic being left in a scary place like a hospital, not knowing why you hurt physically and emotionally. All sense of security and love are taken away. It's a very confusing time to a child. Amy again saw her mom's fear and vowed to herself not to cry. She didn't know why. As the session went on, she allowed herself to cry for herself and her mom. Her pain and fear expressed itself in her heartrending sobs.

Amy had been carrying the sadness and fear inside and had never allowed herself to express it. Now a flood of emotions surfaced and she felt cleansed. She said it was as if a huge weight had been lifted off of her. She said that perhaps the reason she didn't want to cry was to prevent her mom from being sad and fearful, but now she realized that she no longer had to hold the sadness in. Amy also said that this explained why she had always tried to be perfect for her mom (which created feelings of pressure and resentment).

As a result of these experiences, whenever Amy felt that she had let down her mom, she would reach for alcohol and pot to numb her feelings. Tired of being sad and fearful all the time, she had thought alcohol would make her happy. As she got in touch with these feelings of sadness and fear, understood and expressed them, and comforted her three-year-old and five-year-old self, Amy began to feel free, happy, and secure. She realized that there was no need to drown the pain and fear with toxic substances now that she had resolved the issues surrounding these feelings. She began to trust in life, speak her truth, express her feelings, and go for her dreams. That was a year ago, and Amy continues well and happy.

## PERSONAL FITNESS

Personal fitness plays an important role in your recovery. It will give you a feeling of strength and confidence. Ideally, you should exercise so that you are out of breath at least once a day—that is, breathing hard for at least five minutes. Jogging (even jogging in place), exercising, or bike riding (either moving or stationary) will work. In addition, where you choose to get yourself out of breath is important.

Preferably, exercise out of doors or at least in front of an open window or door. If you are out of shape, start slowly and work up to your five minutes. If you feel any pain anywhere, stop. Only work at a level where you are completely comfortable. In addition to moving your body, it's important to stretch. You can go online or to your local bookstore or library and get a book specifically on stretching. (Be certain that the book is about stretching rather than exercising or yoga, although those books will also enhance your exercise routine.)

In the section below, David Appell, Director of Physical Fitness at Passages Addiction Cure Center, explains why a good exercise program, tailored to your body's own needs, will boost your energy and assist your recovery. A certified fitness trainer and founder of Athletic Performance Center, David also discusses how to find the right program and the right trainer for you.

### Questions and Answers with David Appell

**Q:** How does exercise help in curing chemical dependency?

**David Appell:** Like the mind, the human body needs to "feel right"—to feel as if it can and will perform. Exercise gives the physical body the feeling of health, supplies vital blood flow through the muscular system, promotes good sleep, and improves bone density. With correctional exercises, poor posture (a major source of back pain) can be improved to regain the confidence associated with perfect posture. All too often, those who are being treated for dependency will say, "I feel tired or depressed today." That's a sign that they need to boost their energy system through exercises that tax their muscular and cardiovascular systems during the same workout.

**Q:** What kind of exercise should I be doing? Is walking good enough or do I need a more rigorous exercise routine?

**David Appell:** At the start of your conditioning program, walking is often good enough. At some point, through "adaptive response," your body will become accustomed to walking and will want a more rigorous routine. As you become increasingly fit, activities such as tennis, golf, hiking, biking, horseback riding, and resistance training (weights, bands, machines, body weight) can be added. These are all great ways to develop hobbies and at the same time incorporate lots of breathing.

Stretching should also be added to your program. An individual's flexibility can be dramatically improved with a proper program. The benefits of stretching are numerous. It increases and maintains range of motion in joints, aids the recovery process by increasing circulation and decreasing muscle tension, and reduces muscle cramping, tightness, and pain.

**Q:** How important is it to get out of breath when I'm exercising?

**David Appell:** Having your body recover from getting out of breath becomes a rejuvenating experience where your physical systems work together—a concert of strengthening, stretching, hydration, nutrition, and confidence. It also helps you develop increased functional movements and the ability to improve daily activities with a decrease in pain or discomfort. The end result is a greater ability to enjoy a walk, to complete sport-specific movements like playing tennis, to play with a child, or to get in and out of your car with greater ease.

**Q:** Should I look for an exercise program or coach, or should I exercise on my own?

**David Appell:** Exercise programs work best with a coach. A good trainer can ensure proper techniques to prevent injuries. They can also create a personal blueprint for you to develop a functional body. Your program should consist of corrective exercises, preventative exercises, exercises for core conditioning, strength, and balance, and exercises that are proprioceptive (exercising muscles that help you maintain balance such as those in your knees and feet) and work with the energy system and regeneration. You can find many of the best personal trainers at your local physical therapy or sports therapy clinics. Look for a certified personal trainer, certified fitness trainer, or certified athletic trainer.

The most important quality in finding the right trainer for you is "movement." It's all about getting you moving and keeping you going! When meeting with a trainer for a consultation, look for the person that motivates you. After all, you want to have fun with your workouts. It is important to note that physical appearance (good or bad) and age are not good indicators of their training skills. No matter how they look, if they help motivate you to work out three or more times a week, they may be the right match for you.

**Q:** How long should I stay on an exercise program?

**David Appell:** Once you have a program that works for you, the one that taxes your system and lets your body enjoy the rejuvenating experience of having all your physical systems work together, you'll never want to stop. At this point, maintaining good health, posture and energy will become a life habit—one that you can continue forever by using six-week to eight-week cycles to modify your conditioning. Some cycles may be geared more for getting ready for ski season (lots of legs and balance) and others might be geared to get you ready for the beach.

## VISUALIZATION AND MEDITATION

The practice of visualization can give you the extra edge and enhance all the other practices I've covered so far. Keep your practice simple—two minutes a day. If you go a little over, that's okay.

When you first awake, while you are still in that drifting mode, visualize what life would be like for you if you were not dependent on addictive substances or behaviors. See yourself moving through your daily activities in this state of freedom from dependency.

Meditation also enhances healing, and it is different than visualization. I suggest meditating for five minutes a day. After you're awake and have finished your visualization, find a comfortable position, sitting up. Close your eyes and concentrate on your breath. Just follow it in and out for five minutes. If you find that you have started to think of something other than your breath during those five minutes, just gently pull yourself back to concentrating on your breath. What you are seeking is five minutes of relaxed, easy focus on your breath. In, out, in, out, in, out. Use a clock or a watch. Again, if you go a little over the five minutes, that's fine.

Visualization acts as a compass for your efforts toward recovery, and meditation brings in wisdom that goes beyond the rational mind, says Gert Basson, meditation teacher, life coach, and writer. Gert is Activities Director at Passages Addiction Cure Center, where he teaches meditation and visualization. In the section below, he explains why these techniques are so effective in helping achieve a cure.

### Questions and Answers with
### Gert Basson

Q: Why is visualization essential in my recovery?

**Gert Basson:** Because that is where everything starts, including recovery. Most ancient spiritual and esoteric teachings agree on the potency of visualization. A vision held steady in one's mind becomes the "thought form," the blueprint for the universal energies to manifest in the physical realm. Visualization also acts as the compass for your own inner and outer efforts towards recovery.

Of course, just visualizing is not enough to bring about recovery. You also need to do what needs to be done in the physical world. It may be the simple act of not walking down the liquor aisle in the supermarket or going for a run rather than watching a movie that celebrates addictive behavior. In recovery, there is a subtle balance between the inner and outer work required. The act of visualizing yourself healthy and joyful announces to the Universe your highest vision of yourself. It assists in and gives direction to your efforts in the physical world that are in alignment with the divine plan for you.

**Q:** Why is meditation important for my recovery?

**Gert Basson:** Initially, the novice student of meditation will strive only to quiet the chattering mind. That in itself is a very rewarding endeavor. Continuing the practice will open you to a realm of wisdom and experience that lies beyond the capabilities of your own rational thinking. It is impossible for even the most sane and logical mind to bring into consideration the infinite number of variables as it attempts to plan a person's journey to health and happiness. Meditation circumvents the mind, ultimately connecting you to the Higher Self (Soul), which is the conduit to the vast wisdom and perspective that comes from All-That-Is and that goes by many names. The more time spent in conversation with the Higher Self, the more impossible it becomes for the personality to tolerate addictive or any other self-defeating behavior that is so contrary to our divine nature.

**Q:** How are visualization and meditation different?

**Gert Basson:** Visualization and meditation are different but complementary. Meditation is the art and practice of listening and observing. Visualization is the divine art and practice of creating. It is now scientific fact that our thoughts and our expectations affect the quantum domain—the "stuff" that constitutes the physical world. When you visualize, you galvanize Universal law and all its elements to produce what you want. Through the practice of meditation, you come to understand and know who you really are and what you truly want.

**Q:** How will meditating on my breath help me achieve a cure?

**Gert Basson:** There are many techniques of meditation. It is worth your while to investigate and experiment with those you feel intuitively attracted to. Continually bringing your attention back to your breath is just one of many techniques to assist your mind in releasing the ongoing parade of thoughts marching through your head. In time, the "gaps of silence" between the thoughts becomes evident, providing space for the more subtle communication and influences from the higher realms.

**Q:** Can you share an example of how meditating enhanced someone's recovery?

**Gert Basson:** This story shows how one client I worked with used meditation to break the cycle of dependency. This young man was initially unable to spend more than a few minutes sitting in meditation. Beyond the physical agitation he experienced trying to keep his body still, he had a great fear of meeting his real Self and was reluctant to do so. Notwithstanding his many talents, he had extremely low self-esteem and suffered from chronic insomnia. I explained to him that a beginning meditator can be like a wannabe jogger who gives up before he experiences the enjoyable "burn" that a fit runner does, feeling instead only the discomfort and exhaustion that accompanies the first few attempts.

He realized that there would come a time, maybe initially only lasting a few seconds, when he would "get over the hump" and glimpse what was to come should he continue the practice of meditation.

So he persisted, and over a period of time established a routine. He said his meditation practice, albeit sporadic at times, was responsible for his being able to establish a greater sense of self-worth and get over insomnia.

More than a year later, I met up with him again, and he related to me a breakthrough he had experienced. He told me that one day he found himself severely strained emotionally. He had been watching the life of his mother, once a successful person, quickly fall apart because of alcoholism. Feelings of guilt and an inability to "save" his mother were driving him to the brink of relapsing into his old coping mechanism of using drugs.

His girlfriend (whom he had introduced to the practice of meditation) convinced him to join her in a short session before choosing to go out to get drugs. Because of his previous experience with meditation, he was able to sit quietly, still his mind, and see the bigger picture from the Soul's perspective. While in meditation, his options and their ultimate results became crystal clear. Instantly, his guilt fell away, and his desire to use evaporated within minutes. Not only that, but his mother finally booked herself into a rehabilitation facility. Her recovery was greatly enhanced by her son's stable life and evident happiness.

## SPIRITUAL THERAPY

"Happiness is a practiced skill. Health is a strong choice. Love is the healing force," says Audrey Hope, a spiritual counselor and the host and creator of *Real Women*, an award-winning TV talk show dedicated to life-altering perspectives. Audrey is the Director of Spiritual Counseling at Passages. In her answers to the following questions, Audrey describes how recovery from dependency involves spiritual recovery as well. She explores the inner dynamics of healing and shares some tools you can use to promote your own spiritual health and healing.

### Questions and Answers with Audrey Hope

**Q:** How important is spiritual therapy in a recovery program?

**Audrey Hope:** Spirituality is the path to self-love, self-esteem, and self-rule, which is at the heart of any healing program. Like giving air to someone who needs to breathe, spiritual counseling is the power, foundation, and root from which all healing stems. Trying to help someone without a spiritual context is like trying to bring up a child without love. I am astounded by the number of treatment programs that leave out spiritual counseling. One client had been to sixteen treatment centers, and she was still looking at her alcohol problem with shame and guilt. She did not show a hint of self-love, which is what she needed most. This was the missing piece she received at Passages.

**Q:** What is spiritual counseling?

**Audrey Hope:** One must begin to define spiritual counseling by saying what it is not. Spirituality is not a religion, a doctrine, a faith, or a system of rules to live by. Spirituality must be redefined as the return to our higher consciousness of love. Spirituality takes you to the destination of unconditional love. The different ways one may travel to get there are not important. All spiritual paths lead to the same home.

Spiritual counseling is a powerful healing paradigm that goes beyond the five senses into the deeper soul, where true healing takes place. It is a dynamic process that inspires you to follow your own heart and your own path. Spiritual counseling commands "to thine own self be true ... and be loving." On higher ground, we know who we are and what we are capable of becoming. In higher law, we are lifted beyond mediocrity into the powerful truth that we are spiritual beings with the ability to heal ourselves and others.

Spiritual counseling is a deep healing modality that is about the freedom of the soul. It is different than psychology because it invites you to go beyond the rational mind, to enter the divine energy vibration of love and peace. This is the basis of the ancient spiritual teachings and the wisdom of past ages.

**Q:** Why does spiritual counseling help healing take place?

**Audrey Hope:** Einstein said, "You cannot solve a problem with the same thinking that created it." Healing is not done in the rational mind. Some people have been in therapy for years and can write a thesis on their problems, but they don't heal. Healing must take place on a deep energy level in the soul. We need an alchemist, a transformer, someone who knows how to look down into the cave, and the maze, and to solve the puzzle of the soul. A talented healer has radar into your soul, eyes that know where to look, and wisdom to ask the right questions.

Spiritual counseling seeks to clear problems at a profound level. It works because it answers the questions of what *really* makes us suffer as human beings. We all feel pain for wounds not processed, truth not spoken, anger not expressed, unconscious beliefs that kill, low self-esteem, self-abandonment, and longing for inner peace.

Spiritual counseling looks for answers in damaging belief systems, loss of personal power, energy blocks, thought processes, attitudes, life purpose, choices, boundaries, and commitment to truth and integrity. We are asked to take control of our own healing, make conscious, active, and positive decisions, create boundaries, take responsibility, end victimhood, and emerge into our true identities.

**Q:** How can I use spiritual therapy and spiritual counseling to achieve recovery?

**Audrey Hope:**

1. Begin to view alcoholism or addiction, what we call dependency at Passages, as a divine wake-up call. Dependency is never just about the alcohol, drugs, or addictive behaviors. In a higher spiritual context, these substances or behaviors are a signal, a guidepost, to show you where you need to look to find the pain and the potential jewel. They help chart the story, the wound, the unexpressed cry in the soul. The dependency is a call for transformation. As Joseph Campbell has said, "Where you stumble, there lies your treasure."

2. Heal the soul wound. Spiritual counseling looks to heal the long-ago wound that has emerged into your present-day life so it can be healed. It is the deep core pain, or issue, that was reinforced in early childhood. Unless that deep loss of soul is retrieved, you will follow the same patterns again and again. You will spin in a never-ending circle and meet the same characters in a divine play. Life and relationships always form patterns and themes. We can activate spiritual sight by learning to view life as a mirror that reflects back to us lessons we need to learn.

3. Understand energy. As energy beings, we need to scan the invisible energy that steals our life force. We need to know to whom we gave our power and also who took our power from us. We must reclaim our power by removing the hooks, the chains, and the cords that bind us to others.

   Spiritual counseling helps us locate where our boundaries have been invaded and identify the negative energy that makes us tired, angry, confused, and full of self-doubt. We then learn how to protect ourselves from all kinds of energy drain and use spiritual tools as an armor of protection.

4. Learn to listen to and interpret your cellular memory. People carry pain in their bodies and the past in their cells.

   The soul will give us messages to show us about this pain, if we know how to listen. The soul will talk as a child, in simple colors and pictures. For example, a client might say, "I feel like there are hooks in my back," "I feel like a monster is living in my stomach," or "there is a hand choking my neck." This language is full of information that can teach us what is hidden in our inner being. Learning how to listen and interpret these sacred messages of the soul can lead to transformation and save years of therapy.

5. Investigate unconscious belief systems that kill. The most powerful spiritual principle is that "thought creates reality." Unconscious cultural, family, and religious beliefs need special attention in healing dependency. In my years as a counselor, I have been astounded by the pain people carry because of the "hidden rules" they live by. Their unconscious ideas of sin and punishment produce guilt and shame and gnaw at the soul. By uncovering the dark

beliefs and bringing them out to the light of day, you can begin to heal in a moment.

6. Work with your inner child. People hurt us. We may work on our pain and anger for years, and it may ease, but the most damaging part is the way we abandon ourselves. We all have an inner child. What your inner girl or boy needs most is you and your approval. Your inner child is waiting for you!

7. Find the aha moment in healing. In this "now" moment of transformation, we can find the deep spot where the pain began. If you know how to travel to this sacred place, you have an opportunity for real change. Someone has to know how to take you there, and you must have the courage to walk through, to get to the other side. In this spot, I say, "Ring the bell." It is a time of celebration.

8. Realize that healing is not complicated. Spiritual healing asks you to look at truth in the light of day. The most profound part comes after the exploration and recognition of the problem. In spiritual power, you can then decree, "*I am now letting this go!*" All healing eventually becomes a command and a choice—a conscious, active decision to change. (Sometimes, I refer to my healing process as New York Spirituality—get real, get to the point, and be the best you can be, NOW!)

**Q:** What is the major spiritual issue you find when working with those who are dependent on alcohol and drugs?

**Audrey Hope:** Everything is energy and we are energy beings. All spiritual work is truly about raising the energy level, or vibrational frequency, of the body. On the path to self-realization, we are challenged by negative forces that try to lower our vibrational frequency. Negativity is magnetized to a low vibration of fear and self-doubt, and your self-abandonment opens the portals for negative energy to invade the mind and body. All great healers are aware of this truth. *There is no greater opening for these energies than drugs or alcohol.*

Negative energy is dangerous. It can come in the form of tiredness, dizziness, self-hate, confusion, depression, anxiety, and, in its extreme form, the desire to commit a crime or hurt another or oneself.

What makes us vulnerable to this energy is what I call our "Achilles Heel"—our deepest wound, which is the spot that activates our greatest fears. Everyone has one. It is the part of us that was wounded from childhood, is still in pain, and is therefore frightened and vulnerable. It is our shadow self that follows us around and haunts us wherever we go. We will go to any length to hide our shadow and weaknesses from ourselves and others.

Spiritual counseling can help you discover your "Achilles Heel," seal the portal to keep out negative forces, and clear yourself of the negatives that may have entered your world. One way you can free yourself of unwelcome negative energies is by simply knowing and declaring your spiritual power. You can say in a commanding voice: "*In the name of the pure white light of God, I now command all negative energy to leave me immediately!*" Miracles happen when we approach healing from this level of positive and negative energy.

**Q:** Where can I find someone who can be an appropriate spiritual counselor?

**Audrey Hope:** It would be wonderful for you to find a good spiritual counselor in your area. This is not always an easy task. Do extensive research in spiritual magazines and bookstores and ask professional counselors.

Be sure to look for a counselor who is loving and wise and has a high goal to lead you to your best self. Spiritual counselors are not to impose doctrine and belief systems on you. They certainly should not convert you to any form of religion.

**Q:** Can I create my own spiritual healing?

**Audrey Hope:** You can always choose to put a spiritual program together for yourself. The program must include the elements of support, inspiration, positivity, hope for the future, and intention to manifest your dreams. You can take these steps to design a spiritual program for yourself:

1. Look at resources in spiritual magazines. Look at the back of magazines to find teachers, classes, groups, and other resources in your area.
2. Read spiritual books or listen to recordings of books. The sacred information that was once hidden from the public is now abundantly available in bookstores, libraries, and on the Internet.
3. Engage in home practice. Buy or create your own home study course with guide books and journals.
4. Listen to audiotapes, videos, or DVDs of great teachers of the past and present.
5. Join a support group. If you can't find one that's right for you, create one. Meet once a week to discuss a new topic and mark progress.
6. Attend events. See who is coming to town, attend special events or weekend retreats, or take some classes.
7. Enjoy art, music, and drama. These are great for the soul and for inspiration.
8. Work with a good counselor either in person or long-distance on the phone.

9. Join a nature group. Being in nature will get you in touch with your Source.
10. Travel. Look for a tour to a sacred site in the United States, India, Egypt, England, or other parts of the world.

**Q:** What can I do to begin this spiritual healing?

**Audrey Hope:** One can begin a spiritual journey by whispering your intentions to the wind, to your spiritual source. Say, "I want to live a true, great life. Show me the way." The universe hears the call. The doors will open.

You can begin a spiritual journey right now by asking yourself deep questions like these:

- What is my life purpose?
- Why am I here on earth?
- What really makes me happy?
- What am I most proud of in myself?
- What am I least proud of in myself?
- Am I living by my own rules or someone else's?
- What if I only had one year to live?
- What do I want people to say about me when I've left this planet?
- Am I truthful with myself and others?
- Do I have regrets, shame, guilt, or fears?
- Who do I need to forgive?
- Do I believe in miracles?
- Who or what is God?
- Where can I begin to find out?

**Q:** Can you share an example of how spiritual work helped someone break free from an addiction?

**Audrey Hope:** I worked with a client at Passages whose break-through came when she was able to discover the real source of her pain through deep soul work. Susan was happily married, with three beautiful children and a thriving career in the arts. Everything seemed fine, except Susan wanted to die. She was suicidal when she came to us and addicted to pharmaceutical drugs. She had been in therapy for many years, but nothing helped her depression.

The one area of real concern for Susan was her relationship with her business partner. Susan's business partner was controlling and critical, and Susan was concerned that this relationship was causing her to make poor decisions regarding her family. Her loss of power in this situation was unbearable, and Susan could not understand why she was so obsessed with pleasing her partner.

Through spiritual work, Susan discovered a deep wound pattern that explained the issues that were at the bottom of this unhealthy relationship. In a process known as "reframing," Susan revisited the moment the pain began. She changed, or reframed, how it played out. She was able to say what she could not say in the past in order to release her anger, frustration, and fear. This deep level of exploration and expression turned out to be Susan's salvation. Once she understood the source of her obsession, everything finally made sense. She was able to let go of the pain and as a result was no longer dependent on drugs to cope.

## CREATING A HEALTHY CIRCLE OF FRIENDS

Another key factor in the success of your program and your lasting recovery is your environment. In the same way that a formerly dependent person must say goodbye to alcohol and drugs or risk addiction again, sustained sobriety depends on ending unhealthy relationships and choosing to be in healthy relationships with those who share your intentions and new lifestyle.

Who you allow into the circle of your life will make the difference in the quality of your life.

It is not enough to make profound changes in your life and then return to the same environment, says Mary Van Lent, a certified alcohol and drug abuse counselor who also owns and manages a transitional living home. Mary works at Passages in the area of counseling and aftercare programming. In her answers to the following questions, she shows why our choice of friends is crucial and how old drinking and using companions can be triggers for relapse.

### Questions and Answers with
### Mary Van Lent

**Q:** Once I'm recovered, can I see friends who are still drinking or using?

**Mary Van Lent:** I cannot emphasize enough the essential role of friends for the individual in early recovery. More often than not, the recovering person's circle of friends can mean the difference between failure and success. The old expression "water seeks its own level" aptly describes what can happen to a person fresh out of rehab. That is why twelve-step support groups suggest that the newcomer "stick with the winners."

In order to manifest your desires, your intentions and your actions must be in line with each other. If you want to be a musician, you wouldn't surround yourself with people who hate music. Likewise, if it is your desire to live a life that is free of drugs and alcohol, it makes no sense to be hanging out with friends who are drinking and using.

**Q:** Are friends really that influential in my recovery? Isn't my sobriety based on my own willpower?

**Mary Van Lent:** Companions who drink and use drugs are "triggers." A trigger is a cue or stimulus that creates a conditioned response. In the case of the person who was once alcohol or drug dependent, this response is an urge to drink or use—a craving. Studies have demonstrated that even after seven years of being abstinent from cocaine, a person's brain still "lights up" when exposed to stimuli, or triggers, associated with past cocaine use. The body then experiences a physiological response—rapid heartbeat and sweaty palms followed by cravings.

Speaking as a person who was once alcohol and drug dependent, it was not enough for me to change and then go back into the same environment. For this reason alone, I relapsed many times before I recognized the problem. It was not until I was willing to set out on a new path, with new friends and a new environment, that I was able to sustain sobriety. In short, I had to find fellow travelers who were of like mind and spirit and were headed in the same direction I was going.

■ ■ ■

Remember to have all of the practitioners on your personalized recovery team read this book so that they will have the same goal and will understand how to reach it.

■ ■ ■

## Can I Ever Drink or Use Addictive Drugs Again?

Now that you have explored each of the therapies that will assist you in achieving your cure, I must add a final and essential element to the success of your recovery program. The two most common questions I'm asked about cures are: "If I'm cured, does that mean I can drink again?" and "If I'm cured, does that mean I can use addictive drugs again?"

The answer is "No, you cannot ever use addictive drugs or alcohol again." That means not even one sip of wine, once, not one toot of cocaine, not one toke of marijuana, not one pain pill—*nothing*. Of course, if you have an operation or a medical emergency and you need pain medication, take it, but you must discontinue it immediately when the pain has reached a level you can tolerate. If a doctor prescribes an addictive drug for an illness and you feel it's appropriate, take it, but you must discontinue it the moment the illness is over.

Being cured means that the underlying causes that drove you to drink or to use addictive drugs in the first place have been healed and that you'll no longer crave those substances to self-medicate those underlying causes. It means that your dependency on addictive drugs or alcohol will be ended. Cure means that you can feel physically and mentally good without the use of addictive drugs or alcohol. You can live a happy, fulfilling, and substance-free life without the daily, paralyzing fear of relapse.

Cure does *not* mean that you can use addictive drugs or alcohol again, not even in the distant future. If you start believing that you can drink socially, or maybe just have a glass of wine with dinner, or have one little night of cocaine or marijuana, you're on your way back to dependency. I know of no one who was dependent on alcohol or addictive drugs who has succeeded in going back to using either one moderately. All who have tried have immediately become dependent again.

The reason for complete abstinence from addictive drugs and alcohol is abundantly clear and simple: they are addictive, particularly for you. There are many people who can drink alcohol or use addictive drugs recreationally. You are not one of them. You've already demonstrated that when you use addictive drugs or alcohol, you become dependent on them. I'm showing you how to cure your dependency, but I cannot show you how to take the addictive quality out of addictive drugs and alcohol. Why would you want to use addictive drugs or alcohol anyway? They are destructive to life, and life is far better without them than with them.

Do not rely on outside substances to deal with life. They only bring more problems of their own. They complicate life rather than smooth it out. It's like trying to soothe a poison ivy itch by scratching; it only makes the itch worse and it spreads.

## The End Can Be Known from the Beginning

Another way of looking at this is that becoming dependent on addictive drugs or alcohol is not like getting the measles, mumps, or chicken pox, which are one-time illnesses. As many times as you go through withdrawal from an addictive drug or alcohol and then start using it again, that's how many times you'll again become dependent.

Louise is a perfect example. When Louise came to us for treatment, she had been an alcoholic for more than thirty-five years. She was a professional bartender, and when she walked through the doors of Passages, she said, "Boys, I'm not here to stop drinking. I drink, my husband drinks, our friends drink, I'm a bartender, and my life revolves around drinking. No way am I going to stop drinking. My mom died and left me some money, and I'm here to dry out, get healthy, and get the benefits of your program, but then I'm going back home to drink some more."

Passages has a large covered verandah that overlooks a Zen garden, the lawns, and the Pacific Ocean. After the evening meal, a group of six women from various parts of the world, including Louise, and all of them in treatment, would sit on dark-blue canvas lounge chairs and talk. A strong bond grew among them and they began calling themselves "The Blue Chair Club."

One evening, about three weeks after Louise had begun the program, she was sitting outside talking with her friends when something I had said to her the day before hit home and she started crying. I had told her that she was literally trying to kill herself by drinking. The realization hit home and she came in and found me and said, "I'll never drink again." She finished the program, graduated, left in sparkling condition, and went home. She called regularly and told us that she was wonderfully happy, that she had discovered she could have just as good a time not drinking as she had ever had when drinking, that she had her husband down to one glass of wine a day, that she was drinking cranberry juice at the bar, and that she felt wonderful. For just over a year she maintained complete sobriety.

Then her friends convinced her that she could drink one glass of wine a day and still maintain sobriety. The end can always be known from the beginning; within a few weeks, she was again a full-blown alcoholic. After six months of drinking, she returned to Passages for treatment and is now sober again.

Louise's story is a reminder that once dependency ends, it must end forever. Once cured, you must remember the "never again" rule—and so must everyone in your support network. If someone tells you to have a drink, that "one won't hurt," do not be deceived. One is all it takes to get the brain chemistry going again.

The same vicious cycle happens with all addictive substances. For seventeen years, I was addicted to nicotine, which is at the top of every list of the world's most addictive substances. Quitting smoking cigarettes was perhaps the most difficult task I've ever undertaken. Every day for five years was a fight to remain free of nicotine. It nagged at me constantly. During those five years of brutal, concentrated effort, I relapsed three times, followed by another year before my cravings ceased and I could safely say I was past my addiction.

I haven't smoked a cigarette now for more than thirty years. I'm no longer a nicotine addict. I'm cured. But even though I abhor the thought of smoking again, if I were to resume smoking, I would again become addicted to nicotine. Why? Because nicotine is addictive. When I feed it to my body, my body builds up an appetite for it; and when I deprive my body of it, my body puts up a fight. It demands it. That's how it will be for you if you use alcohol or addictive drugs again.

Another word of caution: You cannot think that you can use alcohol if you were once dependent on drugs because alcohol *is* a drug (ethanol). Neither can you use drugs if you were once dependent on alcohol—for the same reason. I have heard many people say, "Oh, I can drink. Alcohol was not my drug of choice." It always leads directly back to dependency. Once it's over, it must be over forever.

## Your Brain Can Play Tricks on You

Another aspect of dependency and relapse that you should understand is that when you are using drugs or alcohol, your brain will play tricks on you, causing you to make decisions that are totally the opposite of what is in your best interest. In the center of your forehead, about an inch in from the front, lies a part of your brain known as the ventral medial prefrontal cortex. This is the part of your brain that takes in information, sorts it out, and decides what action you should take. It's the decision-making part of your brain. Most of the time it works well—you assess each new situation, decide what needs to be done, and then take the appropriate action to accomplish your goal.

However, in clinical studies, patients with damage to the ventral medial prefrontal cortex have been found to show excessive risk-taking behaviors, an unusual detachment from their problems, and difficulty following through with plans. With every addiction—no exceptions—that part of your brain suddenly takes a topsy-turvy spin and issues decisions that are completely the opposite of what they should be. Instead of providing you with the conclusion that you shouldn't do harmful things to yourself, it tells you that it's okay. For instance, it will tell you that it's okay to smoke cigarettes, it's okay to use addictive drugs, it's okay to drink alcohol, it's okay to drive a hundred miles an hour. You know that these things are bad for you, that they'll eventually kill you, and that they'll make a horrible mess of your life in the process. You read about them, you heard about them, and you know in your heart that they are not okay for you. Yet this part of your brain is telling you that it's okay to do them anyway.

This comes from a malfunction of the ventral medial prefrontal cortex area of your brain. It's like an autoimmune disease that tells your immune system to attack healthy parts of your body instead of only the invaders. It's a betrayal of your own mind, and there's only one way to correct it: by abstaining from alcohol and addictive drugs. After you've been away from alcohol and addictive drugs for some length of time (the length of time will differ for everyone), the ventral medial prefrontal cortex begins functioning properly again and protecting you from making bad decisions with regard to drugs and alcohol.

Now that you know that ingesting alcohol or addictive drugs causes the ventral medial area of your brain to malfunction and causes you to make decisions that are harmful to you, you should also know that simply having that information won't stop you from using alcohol or addictive drugs—because the ventral medial frontal cortex area of your brain will tell you that it's okay to continue. However, at least now you'll understand *why* you're making such foolish and potentially fatal decisions. I know that may not be much comfort, but by reading this book you are taking the first important step toward reversing that trend.

## CHAPTER EIGHT

# YOUR
# PERSONAL PHILOSOPHY

ONE OF THE MAJOR CAUSES OF DEPENDENCY HAS TO DO with your personal philosophy—what you believe about life and how it works. You learned in earlier chapters that what you believe, think, and feel actually determine the makeup of your body at the cellular level. Now it's time to learn *how* to think and feel so that *what* you think and feel will create happiness and vibrancy in your life rather than gloominess and despondency.

Step 3 on your path to total recovery focuses on this crucial area of your life. This step is equally as important as the other two steps. It will take you to freedom from dependency and beyond. *In my own life, this is the most important information I have ever discovered.*

**Step 3:** Adopt a philosophy based on what is true in the Universe

That you have a personal philosophy is indisputable—we all have one. Although you may have never sat down and defined what your philosophy is, it is fully operative and working in your life all the time. It deals with what you believe about the world in which you live, about its people and events, about how events and circumstances affect you, and about how you affect them.

If you were asked about your philosophy of life in general, you might say, "Life is great, good things happen to me, I'm a lucky person, and I believe the world is a wonderful place with wonderful people in it." Or you might say just the opposite: "I'm unlucky, bad things happen to me, the world isn't a very nice place, people take advantage of me, and they're just out for what they can get." You might believe that Murphy's law—"If anything can go wrong, it will"—is in full operation. Whatever your personal philosophy is, it determines how you respond to events that come into your life. It is *completely* responsible for your state of happiness and well-being.

The future may seem to you to be something unknowable, indeterminate, perhaps scary or hopeless, as if you're sitting in a buggy being pulled by a team of high-spirited horses without knowing how to control them. You don't know if those horses will turn your buggy over and spill you to the ground, drive off a cliff, become lost, or take you to your destination. Not knowing how to handle them, direct them, or stop them, you're probably terrified. But once you know how to rein in the horses and control them, they will follow your directions and take you where you want to go. You'll be relaxed and confident because you know you're in control of your journey. That's how life is when your personal philosophy is based on what is true in the Universe; you know what actions to take to bring about the circumstances you desire, and you are not disappointed.

If this chapter seems off the beaten path to you, that's only natural. It may seem as if I've reached into a grab bag of strange concepts and pulled out some that are truly unusual. On the other hand, you may find that what follows isn't unusual at all. In either case, if you put these concepts to use, they'll work for you in a way that will completely change your life. These concepts have been in use for thousands of years, and they have survived because of their immense benefit to people all over the world. I've been teaching people of all ages about them for many years, and I've seen great success come into the lives of those who have embraced them. The success of your cure and your future happiness will depend in a large part on how well you can apply these concepts in your life.

## Aligning Your Beliefs with What Is True

What I mean by "adopt a philosophy that is based on what is true in the Universe" can best be shown by a ridiculous example. If you believed that the way to rid yourself of a headache was to repeatedly smash your head with a hammer, you would soon discover that what you believed was not how the Universe worked.

Because your belief was based on an assumption that was not in accord with Universal law, not only would your efforts fail, but you would also incur additional injury that would complicate the matter rather than resolving it. The same thing applies when we believe that using alcohol or addictive drugs or behaviors will better our life; it just isn't so and we only injure ourselves further by relying on them. Ultimately, by the consequences you experience, the truth will make itself known to you.

There are Universal laws that were in place and fully operative before you were born, and they'll remain so during your lifetime and long afterwards. One such Universal law is the law of gravity. That law, as stated by Sir Isaac Newton, says that every particle in the universe attracts every other particle with the force that is directly proportional to the product of their masses and inversely proportional to the square of the distance between them. Cause and effect is another Universal law. I've mentioned this one before. It states that every action produces a result, and that the result is in exact accord with the action. If you plant an acorn, you'll get an oak tree, not a willow. If you overeat, you'll get fat. If you're a mean person, you'll lack friends. If you fail to nourish yourself, you'll become ill.

Knowing the laws of the Universe will save you from making costly errors of judgment. If your personal philosophy is in accord with what's true in the Universe, your actions will be successful as a result of natural law, and your efforts will produce the results you desire. If your personal philosophy is not in accord with Universal law, can anything happen but that you'll fail in your efforts to be happy or successful or healthy or free of dependency? Just as you will fail to achieve a goal if you set out to accomplish it in the wrong way, so you will fail to achieve freedom from dependency if you go about it in the wrong way.

Don't be concerned if you haven't been aware of these natural laws before. Once you begin to incorporate a philosophy into your life that is in accordance with Universal law, your life will bring you such joy that you'll laugh in amazement. It will be as if you've spent your life driving a car in reverse and you've suddenly discovered that there are gears that make it go forward—and fast!

## Face Down in the Mud

A personal philosophy that's based on what's true in the Universe will sustain you through every occurrence that life brings to you. It will make even your best days brighter and will save you countless hours of misery and needless suffering. It will help you see that events you may have lamented for weeks, months or even years may turn out to be the best events that could have happened to you.

In 1993, Pax and I were out gathering rocks for a landscape project. We were driving through a canyon in Malibu when I saw what looked like an interesting rock projecting eight or nine inches above the edge of a ravine. I got out of the truck and looked down into the ravine and saw that the rock was about twenty inches long and embedded in the side of the ravine, which was about thirty-five feet deep. Holding onto the rock, I climbed into the ravine and kicked a place into its earthen wall to give myself a toehold so I could get under the rock and push it up. I was wearing tai chi shoes with smooth cotton soles, and the surface of the dirt was still moist from the morning dew.

The rock weighed well over a hundred pounds, but I managed to dislodge it. Then I heaved and pushed until I had it at its balance point, just ready to topple onto the road, when my feet slipped out from under me. I slid to the bottom of the ravine, still standing erect but supporting myself against the side of the ravine with my outstretched hands. What I didn't know was that the rock hadn't fallen onto the road but was hurtling down into the ravine, bounding into the air because of its triangular form. The flat part of the rock hit me squarely on the top of my head. I was slammed into the ground with such force that two bones were broken in my left hand and my knees were bruised from the terrific force with which I hit the ground. I was lying face down in the mud, unable to breathe and unable to move because all my vertebrae had been compressed and I was paralyzed.

Now, what do you think was going through my mind as I lay in the mud, paralyzed and unable to breathe? Before I tell you, I must go back in time so my answer will have some meaning for you and so you can begin to understand what I mean by a philosophy that is based on "what's true in the Universe."

When I was in my teens and early twenties, I had no moral code whatsoever. My mother, Bea, was born in New York in 1900 to a poor German family. When she was fifteen, she was raped and became pregnant. They forced the older man to marry her and it began a life of hell. My mother hated him for what he had done to her, and he hated her because she immediately became as tough and as hard as was necessary to defend herself from him. During the first two years of her marriage, she sewed buttons on shirts to earn a few pennies. After three years, she divorced him, but by then she had become totally hardened and she turned to a life of crime. Within a few years, she was leading a stolen car ring in New Jersey and had a crew of con artists working for her in New York. When prohibition began, she became a bootlegger and supplied whiskey to the local clubs.

Later, when I was born, she brought me up the only way she knew—to be like her. She always insisted that I call her Bea, never mom or mother. The first rule she taught me, when I was about three-and-a-half, was "Never tell the truth." She said, "Only fools tell the truth. If you do, it will only get you into trouble." Her motto was "Never tell the truth when a good lie will suffice." So I lied and cheated and stole, and I was highly praised for it.

She taught me shoplifting when I was four. It was one of her favorite games. She also told me that no one could be trusted, particularly women, and she taught me not to respect authority. Regarding rules, she explained that the main rule was that there are no rules—except the golden rule, which was "Those who have the gold make the rules." When I grew older, my business dealings were always shady.

Fortunately, I was an insatiable reader, and in the many hundreds of books I read, I perceived a different way of life. When I reached the age of twenty-five, I began to realize from the books I had read that Bea, that marvelous woman whom I loved dearly, had programmed me one hundred and eighty degrees in the wrong direction. I was following a path that would unerringly lead to unhappiness for me and for everyone around me. It was hard to see that at first, because she was so successful and had become something of a minor political power. Besides that, Bea was fun-loving and generous to a fault. I, too, was successful, although I had obtained my success in a deceitful way.

So I set out to change my ways. I realized that I couldn't do that living near Bea, so in 1965 I packed up and moved to California. I was determined to turn my life around. My first resolve was that I would always speak the truth. My second resolve was that I would never again take advantage of anyone. That wasn't easy for me in the beginning, since I had lived my whole life up to that point lying and without a moral code, so I had to make one up as I went along.

## Understanding Universal Laws

As the years passed, I made some progress. If I lied to someone, I would force myself to go to that person and tell him or her the truth. I made a trip back to New Jersey to make whatever amends I could to the people I had wronged and cheated. That part was very difficult, but I forced myself to carry on until I had seen everyone I could remember having hurt in some way.

When I was about thirty-three, I came across an ancient Chinese book of wisdom called the I Ching. When writing came to China five thousand years ago in 3,000 B.C., the I Ching was the first thing to be written. Before that, it had been passed along in the oral tradition for thousands of years. The I Ching may be the world's oldest known wisdom. It survived all those years because it was of such great value for the people. I studied it not only because of its wisdom, but also because it contained many

Universal laws. As the I Ching was written so long ago, much of its language and meanings were unclear to me, and I yearned to know what its phrases meant. I felt certain that some of the secrets of the Universe were locked away in them.

Over the years, I grew in my understanding of Universal laws such as cause and effect, and I became ever more careful of my words and actions. I began to build character. I learned that character is the bow from which we shoot the arrows of the future. During all those years, I spent several hours each day studying the I Ching, and I still spend a few minutes each day reading it.

I came to see that Universal law governs everything. Once I understood that, I was able to perceive and understand a great many other aspects of the world in which we live. For instance, I learned that *all the laws of the Universe are in favor of the continuation of the Universe.* How do I know that to be true? Because the Universe continues. That truth is self-evident. Astronomers and scientists tell us that the Universe has been around in its current state for about 13.7 billion years. If there was even one law that favored discontinuation, surely it would have come to pass by now. Since it hasn't, I feel it is safe to believe that all the laws are in favor of continuation.

Carrying that thought further, I assumed that *the Universe is perfect.* If you believe that God or a Supreme Being of any other name is the cause of everything, and if you believe in the popular conception of a Supreme Being that is all-knowing and all-powerful, it follows that whatever comes from that Supreme Being, such as the Universe itself, has to be perfect as well. (Incidentally, validating everything that happens as "perfect" puts you in step with the Supreme Being whom you believe is causing it. If you believe in God, but you believe that we live in an imperfect Universe, then it necessarily follows that the God you believe in must also be imperfect.)

The next step in my thinking process led me to understand that *whatever happens is the best possible event that can happen*. If one thing could happen that was truly bad—one thing that was imperfect—so could three, four, five, and more imperfect, bad events happen, which could possibly lead to destruction. But that doesn't happen. The Universe continues to be perfect at every moment and never permits even the first imperfect event to occur. It goes from perfect to perfect to perfect—endlessly.

Carrying that thought still further, I came to believe that *I was a part of the Universe, an integral, inseparable part, and therefore everything that happened was for my complete benefit*. Even if an incident hurt me or took something from me, it would always work to my benefit since the Universe will not let anything bad happen to itself, and I am part of "itself."

I came to see the entire Universe as alive and aware, a living, breathing entity that has consciousness—that *is* consciousness. That is why I capitalize the word *Universe*. What most people refer to as God, Allah, Jehovah, Buddha, or any of a thousand other names people use to refer to a supreme entity, I simply think of and refer to as "The Universe," a vast energy source of consciousness. As the decades moved on, I continued to live with my philosophy and it has borne itself out through every circumstance of my life, even when what I believe has been put to the fire, sometimes on a daily basis.

Now that you know my state of mind when the rock smashed me to the ground that day, I ask you again: What do you think was going through my mind as I lay in the mud, paralyzed and unable to breathe? I suppose I've given you too many clues for you not to have some inkling of what was going through my mind, but what I was thinking was, "I wonder what good thing will come from this?"

## What Good Thing Will Come from This?

Pax had seen the rock disappear over the side of the hill. He ran to the ravine, looked down, and saw me lying in the mud. He slid down, turned me over, and asked if I was okay. I was able to speak, because my paralysis was from the neck down, and I told him I didn't know. As I lay there, I began to get a tingling sensation all over my body, the kind you feel when your foot goes to sleep or you hit your funny bone. My vertebrae began to decompress and I was slowly able to move. I didn't want to reach up and examine my head because I was afraid I would put my hand through the hole I thought must have been there and kill myself. When that rock had landed on my head, it sounded as if someone had broken a baseball bat over my head. I didn't think anyone could get hit that hard and survive.

One week later, as I was lying in bed recovering, I picked up the I Ching and the passages that had earlier baffled me were now understandable. Somehow, that blow to my head had opened the channels that allowed me to perceive the meanings of what had before been unintelligible. Since that time, I've written ten books on the I Ching, including my own popular version of it called *The I Ching: The Book of Answers*, written under my Chinese pen name, Wu Wei. All that was a result of the rock smashing my head.

We can speculate forever about whether that rock falling on my head was divine intervention or an accident without any significance, but the benefit to me was beyond calculation. My main study up to that point in my life had been to try and fathom the information locked away in that ancient Chinese volume and suddenly I could understand it! For that kind of gift, I would willingly be hit on the head many times.

Because the core of my personal philosophy is that everything that happens benefits us, I was also spared the futility of cursing my bad luck, lamenting the occurrence, or feeling as if I was a victim. Never for an instant, then or now, did I think anything other than that this so-called accident was for my total and complete benefit. Oddly enough, to this day I have no neck pain, nor have I lost mobility of any kind, and I even get to put the incident to good use by writing about it these many years later.

The reason I was able to benefit from my accident was because of the way I looked at the event. If I hadn't viewed it in a positive light, I would have been looking for all the bad outcomes, and in so doing I could have actually created problems for myself. My stress over what had happened could have led to sickness and further complications with my neck. I could have been depressed and cursed my bad luck. Yet none of those things happened.

I want to give you another example of how looking at events in a positive light can create a positive outcome. Twenty-four years ago, I bought a brand-new car and it was parked in the alley next to my house. I walked out of the house just in time to see an old VW bus scrape the front fender of the car. The driver got out, threw his hat on the ground, then held his head in his hands and bowed it. He obviously had no money to pay for the damage to my car and he almost began to cry. His wife was in his car and his son was in the back seat crying. When he saw me coming, he looked even more distraught. I walked up to the car, looked at this man, and said, "Perfect. That's just what my car needed."

He couldn't believe what he was hearing. I told him to have a nice day and not to worry about the scrape, that now I wouldn't be so worried about getting a scratch on my car. He began crying tears of happiness and hugged me. He danced a little jig and ran around to his wife and hugged her. He got them out of the car and introduced me to them. He told me that he had just arrived in town, that he was a carpenter, and that they were looking for a place to stay until he could find work. I gave him the phone number of a friend of mine who was in the construction business, and the next day he began working for my friend.

Three weeks later, this man showed up at my house to give me two hundred dollars to repair the scratch. I told him to keep it, that I liked the scratch because it reminded me of what a wonderful place the Universe is. To me, it was worth the damage to my car just to see how happy that man was when I told him it was a perfect event. I still think about it to this day and it still makes me happy.

I never did repair the damage. When people would ask me how I scratched the car, I would say, "It's a gift from the Universe." When I was asked to explain what I meant by that, I would tell them of my philosophy, and I was able to lead many people into a new way of understanding that stood them in good stead. On several occasions, the people I've spoken to have told me that they've come to see seemingly bad events in their lives as a "scratch on the fender."

Suppose I had not reacted the way I had when my car was scratched. Suppose I had instead punched the driver of the VW bus and after a violent fight we had both wound up in jail. Suppose I had been sexually molested in jail, had gotten into another fight, had seriously hurt someone, and had been sentenced to twenty years in prison. All of life presents us with two basic ways to treat events. We can either label them "good for us" or "bad for us." How we treat those events determine what they become in our lives. It is not the event that determines the outcome. The event is only an event. It's how we treat the event that determines its outcome in our lives.

I have learned that bad events simply do not happen. Pax tells me that the most important thing that I have ever done for him was to pass on to him this philosophy, because it saves him from feeling bad when things happen that seem bad. He immediately knows "this is for my benefit and I will use this event as a springboard for further success." That philosophy was of immense benefit to us both in the time of his dependency.

## A Strong Philosophy Sees Us through Difficult Times

Earlier, I mentioned the workshops I led from 1984 through 1986 for people who wanted to change their lives. Those workshops showed me once again how important it is to have a strong personal philosophy that can sustain us through whatever life brings our way. There were two rules that participants had to follow: they had to attend every workshop and they had to be on time. If someone was not in the workshop when the door closed, he or she was out of the workshop, no exceptions. About forty percent of the participants had to drop out of every workshop because they missed a class or arrived late.

After a week or two, those who remained in the workshop were making such extraordinary changes in their lives that some would leave home with enough time to walk to the workshop in case their cars broke down. The workshops were incredibly successful in that the participants made lifestyle changes and accomplished deeds they had previously believed were far beyond their capabilities. They made advancements in their chosen field of work, they moved out of apartments and bought houses, they overcame lifelong fears, they ended dependent relationships with family members and friends, they accomplished long-sought goals, they became happy and free of bad habits, they discovered their passion for life, and they found peace.

Because the workshops were so successful, I was invited to do a number of TV and radio shows. The response was so great, thousands of inquiries, that I couldn't accommodate all the people as attendance was limited to thirty-five participants.

I decided to discontinue the workshops to write a book that would accommodate the needs of a great many people rather than just a few. It would incorporate the principles responsible for the extraordinary changes that the people in the workshops were making in their lives, but first I had to discover what those principles were.

All the workshop sessions had been recorded and transcribed into ten large volumes. I sold my business, sold the building where I had conducted the workshops, and spent the next two-and-a-half years studying the transcripts to find out what was behind the mind-boggling accomplishments of the attendees. The principles didn't make themselves known immediately, but gradually, as I persisted, they became clear.

I learned how essential it is to live according to an empowering personal philosophy, a lodestar, a guiding light that will see us through the difficult times of despair, hardship, grief, and despondency that seem to regularly occur to us all. It became clear that those who led fulfilling lives had adopted a philosophy that changed their down feelings into cheerful feelings and brought a smile to their faces, a smile that was more than just a brave veneer in the face of adversity.

I understood that a strong philosophy, based on what is true in the Universe, is powerful, joy-giving, and happiness-sustaining, and it withstands all the rigors and tests of time. Further, I came to realize that a weak philosophy is a weak way of life. I saw that the failures that had dogged the footsteps of my workshop participants had always been due to a weak or misguided philosophy. Once they adopted the new philosophy and put it into action, their lives took an amazing turn for the better. As their outlook changed, all the circumstances of their lives changed.

Just as it was true for those workshop participants, it is true for you: how you conduct yourself along the path that is your life determines how your life unfolds. That's a basic law of the Universe. Imagine yourself being angry most of the time. Your anger would affect everything and everyone around you. People wouldn't want to be near you. The anger would also produce an acid reaction in your body that would slowly destroy you. It would influence your thinking so that you wouldn't have the state of calmness necessary to produce clear, rational thinking. Your friends would be few, if any. You wouldn't enjoy eating or recreational activities. Harmony would be absent from your life. You wouldn't be able to feel happy, and it would probably be difficult to get a good night's sleep. In business, success would be hard to come by, or it might not come at all. If you worked for others, it would be hard to keep a job. You, and you alone, determine what your world is like. You are the doorway through which your life unfolds.

## You Determine How Your Life Unfolds

The path that has led to your current condition and situation was not a few days or months in the making, but a long and arduous path that spans many years. Actually, it has taken you as long as you've been on the planet to become the way you are. It has also taken you that long to achieve what you've achieved, to possess what you now possess, and to arrive at your current condition. Your life today is the result of a series of decisions you made that have caused you to arrive where you are.

If who you are and what you have is what you want, if you're satisfied with the conditions of your life, congratulations—do more of what you've been doing and you'll get more of what you already have. But if who you are, what you want, what you have, and your current conditions are less than what you want, or are different from what you want, you have to make some changes—basic changes, inner changes.

Each of us has suffered in our lifetime. We've been lied to, we've been betrayed and cheated, and we've been taken advantage of. Many of us, perhaps you, have been beaten, raped, mistreated, forced to do things against our will, or sexually molested by parents, siblings, or strangers. We've had our hearts broken and we've suffered great financial, spiritual, and physical losses. We've grieved over the loss of loved ones and we've been born with physical or mental deformities. How we deal with those traumas and others like them will determine our state of happiness today or, for that matter, any day.

A few years ago, Peter, a twenty-five-year-old athlete, checked into Passages. He had been using marijuana. Peter was particularly interested in my weekly metaphysics sessions. He loved the philosophy portion of those groups and took it to heart. He and I also had several one-on-one sessions. In those sessions, he learned what you're learning here. At the end of his thirty-day stay, his marijuana addiction was over. A few months after he left Passages, Peter had an accident and is now paralyzed from the waist down and confined to a wheelchair.

Two days after his accident, I went to see him in the hospital. When I walked into the room, his eyes lit up and he said in a quiet voice, "Don't worry, I know this is the best thing that could have happened to me." Today, he persists in that belief. We talk every few months and he tells me of the heights to which his enlightenment has soared. He says that his spiritual growth could never have come so far in such a short time without his accident. He's an inspiration to all who meet him and he occasionally visits us and speaks at meetings of Passages alumni.

How did you feel about Peter's response when I walked into his hospital room and he said, "This is the best thing that could have happened to me"? Did you say to yourself, sarcastically, "Yeah, right!" as if nothing could possibly be further from the truth? To the degree that you reacted that way, your personal philosophy is different from the one that's sustaining Peter and his peaceful feeling while he sits in his wheelchair. It means that you probably regard all incidents that seem unlucky as actually unlucky. But it's mainly because of that thinking that your current circumstances have come about.

A strong philosophy that's based on what's true in the Universe saves us from playing the role of the victim—a person who's been ill-used, a person who's suffered bad luck, or a person whose life is one of despondency and unhappiness. A strong philosophy sustains us through adversity because we know that the mystery will unravel itself and reveal a happy and perfect ending. Do you think that you could maintain Peter's joyous outlook if you became paralyzed? If you don't have a personal philosophy that will see you through the times of hardship, tragedy, and despair that comes to us all, it's unlikely.

## Freedom from the Tyranny of Events

A personal philosophy that's based on what's true in the Universe does more than sustain us through the tragedies of life. It also sustains us daily in everything we think and do. It gives us optimism and hope. It frees us from the tyranny of events. Here's a story from those workshops I used to offer that shows how liberating it is to be free of the events that knock on our door. (It's a little like the story I told earlier about my car but with a slightly different twist that shows how this philosophy can help lift you up in so many ways.)

Doris was a waitress in a coffee shop. She came to the workshop because her son had been there the month before and the results he had experienced amazed her. One day after she had been in the workshop for about three weeks, I arrived and saw fifteen or twenty of the workshop participants in the parking lot looking at a new car. They were laughing and talking excitedly. When they came in, I asked what the excitement was about and they all laughed.

Doris had bought that new car the day before, and when she had gone down to the garage in her condominium complex that morning, her new car had a dented fender. Doris said that ordinarily she would have cried and gone back upstairs, gotten back in bed, pulled the covers over her head, and stayed there all day so no more bad luck could come her way.

However, she remembered what she had learned in the workshop, and she looked at the car with new eyes. That dented fender no longer had the power to ruin her day. She said that she had just experienced one of the *best* days of her life because she was no longer tied to what she called "the tyranny of events," those incidents that come to all of us—the lost watch, the stolen wallet, the missed bus or plane. She was free, and everyone outside looking at her dented fender and seeing her reaction to it was rejoicing in her freedom and in their own. Doris said she might not even get the fender fixed because it had such great meaning for her.

Have you ever had anything happen to you that seemed really bad at the time but later turned out to be beneficial? Everyone I've ever posed that question to has been able to remember several events like that. It's time to look at *all* events in the light of that information.

Don't start with what's most difficult—infant death, the tragic loss of a loved one, Hitler, or 9/11. Start with something small like a stubbed toe.

Say, "Thank you for my stubbed toe. Right there is an acupuncture point that needed release. Now I'll have more energy!" If you bump your head, say, "Ouch, I bumped my head! I must remember to pay attention and stay present in the moment.

Thanks for the reminder." At least you'll get a laugh out of it. Practice on little things, and what seemed impossible will soon be just as easy. If you feel I'm stretching my credibility too thin here, stay with me a little longer and I'll show you what I mean about seemingly bad events having a benefit.

## The Traumas Locked in Our Subconscious

Pax tells me I am running a risk by including this next case history, the story of Sally. He thinks the story may be too much for most women and also for many men to encompass within their brand-new philosophy that labels everything as "good" and as "a benefit." His concern is that it may be "too much, too soon."

His concern has merit. When I have discussed subjects like this in my metaphysics groups at Passages, it is not unusual for a woman or a man who has been raped to react as though I'm insane to suggest that what happened was for their benefit or that any good thing could come out of it.

One woman in her forties who had been raped by an uncle called my suggestion "the stupidest, most ridiculous utterance I've ever heard." People have gotten up and walked out of the room after hearing my viewpoint that all events benefit us in some way.

However, before the end of their stay at Passages, after they have come to understand the reasoning behind that statement, the same people invariably grasp the concept. They understand that if they are ever to be truly happy, they must put to rest that hurtful incident in their lives. The real turnaround comes when one of the women says in an angry tone, "You wouldn't say that if it was you who was raped!" Then I reply, "I was raped when I was in the sixth grade." Then there's a silence. I wait while the information is absorbed and add, "But I'm not so foolish as to let that event ruin the rest of my life."

Of course it's hard to live with, of course it's shameful, of course it's degrading, of course we're filled with images of what we'd like to do to the person who raped us. But in the last analysis, we'd better learn to deal with it or it will be there to greet us every morning when we awake.

One woman who had been raped, and who was still carrying the anger, hurt, humiliation, and outrage of what had happened, couldn't even vent her rage on a physical person because the man who raped her had died a few years afterwards. I told her that if she loved herself, she would treat herself to the relief of seeing what had happened to her in an entirely new light, a light that would relieve her of all pain and resentment. "If you could do that for me," she said, "I would be forever grateful." It took only one more conversation, just the two of us, for her to achieve that goal.

So I have decided to run the risk of including Sally's story because if you are ever to become whole, free, and without fear, you must one day, like Sally, let go of the weak philosophy that makes you believe that events have hurt you, taken something from you, shamed you, or in some way diminished you. Read carefully, stay open to the words and the concepts, and you too will be able to live pain free and happy.

Several years ago, Sally checked into Passages for treatment. She was fifty years old and heavily dependent on alcohol. She had been drinking for many years and it had gotten so out of hand that her husband would no longer tolerate it. Her drinking had upset her entire family, and their four children were acting out because of her drunkenness. No one knew the source of her dependency on alcohol, including her.

During Sally's first two weeks at Passages, we were unable to discover the cause of her drinking. Finally, in a hypnotherapy session when she was deeply under, Sally was able to recall that when she was five, her next-door neighbor had abducted her, tied her to a bedpost, and raped her. He had told her that if she told her parents, he would kill them and her too. During the next three years, Sally had lived in terror as her neighbor repeatedly stalked her, took her back to his house, and raped her. When Sally was eight, the rapes stopped. After that, she had lived in terror for a few more years and then completely blocked everything that had happened from her memory.

When we suffer from a trauma like that, or even one that's less severe, we don't want to remember it because it brings us so much pain. One of the only defenses a child has is to forget. Every time the memory surfaces, we block it out so that we won't feel the pain, the fear, and the shame. After we've done that enough times, we succeed in blocking it out completely. At that point, we can no longer recall the memory, even if we're asked specifically if such an event ever occurred to us, but it still lurks in our subconscious minds. That's what happened in Sally's case.

Whenever we live through trauma, we're also recording many sensations: birds singing, a siren going by, the smell of chicken frying, a particularly bright shade of red, or perhaps a rainy day.

We're also recording the physical sensations of what it's like to be forced to do something terrible against our will. As the years pass, even though we have successfully blocked out the memory, what we recorded while the trauma was occurring is still locked in our minds. When we hear a siren or see that shade of red or smell chicken frying, we become uneasy and frightened, and we need to do something to alleviate our fear and the uncomfortable feelings. Many times, we turn to addictive drugs or alcohol to alleviate those feelings. We'll also rebel strongly if someone tries to get us to do something we don't want to do. We may even react violently, much more so than the situation would call for.

## The Worst of Times Can Lead to the Best of Times

When Sally remembered the rapes, it triggered a major emotional upheaval. She cried for several days and began having terrifying nightmares. She was afraid to be alone. All the therapists talked with her about her tragic childhood, and each one approached it from a different perspective. In my metaphysics groups, I spoke about carrying hurts from the past into the future. I told the group that every ounce of sadness, pain, or terror that a past event inflicts on us today is made possible only because we have given it the power to do that. The event is over—we can't change that—but we *can* change how we view and relate to the event. Once we realize that we're the ones who are giving that past event the power to hurt us today, we can remove that power. What we give, we can take away.

In the metaphysics classes, Sally also learned that she was an integral, inseparable part of an eternal Universe—that she was not an insignificant part, but as important a part as anything can be. She saw her life as an unbroken chain of events that had led her to the moment where she could come to terms with what had happened to her. Over the following few weeks, Sally explored her personal philosophy and how it was causing her to see events from the past in a negative light.

Now, this is the part that will most likely be difficult for you; you'll wonder how it's possible to see such a terrible trauma in anything but a negative light. Yet with the help of her therapists, Sally did get to a point in her thinking where she learned to see the rapes from a new perspective, a perspective that no longer terrified her. She was in some ways even grateful for the event because it had given her strength, understanding, and insight. It had led her to develop a new, empowering philosophy—one she could now teach her own children.

Sally learned how to be happy, not in spite of what had happened to her, but because of what had happened. She understood that everything was part of her soul's journey, that the events were over, and that she could do nothing to undo them. She was faced with the same option you face regarding the events in your past—she could choose either to continue to suffer over them or to use them as stepping-stones to happiness. Sally chose happiness.

That was almost four years ago. Today, Sally is completely sober. She applies her new philosophy to everything in her life. Her marriage is happier than ever and her family is whole again. Her husband has his wife back, her children have their mother back, and Sally has her happiness back—happiness that had been lost for forty-five years. That's what we do best at Passages. We give back.

Not everyone has to live through experiences as severe as Sally's; but should they happen, you'll suffer greatly and needlessly if you don't have a philosophy that will see you through those bad days, if you fail to grasp the inner significance of events. If you have not grown up with a philosophy that would help you put events in a proper perspective, it's understandable that you would then turn to addictive drugs and alcohol to alleviate your pain and suffering. When these things happen to little children, we wouldn't expect them to grasp such a philosophy. But when they reach the age of understanding, someone must guide them into a correct understanding and help them put the events of the past into a perspective that they can not only live with but thrive through, as Sally did and as you can.

Pax's story, which you have read, is another excellent example of how good things can emerge from hard times. If you were to ask Pax how he sees the ten years of his addiction—the beatings, the degradation, the humiliation, the loss of friends, the loss of his college years, the loss of respect, the lost years—he would tell you that it was the most terrible experience of his life, and also the greatest. He would tell you that those ten years led him to his life's work, that without them he would never have had the idea or the drive to create Passages, and that the Universe was preparing him for a brilliant future where he could save the lives of many people. He would go on to say, and I've heard him say it, that if he had to go through it all again to achieve what he has now achieved, he would do it. It was the worst of times; it led to the best of times.

## Everything That Happens Benefits You

Learning to live, and live happily, with trauma, even one as serious as Sally's, is possible if you possess a strong personal philosophy based on what's true in the Universe. And what's true is that *everything that happens benefits you*. Even though events may hurt you, take something from you, or bring you pain, they're there for your growth, for your understanding, and for your total and complete benefit.

Another client, Samantha, came to learn this in such a potent way that, like Pax, she is now using her life experiences to help those who are chemically dependent. She was born and raised on Nob Hill, one of San Francisco's most affluent areas. She was an exceptionally beautiful child with lustrous brown hair and blue eyes that would delight any parent. She had a sparkling personality and an infectious laugh—and a deformed back that gave her a hump. It wasn't a large hump, but it was there.

To other children, Samantha's affluent life probably seemed perfect because she had everything that most children long for—a beautiful home, all the toys she wanted, trips to places with wonderful-sounding names, club memberships, and everything else that plenty of money can buy. But to Samantha, her life was anything but perfect. Both her parents were alcoholics, and she witnessed physical abuse between them that would later include her. Starting at a very early age, other children made fun of her deformity. Her earliest recollections of school were being made fun of by other children. In her class, they read the story of the hunchback of Notre Dame in Victor Hugo's novel. After that, she was called "Modo," after Quasimodo, the hunchback in the story. Children can be cruel. In addition, her parents treated her deformity as though it didn't exist, which left her feeling ashamed and terribly self-conscious.

Samantha masked her feelings of inferiority with a fierce determination to be the best at everything while at the same time wishing to be invisible. By the time Samantha was ten years old, her parents divorced and her world became even more abusive and horrific. Her mother took up with many alcoholic and addicted boyfriends, who stayed in her home. At various times, they sexually abused Samantha. Her mother seemed not to notice, but Samantha knew that her mother was aware of what was happening. She suspected it was one of the ways her aging mother kept her boyfriends interested. To fill the void inside, Samantha focused on getting A's in school and on being "perfect" with external accomplishments.

At fourteen, Samantha's days began and ended with marijuana. In high school, alcohol and pot were sufficient to dull her internal pain. When she was in college, she added other addictive drugs. That "solution" continued for several years before she had a mental breakdown and was forced to leave college. She received therapy, but it wasn't enough to keep her demons away, and her drinking and use of addictive drugs continued.

Samantha went back to college and graduated. She thought she had found the real solution to her problem when she fell in love, married, and had a child. She loved her little girl, but her husband turned out to be abusive to Samantha, and he ended up in jail for assault as well as drug possession. She divorced him and started a relationship with a new boyfriend, but he also abused her brutally. It seemed to her as if the hump on her back gave them permission to despise her and to physically and mentally abuse her.

Eventually, her alcohol and drug use escalated to the point where she lost her home, her child, and her job. Over the years, her downward spiral continued. Her affluent mother sent her to many different treatment centers, but she would relapse within a few days of leaving. Her mother was also taking care of her child, and Samantha was in agony, knowing that her little girl was likely being exposed to the same kind of sexual environment that she had experienced.

Just before Samantha came to Passages, she was living in her car, smoking other people's cigarette butts, and drinking stolen cheap wine out of the bottle by holding it up and pouring it into her mouth because the glass was jagged where she had smashed it to get the bottle open. Drug dealers had slashed her tires while she was in the car and taken her only possession, a small suitcase. She had two black eyes and a broken nose—the result of yet another confrontation with her latest companion. She had recently been in six different renowned treatment centers that had done nothing to help the deep depression that had caused her to be on suicide watch several times.

Then Samantha came to Passages. During her first month, she opened herself up to the possibility of healing the painful experiences that were causing her so much anguish. At the end of the month, it was clear to all her therapists that she needed more work, but she left and relapsed after a few days. She came back again a few weeks later and that time stayed for two months. We were able to help her delve deep into her tortured psyche so she could release the terrible memories that were destroying her, repair her terribly flawed self-image, and bring herself back to life. Samantha left Passages fully cured.

During her time at Passages, she said that after each of her individual sessions with our various therapists, she would walk away feeling a little more sense of herself and a little less damaged, until finally she could connect to herself and even to other people. Samantha began to feel as if she was a meaningful part of the Universe—that she had a right to be here, that she wasn't a mistake. Her shame and feelings of unworthiness were disappearing. Samantha was learning to see her physical deformity in a new light. She learned that to be happy today, we must leave our old baggage behind and see ourselves as we are—golden children of an indestructible Universe.

Several years have passed. Samantha is now a licensed therapist who works in the field of addiction, has a beautiful home, and has her daughter with her full-time. Her external success is just a reflection of her internal feelings of well-being and inner peace. She's an inspiration to all who know her. As you can imagine, with her background and experiences she is an expert and gifted counselor.

## The Universe Doesn't Make Mistakes

What saved Samantha, as well as Peter and Sally, was that they adopted a new way of viewing life and events. Their story is not uncommon. Every new client who comes to Passages has what these people once had—an inadequate personal philosophy that could not sustain them through the rigors and traumas of life. Those who have turned their philosophy around have turned their lives around. They have come to see that the Universe is not a place of nasty tricks and random events.

You may still be asking yourself, if the Universe doesn't make mistakes, why do seemingly bad things happen to good people? The answer, as you've been reading, is that they don't. Events happen and we label them as bad. Many people view death as bad and label it that way when someone close to them dies. They become depressed and use it as a reason to drink. Yet there is nothing more natural and part of the Universal plan than dying, separating from your body, and being absorbed back into the Universe. I remember when my mother died, I celebrated her death by having a beautiful dinner, knowing that she had left her old, tired body and gone home.

The Universe doesn't make mistakes. Everything is happening just as it should. It's only our perception of difficulties that causes us the distress and the difficulty we experience. Furthermore, when we label events as "bad," we fail to receive the benefit that is waiting for us.

I once knew a man who lost his job, cursed his luck, and began to drink alcohol and snort cocaine. He went on a three-month binge. One day toward the end of the three-month binge, he received a phone call from a company he had always wanted to work for. They had heard that he was available and wanted him to start right away. Before he could start, however, they asked him to take a drug test. They had high standards and didn't want anyone working for them who was using drugs.

He couldn't pass the drug test, so he never got that job. But the real reason he didn't get that job was that he had lost faith in the Universe, cursing his "misfortune" for having lost his job rather than expecting that the Universe had something better in store for him. In reality, when he lost his old job, it wasn't a mistake or a misfortune but a purposeful event. It was a graduation certificate that would allow him to move on to something better. He just didn't know it.

If you and I were living in a Universe that was not alive, conscious, and fully aware of us, it might be the case that "things just happen." But we are an integral part of a Universe that is fully alive, fully conscious, and *totally* aware of us, and that provides *exactly* what we need to achieve our full potential.

Just as we tend to label events as "bad," we also tend to label difficulties as being outside of us, which makes us feel that there is nothing we can do about those difficulties. Take the story of Max. Max owned a thriving sandwich shop. There were almost always people waiting in line to eat at his little shop. He gave away free pickles, free potato chips, sometimes a free soft drink, and his sandwiches were famous for being overstuffed.

One day his son, who lived in a distant city, came to visit. They had a good visit, but as the son was leaving, he told his father, "Since I've been here, I've been observing how you run the sandwich shop, and I have to tell you for your own good that you're making a big mistake giving away all those extras. The country's economy is in bad shape. People are out of work, and they have less money to spend. If you don't cut back on the free items and on your portion sizes, you'll be in a bad way before long too." His father was amazed, thanked his son, and told him he would consider his advice.

After the son left, the father followed his advice. He stopped giving away free items and he cut back on the generous portions of food in his sandwiches. Before long, after many of his disappointed customers had stopped coming, he wrote to his son: "You were right! The country's economy *is* in bad shape, and I'm experiencing the results of it right here in my sandwich shop!"

The poor economy that the man's son saw all around him was real. Despite the poor economy, though, the father had been running a successful sandwich shop. He didn't realize that times were hard, that many people were out of work, and that money was scarce. He was treating everyone with great abundance and he was reaping the rewards that such actions always bring. But after his son told him about the "bad shape" the country was in, he began to act as if it were so, bringing about the only possible result—a negative, fearful, ungenerous experience of life, an experience that he believed was "out there." Was it "out there"?

In reality, all addictive behavior is a search for relief and answers outside yourself, but the answers are never to be found "out there." *All the answers are "in here," inside you, waiting to be discovered. What you've been doing with drugs or alcohol or any addictive behavior is suppressing your own ability to overcome the difficulties that surround you.*

## Distress Comes from Imagining the Future

Often what causes you distress today is only the imagined events of the future. For you to feel distress, fear, or anxiety over a future event, you must use your mind to imagine a bad outcome. If you don't use your imagination, it's impossible to feel fear or stress. You should get a great deal of comfort from that information because your imagination is entirely under your control. You can just as easily imagine a good outcome. Here's an example so you can see what I mean.

Let's say that you and I are living in a house that's in foreclosure. We haven't made our mortgage payments for six months, the bank has foreclosed on us, and the sale is set for next month. After the sale, we'll have to move out, and we have no place to go. Over the past months, we fretted and anguished, moaned and lamented. Every bit of the discomfort we're now feeling has been caused by our imagining a bad outcome.

Now, suppose that unbeknownst to us, Aunt Agatha passed away a year ago and left us a fully paid-for house in the country along with enough cash to keep us living quite comfortably for the rest of our lives. When we find out about Aunt Agatha's bequest, we suddenly use our imagination to create a wonderful future for ourselves—a life of ease in the country. We couldn't care less about the impending foreclosure. We go out and celebrate for several days.

Then Aunt Agatha's lawyer calls and tells us that there's been a mistake. Aunt Agatha didn't leave the house to us; she left it to our sister. Now we're back to where we were in the first place, imagining a very bad outcome. On top of that, we have the loss of Aunt Agatha's house to lament.

For a week, we imagine all the bad things that will happen when we're thrown out onto the street with no place to go. Then the lawyer calls again. Our sister, who hated Aunt Agatha, wants no part of the house. She wants us to have it, along with all the cash.

Now we're back to joyously imagining a good outcome. We move out of our foreclosed house and into the country house—only to find that it's uninhabitable and in a bad neighborhood. The lawyer calls again. There's been a glitch in the will, and the cash is going to be held up indefinitely. We go into a slump and start imagining the terrible time that lies ahead. The next day, we get an offer from a developer who wants to develop the entire area. He offers us a huge sum of money for the house. We're elated, imagining that our troubles are finally over. . . .

Well, you get the picture. What has caused us our grief and our joy? We have! By using our imagination. We've been bobbing along like corks on the ocean, rising and falling as events have gone up and down. Just for a moment, imagine what it would have been like in our imagined story if we had known *from the first moment* that everything would turn out wonderfully well for us. *That's the way it is when your philosophy is based on what's true in the Universe.*

## Opportunities to Grow and Gain Strength

One of the reasons any obstacle is in your life is so that you can grow from it and become strong. You know the old saying that a chain is only as strong as its weakest link. Well, you're only as strong as your area of greatest weakness.

You can see these principles at work in nature all the time. A mother bird pushes her young out of the nest so they can learn to fly. She stops feeding them so they must venture forth. Baby lions playfully attack each other, even if the one being attacked doesn't want to play, so they'll learn how to fight for a mate when they come of age. In the animal world, the survival of the fittest is the law. The stragglers and weak animals are driven off or killed. Only the strongest males get to mate with the females. Life in the animal kingdom is hard, and that's what makes animals so strong and so capable. Everyone and everything is alive today only because its ancestors were survivors.

One of the reasons that the circumstances of your life are sometimes so painful, so devastating, and so difficult is that *the Universe always strikes at your weakest point because that's what most needs strengthening.*

Our challenges are, in effect, hand delivered by a loving Universe to make us stronger. In order to get the benefit from the obstacles, we're meant to face and overcome them rather than turning away and giving up. The moment you reach for a drink of alcohol or an addictive drug, it's actually a signal that one of your weak areas has been attacked, but instead of rising to the challenge and overcoming it, which would give you additional strength, you're succumbing to it and letting it roll over you as if you were lying in the middle of the road waiting for a truck to run you over.

Here's an example. One of the most common causes of anxiety is speaking in front of groups of people or meeting other people we don't know. This anxiety comes from using our imagination to foresee a bad result. Many people, including actors, have come to Passages stating that they need Valium in order to speak in front of groups, to go to big meetings, or to perform, and that they've become addicted to it.

They do not *need* Valium, to which they are now addicted, even if it's what the doctor told them. What they need is to work on strengthening the inner weakness that is causing them to imagine a bad outcome and become anxious. Perhaps they simply needed to overcome the fear by practicing public speaking in order to become better at it and more confident. Yet instead of dealing with the real reasons for the anxiety, they are turning to a drug to take the anxiety away. By using drugs, they are depriving themselves of the opportunity to grow into a strong public speaker.

So, how should you deal with the challenges in your life? First, recognize that the situation or event has a purpose and is meant to benefit you. The circumstances may look like problems, feel like problems, and seem to be problems, but that's just one possible point of view. Once you learn to look at your problems as "workout situations," they take on a whole new aspect. I call them "workout situations" because they are just that: situations for you to work out so you can gain strength and understanding. After you have done that, the circumstance is of no further use to you and it passes out of your life. Of course, the relief and the answers won't be handed to you without effort on your part since it is by working your way through the problems that you will gain strength, wisdom, and knowledge.

Realize also that the goals you seek aren't the be-all and end-all of life, even though you may think they are. It's the path itself that's the be-all and end-all. Reaching for your goals and searching for answers and relief is what is leading you along the path you've chosen for this lifetime. The path itself is where the truth is to be found, where your destiny manifests itself, and where your happiness lies. Just now, it has led you to this book. It has led you to a formula for recovery that will help you strengthen your weakest points and take the next steps on your path.

## You Need All Your Power

Earth is a place of discovery and of experience. That should be clear to you. It's no accident that you're here. It's no accident that you're reading this. You're a spiritual creature, here on earth to perfect yourself. Your problems and what you've suffered were and are in your life for that purpose. If you leave the planet without discovering that vital piece of information, your life will have been like driving two thousand miles to see the Grand Canyon and then spending your entire vacation in a hotel room. If you believe that your existence is just life and death and that everything in between is only a struggle, your life will lack the magic that makes life vital, wondrous, and transcendent.

Having said that, you cannot really be off your path to enlightenment—your path to realizing that you are an integral and vital part of the Universe. Enlightenment is like an ocean, and our paths to enlightenment are like rivers. Each river is different, but they all eventually lead to the ocean. No matter what we're doing, or when, or whether it brings us happiness or remorse, gain or loss, we're all on our individual paths to enlightenment. Even when we've done something we consider wrong, we're still on our own path to enlightenment.

The progress we make on our path will either be quick or slow, according to our awareness. If we're lying drunk in the gutter, chances are that our progress will be slow. If we're intentionally seeking enlightenment, which manifests as a desire to discover our relationship with the Universe, we'll use our so-called problems as opportunities to learn, we'll progress quickly, and we'll enjoy the rewards of peace, success, abundance, great good fortune, and well-being.

Using drugs and alcohol only complicates what you're here for. Using drugs and alcohol is giving up, abandoning your quest. Using drugs and alcohol is the road that leads to the loss of your birthright. You need all your mental capacity, all your power, all your imagination, all your drive, and all your faculties to follow your path to realization and enlightenment.

Personally, I love being here. I'm in love with our earth, our sunsets, our moonrises, our creatures, our wonderful people. When I see the broken, hopeless people who come to Passages, and I see the light return to their eyes, it brings tears to mine. It is drugs or alcohol or other addictive behaviors that have brought them to Passages, but what they receive is far more than relief from dependency. They learn how to heal the problems underlying their dependency rather than being a victim of them, and in the process they learn how to live happy lives.

I have received many letters from graduates of Passages telling me how important it was for them to have adopted a strong personal philosophy while they were at Passages. It was the key to their being able to create a happy, prosperous life, free from addiction. One graduate wrote, "What I learned about life and how to live it means as much to me as my sobriety. It's only been six months, but I know it will last. I have no cravings at all. I don't even think about drinking or using cocaine any more. My marriage is saved, my relationship with my children is solid, and I love being me, something that was absent for twenty years or more while I was using drugs and alcohol. Life is so much better without them. It's just what you all said it would be like. Thank you, thank you, and thank you."

Another letter I received said, "When I walked through that fifteen-foot door at Passages, supported on either side by two of your staff, I was hopeless. I had been in six centers, and the last one said that they expected to see me back within two years. Can you imagine that? I guess you can, having seen all that you have seen. Well, I'll never see the inside of a rehab again except to visit Passages. I am cured. I have not used drugs or alcohol in a year, and I know I never will again. Praise God! Praise all of you at Passages. I waited a year to write this, just to be sure, but now I'm sure. For me, it's over. . . . It's tough to live alone in New York, but now I'm not afraid anymore. I live in a safe place inside of me that you led me to. I have hope and I believe in myself after many, many years of hopelessness. I have you and your staff to thank for that and for so many other gifts of the spirit. God bless you all."

I don't mean to make light of your struggle to triumph over your dependency, but as you should realize by now, overcoming drugs and alcohol is relatively simple. A few weeks away from them and your withdrawal symptoms will disappear. What remains, and what is more difficult to heal, are the problems that drove you to drugs and alcohol in the first place. They are the weak links in your chain. Unless you heal the underlying conditions that have created and maintained your dependency, those problems will lead you back to the drugs and alcohol and addictive behavior over and over again.

How to accomplish that deep healing is what is at the heart of the three steps to total recovery I've been describing in this book: (1) Believe that a cure is possible for you, (2) Discover and heal the underlying causes with a holistic recovery program, and (3) Adopt a philosophy based on what is true in the Universe. By making those three steps your own, you can accomplish your task. Once you've cleared away those core problems, sobriety will be easy.

CHAPTER NINE

# THE NEW CHAPTER
# IN YOUR LIFE

W ITNESSING, SOMETIMES DAILY, TRIUMPHANT REAL-
life stories like the ones you've been reading here, I
ask myself over and over again: Why, in treatment
centers around the world and by all types of medical doctors,
psychiatrists, psychologists, drug and alcohol therapists, and
addiction specialists, are people regularly treated for "alcoholism" and "drug addiction" when the use of alcohol and drugs
is merely a means of coping with an underlying condition? Why
are symptoms being treated instead of causes?

Isn't it obvious that people who have become dependent on
alcohol or addictive drugs are using those substances to dull a
chronic pain? To blur the traumatic images of the past that still
haunt them? To ease their anxieties? To go to sleep at night? To
escape the stresses of everyday life? To help them face an
unbearable reality?

Throughout this book, I've emphasized that the word *alcoholism* is a misnomer. It's a made-up word that we've come to
accept, but that acceptance comes with very bad psychological side
effects. I'm surprised someone hasn't started using the word *addic-
tionism* as well as *alcoholism*. As I've shown, what has been labeled
as "alcoholism," "a disease," and "incurable" is merely dependency.

Since I don't even believe in the word *alcoholism*, and I hope by now you don't either, you may question why I chose the title *The Alcoholism and Addiction Cure*. I chose it because it is what you are used to hearing and reading. I look forward to the day in the near future when the paradigm shift has occurred and we will no longer be talking about "alcoholism." What is important is that you now clearly know the difference. This book—and the opportunity that is before you—is about curing yourself of your dependency on alcohol, addictive drugs, and addictive behaviors, not about curing yourself of alcoholism or addiction.

I've also explained in these pages that, without being aware of it, what everyone who is dependent on drugs or alcohol is trying to do is adjust the chemical imbalance in their brain so they'll feel calmness, harmony, and a sense of well-being instead of anxiety, stress, and pain. I've said that when you discover what is *really* making you turn to alcohol or drugs—one of the four causes in Chapter Five—and you take the necessary steps to heal those causes, you will be cured and your dependency will be ended.

I've said that *the greatest of all the healing agents available to you is your own body. And within your body, it is your own mind that is the most powerful activator of healing.* What we think and what we feel activates our healing process. If it seems to you that you remain pretty much the same, day after day, year after year, except that you grow older, that sameness is mostly because day after day, year after year, *you don't change what you think and what you feel.* You plod along, head down, not knowing that you are this wonderful healing instrument, capable of bringing about the most miraculous changes in yourself—changes that can create a whole new you, a person who is healthy, happy, and permanently free of alcohol, addictive drugs, and addictive behavior. You *are* a walking miracle. As you put into action the three steps to recovery outlined in this book, you are activating the miracle-maker part of yourself.

Once your dependency is cured, can you stay clean and sober forever? Yes. Will you? The answer to that has a lot to do with your character and willpower. Can someone who has ingested strychnine and been cured drink it again? Yes, but given all the negative consequences of doing so, would they?

I said this earlier, but it is well worth repeating: You cannot be a casual drinker or user once you have recovered. All you have to do is use alcohol or addictive drugs again and you will reactivate your dependency. I have never heard of one person who has been able to remain a "moderate drinker" or "moderate drug user" once he or she has once been dependent on alcohol or addictive drugs. Even after the underlying causes that led to your addiction have been eliminated, addictive substances have inherently addictive properties, particularly for you since you have a history of chemical dependency. As many times as you use them, you will become dependent on them.

## A Vibrant Reunion

As I was finishing the last few pages of this book, we had our first reunion at Passages for our graduates. They came from all over the United States and from a few other countries. As I greeted them, hugged them, shook their hands, laughed, and talked with them, I thought how wonderful it would be if you could be here to see them and hear them, to look into their eyes and see the joy and happiness that literally flowed from them. Nearly all of the people I have written about in this book were there. They looked like poster people for ads in health and fitness magazines.

They were all so eager to share their stories, their successes, and their accomplishments, including the hurdles they had overcome and the challenges they had faced and used as stepping-stones to gain more strength and understanding. They were brimming over with enthusiasm. It was as if our own children had returned home, which indeed they had.

The greatest feeling was that of love. We all truly love each other. Many of them cried with joy at being reunited with the people who had helped free them from the affliction of their terrible dependencies. Even the men cried. The most common statement I heard from them was "It is just like you and the treatment team said it would be." Everyone at Passages, even those of us who expected it, were amazed at the level of vibrancy in the air.

That vibrancy is what I want for you. I want you to achieve that feeling of great accomplishment, that feeling of joy that comes from knowing you will never again be held in the grip of dependency, that you are forever free.

I know how badly you want to return to a life of health and well-being, free of dependency. I wish I could meet you, talk with you, shake your hand, look into your eyes, and communicate the love I feel for you. We are spiritual beings sharing this magical, wondrous moment on planet Earth. We are fellow human beings. I wish I could be there with you to guide you every step of the way, lending you encouragement and reminding you when you are faced with a challenge that the challenge is only in your life to help you become strong and enduring. Since I cannot be with you, I have done the next best thing; I have written this book. Pax and I, with the help of our therapists, have also created a website to assist you and your treatment team with your detox and continuing sobriety. You can visit our website at www.TheAddictionCure.com.

I offer this transformational information in the hope that it will translate itself into the power to carry you through to the success that awaits you. I want to thank you for reading this book. You are a pure, virtuous, spiritual being. You deserve love, you deserve happiness, you deserve success, you deserve all good things, and most of all, you deserve to be forever free of dependency. As the Chinese sages are wont to say, may you mount to the skies of success as though on the wings of six dragons!

■ ■ ■

## LETTERS FROM THOSE WHO HAVE MADE THE PASSAGE TO RECOVERY

Throughout *The Alcoholism and Addiction Cure*, I've told stories about our clients at Passages and included some of their letters to us so you can see that you're not alone in what drives you to addictive behavior, so you can gain hope from the success of others, and so you'll feel confident following this path to your cure. I assure you that no matter how bad your circumstances are, many people whose circumstances were worse than yours have been cured using this holistic program and approach.

I am closing this book with just a few more of the emails and letters we receive from graduates of Passages and their family members. I want you to hear, through their own words, what they have achieved—and I want you to know what you can expect when you wholeheartedly adopt and make your own the three steps to total recovery from the Passages program.

Dear Chris and Pax and the staff of Passages,
There are simply no words I can use to thank you enough for saving my life. My journey began on September 22, 2003, when I arrived at Passages. Upon my arrival, I was very sick mentally and physically. I felt like a dead man walking. Your kind, understanding staff and techs took care of me in a manner that I will

never forget as long as I live. The demon that I was fighting was literally taking over my entire body. The human compassion and dignity given to me was overwhelming. I never had so many people in my life take care of me at this extraordinary level. It was truly a magnificent display of teamwork on so many people's parts.

I was admitted for a thirty-day stay. The treatment team, after thirty days, made a recommendation that I stay on an additional thirty days. At first I was opposed because I wanted to return to my home. But for the very first time in my life, I was going to listen to medical advice. I've never done this before. They were right on target.

The next thirty days were a blessing in so many ways. The mind, body, and soul-healing experience at Passages was truly a gift that is the best gift that anyone can ever receive. When a person enters Passages, it's unlike any other treatment facility in the world. All of us are so beaten down, and Passages, from the moment you enter, brings you up, giving you the necessary tools to face the reality of life. Those tools that are provided are truly the essence or key ingredients to battle whatever demon or demons you're battling. I've thought many times about this. It's very difficult to thank someone for giving you back your life.

Once again, to Chris and Pax and to every staff member, "thank you for your compassion and understanding." I'm profoundly and eternally grateful to Passages for showing me a better life. From the very bottom of my heart, "I thank you!"

Dear Chris and Pax,
Year upon year, I relapsed due to nerves. I couldn't function. The prescriptions for Valium and Xanax kept me in

the cycle of drug addiction and of alcoholism. I needed
to find a "cure." Through six relapses and sixteen years
of AA, the craving was battled and lost, and lost and lost.
I was a nervous wreck. My blood pressure was off the
charts, and I was as nervous and anxious as one can be
and still function, at least sometimes.

Coming to Passages . . . it was the last hurrah. I was
told I would lose the cravings for drugs and the compulsion for alcohol. I didn't believe it. After sixteen years
of drug addiction and alcoholism, I felt hopeless.
At first, even though Passages was wonderfully beautiful
and the staff was loving and warm, it was just another
treatment facility.

Then I was put on what was for me the correct medication. My blood pressure became perfect and my nervousness miraculously disappeared. The first day of the
new medication, I had a smile on my face all day that I
couldn't account for. It was noninvasive, nonaddictive,
and I had a feeling of neutral peace and well-being, of
love and warmth. And then I experienced the miracle
of your fabulous treatment team. They must have been
assembled in heaven. This was the treatment I needed
and wanted. I needed this balance in my life, and it
happened . . . it really happened, and it was just as it
said in the brochure about Passages. A miracle is I.
I've become me, the real me, the better me.

Dear Chris and Pax,
During the month that my son was at Passages, I spoke
with him several times. In each conversation, I could
hear the hope returning to his voice and attitude. He
has returned home with an accurate assessment of his
past, a committed perspective about his present, and a

positive outlook for his future. All of you at Passages are instrumental in saving my son's life. I cannot thank you enough. God bless you in your continued good work.

Dear Chris and Pax,
My journey to Passages began with a giant leap of faith taken, quite honestly, with my eyes squeezed tightly shut out of fear and apprehension. I came searching for a solution to a problem of a long-standing, daily addiction to alcohol.

What I found at Passages goes well beyond a mere solution. What I discovered and came to embrace was an intense understanding, an awakening, gained through the knowledge found in the very basic fundamentals of the universe and a belief in a higher power bringing all things together.

I thought that my journey began with a coast-to-coast flight and a forty-minute ride along the Pacific Coast Highway. It actually began the moment I crossed the marble threshold of the front door to Passages. In just the first few hours, my eyes and mind were opened to the fact that virtually everything I needed to recover was about to be made available to me in a genuinely caring and nurturing environment. Rarely in my life, if ever, have I felt the depth of gratitude I feel for the circumstances that led me to Passages, for the special people there who were paramount to my recovery, and for the resulting miracle of the power and peace I carry with me today. Passages is not just a place to heal and recover; it is truly a door that opens endless possibilities to the life and person we were meant to become.

Dear Chris and Pax,
I just wanted to take a moment to thank you so much for everything you did for me. I truly enjoyed my stay at

Passages and learned so much about myself and the pursuit of happiness. You've put together an incredible staff at Passages. Each person, each therapist, each tech adds so much to the whole picture and treatment offered at Passages. For those who want it, there's so much to be gained at your facility. I know I personally gained so much. I can't wait to come back for a visit. I'm already looking forward to it. It's been hard to come home, but I feel very confident that all is going to go well.

But damn, I miss Malibu—who wouldn't, right? Keep up the good work. If you ever need me to speak to any prospective clients, I would be more than happy to do so. I only have the best things to say about you and your staff at Passages. Thanks again for everything. I mean it from the bottom of my heart. All my best.


Dear Chris and Pax,
If everything happens for a reason, then I'm glad that God made this happen. After only thirty days, one month, I can say that I've done more growing than I had ever done prior to Passages entering my life. I've gone through a change personally, mentally, and spiritually, and I can say that I have a freedom I've never possessed before. I've learned so much here, and I've taken another step toward the person who I really am.

Inside myself, I'm grateful, not just for being at Passages, but for knowing all of you, and for becoming part of a family, which is something a tad strange to me. Not to sound as if I have never had a family, but not this type of family, where there are so many different people and no names for them like mother, father, brother, or sister—just friends becoming one unified group of people under one roof. This is a fellowship of men and women, and it's an incredible thing. It's amazing how loyal we've become to each other, and no matter what problem presented itself, every one of us in our own ways had an answer and a way to get past the obstacle in front of us.

I've overcome many obstacles going through Passages, one being my addiction, which is completely gone. I'm not dependent on drugs anymore. The other was my anger problem. I never really got angry while at Passages, not to a point where it was a problem. My yelling on the tennis court is one thing, but I find that normal. Even though anger is a natural feeling, with assertiveness and expressions of it through words, nobody will have to see me blow up anymore.

I'm very excited to get back to normal life, but this is also a sad and scary time. I'm sad because I must leave my newfound family, but I'll be in touch with every individual here because I want to keep this alive, just as I hope you all do. The scary portion is that I must get back to normality and realize that I do have a life outside of Passages, but I also need to realize where I'm going with it and how to travel the road of the future.

I can say one thing, though. Heading off to college in a few months will not be as hard for me anymore because I learned so much here, the most important being independence. I learned to fend for myself and not depend on others to do things for me. I also learned the importance of communication. If a problem arose, I went to different people each time and asked what they thought I should do.

Tough lessons were learned here too. I learned how to deal with two of the toughest, which are about trust and betrayal from my family and friends and how to cope with them. There's so much to be said about Passages and what I learned, but I just want to say thank

you, because without Passages I'd probably still be in a
major fight with numerous people, including my parents. I'm extremely grateful to have come here and I
wish all of you the best of luck in the future, even
though I know we will all do great. Thank you for giving
me this time and this graduation. With much love.

Hey Chris,
It's one of your Montana graduates. I just got "home-
sick" for you all and visited the website. I hope you're all
fine. I was glad to see your therapist, Audrey's, picture
on the website. She remains, to this day, one of my
favorite people, and she always will be. What a joy she is,
and what joy she gives. I'm alive, happy, and in a good
recovery pattern. I attend four twelve-step meetings a
week, and I find that I'm finally learning the skills to live
my own truth in this world. My husband and my two
boys are wonderful. The last two years since I graduated
from Passages have been very eventful—not easy, but
I've certainly become a student of recovery.

I just wanted you all to know—Gert, Anna, Ranjit,
Pax, and the rest of your staff as well as yourself—that
I consider my time at Passages irreplaceable. I found
that I wanted to stay alive while there, and that there was
a place for me in this world. My spirituality has grown
into the foundation on which I stand, and my intuition,
empathy, and understanding toward others and myself
is truly a gift that I enjoy now. It helps me to feel joy
instead of wounding me. Thank you from the bottom of
my heart. Continue to do your good works. I believe that
I'll return just to visit someday. If you can share this
with Audrey, please tell her I can feel her from here!
With much love and gratitude.

Dear Chris,

Finding Passages was one of the best things that happened to me in my life. The choice of wanting to live the rest of my life sober was the best. Realizing that it was necessary to find help doing that, I started looking for a rehabilitation facility that would meet my physical and spiritual needs. Chris, you and the staff at Passages are an amazing group of talented and supportive people who treat the cause as well as the effects. To me this is a "Magical Island of Assisted Recovery." I would say to anyone who truly wants to start a new sober life, don't wait, book your "Passage" today. It will be the best gift you will ever give yourself or loved one in need. Many thanks.

Dear Chris,

My God! What a treasure Passages is, and what a treasure you are. I learned more about myself in thirty days than I had in the rest of my life before Passages. I thought I was a diseased alcoholic condemned to a life of drinking—at least that's what everyone had told me at the four centers I was in before coming to your place—but now I know that was just because they didn't know how to cure me.

I wish that everyone could go to Passages to learn about life, love, spirituality, compassion, healing, and the truth about drugs and alcohol—that they aren't the demons. Our own demons are actually what's driving us to use those substances. I'm cured forever, I know it in my heart. My relationship with my family is healed, my self-image is restored, and I'm living my dream again. How I can ever repay you is beyond me.

You and Pax and your staff are among the finest people I've ever met. You and your staff were so nonjudgmental about the things I had done in my past, and your metaphysical groups set me straight about how to see those things in the right light. I'll be forever grateful.

Yo Chris!
I'm back in college, dude! My dad loves me, my mom loves me, my sister loves me, my brother Dan still thinks I'm a sack of shit, but what the heck, you can't win them all! Three out of four is a big win. After what I did to them over the years, I'm grateful that I've won back three of them.

More than that, I've got a new lease on life. I'm going to be a psychologist and help people just as you guys helped me. Oh yeah! My girl loves me too, that's four out of five! When I got to Passages nobody loved me, especially me! I gotta say thanks, Chris. Your metaphysics classes saved my butt. I'm glad to be me for the first time in my life. I love ya, bro!

Dear Passages,
Thank you, thank you, and thank you. That's one thank you for each year of my sobriety. I never believed life could be so wonderful. My boyfriend says thank you too, and so do my mom and dad. I think of you all. I keep my little angel that you gave me at my graduation with me all the time. Love you all.

Dear Chris and Pax:
I've been home for forty-two days. My anxiety and nervousness are completely gone, I haven't had one panic attack, and my migraines have disappeared. It's a miracle. I miss everyone there so much. You're the family I never had. It's the first time I've ever felt truly loved. I keep you all in my prayers and I'll visit soon.

The book I finished just before coming to Passages is a hit, and I have another in the works. I have you and the staff to thank for creating a new life for me. I wish I could have you all with me.

Dear Chris and Pax and the fabulous staff at Passages, I just celebrated my three-year birthday of being sober. I gave a toast (grape juice!) to you and Passages for saving my life. What I learned at Passages gave me not only sobriety, for which I'm grateful, it gave me back my life—but better than it had ever been before—and for being nearly seventy-five, that's quite a mouthful.

My only regret is that I didn't find you earlier. God bless you all. It's a beautiful world when looked at through the "new eyes" you gave me in your metaphysical groups.

# NOTES

## Chapter Two

1. The National Center on Addiction and Substance Abuse (CASA) at Columbia University, *Under the Counter: The Diversion and Abuse of Controlled Prescription Drugs in the U.S.* (2005), ii.
2. Ibid., ii, iii.
3. P. R. Barker, J. F. Epstein, L. L. Hourani, J. Gfroerer, A. M. Clinton-Sherrod, N. West, and W. Shi, W., *Patterns of Mental Health Service Utilization and Substance Use among Adults, 2000 and 2001*, DHHS Publication No. SMA 04-3901, Analytic Series A-22 (Rockville, Md.: Substance Abuse and Mental Health Services Administration, Office of Applied Studies, 2004).
4. Center for Substance Abuse Prevention, Substance Abuse and Mental Health Services Administration, "Trouble in the Medicine Chest (I): Rx Drug Abuse Growing," *Prevention Alert* 6, no. 4 (March 7, 2003).
5. National Institute on Drug Abuse, U.S. Department of Health and Human Services, National Institutes of Health, *Prescription Drugs: Abuse and Addiction*, No. 01-4881 (2001), 10.
6. Pharmaceutical Research and Manufacturers of America, *Pharmaceutical Marketing and Promotion: Tough Questions, Straight Answers* (Fall 2004), 4.
7. Alan Sager and Deborah Socolar, "Drug Marketing Staff Soars" (Boston, Mass.: Boston University School of Public Health, 2001).

## Chapter Four

1. Substance Abuse and Mental Health Services Administration, Office of Applied Studies, *Treatment Episode Data Set (TEDS): 1994–1999, National Admissions to Substance Abuse Treatment Services*, DASIS Series: S-14, DHHS Publication No. (SMA) 01-3550 (2001).

2. Substance Abuse and Mental Health Services Administration, Office of Applied Studies, *Services Research Outcomes Study* (1998).

Chapter Six

1. Andrew Weil, *Spontaneous Healing: How to Discover and Enhance Your Body's Natural Ability to Maintain and Heal Itself* (New York: Ballantine Books, 1995), 6.
2. Candace B. Pert, *The Molecules of Emotion: Why You Feel the Way You Feel* (New York: Touchstone, 1997), 21.
3. Ibid., 21, 22.
4. Ibid., 24.
5. Ibid.
6. Ibid., 25.
7. Ibid., 27.
8. To read more about the work of Norman Cousins, see his books *Anatomy of an Illness as Perceived by the Patient* and *Head First: The Biology of Hope and the Healing Power of the Human Spirit.*
9. G. Ganis, W. L. Thompson, and S. M. Kosslyn, "Brain Areas Underlying Visual Mental Imagery and Visual Perception: An fMRI Study," *Cognitive Brain Research* 20, no. 2 (2004): 226–41.

Chapter Seven

1. The information on the body's organ systems is drawn from the excellent summary of Anthony Carpi, John Jay College, *Basic Anatomy: Tissues and Organs* (1999), http://web.jjay.cuny.edu/~acarpi/NSC/14-anatomy.htm.
2. Andrew Weil, *Spontaneous Healing: How to Discover and Enhance Your Body's Natural Ability to Maintain and Heal Itself* (New York: Ballantine Books, 1995), 250.
3. Genova Diagnostics works with and educates physicians around the world in the use of cutting-edge diagnostic testing. They can be reached at www.gdx.net or (800)522-4762.
4. M. A. Stewart, "Effective Physician-Patient Communication and Health Outcomes: A Review," *Canadian Medical Association Journal* 152, no. 9 (1995): 1423-33; Emil Lesho, D.O., "When the Spirit Hurts:

An Approach to the Suffering Patient," *Archives of Internal Medicine* 163, no. 20 (2003): 2429-32; M.R. McVay, "Medicine and Spirituality: A Simple Path to Restore Compassion in Medicine," *South Dakota Journal of Medicine* 55, no. 11 (2002): 487-91.

5. Nancy Waring, "Mindfulness Meditation: Studies Show Awareness Promotes Healing," *Hippocrates*, July 2000; Jon Kabat-Zinn, *Wherever You Go There You Are: Mindfulness Meditation in Everyday Life* (New York: Hyperion, 1995).

6. See Pert, *The Molecules of Emotion.*

7. *Destructive Emotions: How Can We Overcome Them? A Scientific Dialogue with the Dalai Lama* narrated by Daniel Goleman (New York: Bantam, 2003). The scientific dialogue with the Dalai Lama occurred in March 2000 in Dharamsala, India, with contributions by Richard Davidson, Paul Ekman, Mark Greenberg, Owen Flannigan, Matthieu Ricard, Jeanne Tsai, the Venerable Somchai Kusalacitto, Francisco J. Varela, B. Alan Wallace, and Geshe Thupten Jinpa.

8. R. Davidson, D. Jackson, and N. Kalin, "Emotion, Plasticity, Context, and Regulation: Perspectives from Affective Neuroscience," *Psychological Bulletin* 126, no. 6 (2000): 890-909; R. Davidson, "Affective Style, Psychopathology, and Resilience: Brain Mechanisms and Plasticity," *American Psychologist* 55 (2000): 1196-1214; R. Davidson and W. Irwin, "The Functional Neuroanatomy of Emotion and Affective Style," *Trends in Cognitive Science* 3 (1999): 11-21; R. Davidson, J. Kabat-Zinn, J. Schumacher, et al., "Alterations in Brain and Immune Function Produced by Mindfulness Meditation," *Psychosomatic Medicine* 65, no. 4 (2003): 564-70.

9. "The Downsides of Prozac: Worse Living through Chemistry," *Harvard Magazine* 102, no. 5 (May-June 2000).

10. E. H. Turner, A. M. Matthews, E. Linardatos, et al., "Selective Publication of Antidepressant Trials and Its Influence on Apparent Efficacy," *New England Journal of Medicine* 358, no. 3 (2008): 252-60.

11. Sanesco International, Inc., 1200 Ridgefield Blvd., Suite 200, Asheville, NC 28806, 866-670-5705; NeuroScience, Inc., 373 280th St., Osceola, WI 54020, 888-342-7272.

# INDEX

AA, *see* Alcoholics Anonymous
abstinence, 272–76, 317
acupuncture, 215–16, 218–220, 228
addiction(s):
  to caffeine, 27
  defined, 23–24
  as dependency, 19
  and "dry drunk" characteristics,
    28–29
  to methadone, 87
  Pax's experiences with, 43–127
  to peptides, 165
  as response to underlying
    conditions, 15–17
  thought paradigm about, 15
  trading, 29
addictive behavior, 190–91, 197
  medicating feelings with, 178,
  not the problem, 183–84, 264
  psychological addiction to, 146
addictive drugs, 22–23
  abstinence from, 272–76
  tolerance to, 23–24, 203–4
  withdrawal from, 24–25
ailment, defined, 32
alcohol dependency, 26–27
alcoholics, beliefs about, 12–13
Alcoholics Anonymous (AA), 13,
  134–37
alcoholism:
  connotation of term, 16
  as dependency, 19
  as disease, 13
  and "dry drunk" characteristics,
    28–29
  as response to underlying
    conditions, 15–17
  thought paradigm about, 15

allergy(-ies), 188, 193, 199, 216
  alcoholism as, 13
All-That-Is, 259, *see also* Universe
alternative medicine, 188, 189,
  190–91, 200
AMA (American Medical
  Association), 13
American Association of Integrative
  Medicine, 200
American Association of
  Naturopathic Physicians, 189
American Medical Association
  (AMA), 13
American Society of Addiction
  Medicine, 204
amphetamines, 22
antidepressants, 190, 197, 203, 210–13,
  *see also* SNRIs; SSRIs
anxiety, 38–39
Appell, David, 255–57

"bad consequences" approach, 131
balance, 40–42
Bannister, Roger, 14, 143
barbiturates, 22–23, 187
Basson, Gert, 258–61
beliefs, 159–73
  about alcoholics, 12–13
  based on truth, 281–82
  as cause of dependency, 146,
    153–56
  and cellular communication
    system, 162–65
  in community of support, 172–73
  in effecting cure, 170–72
  and emotions in healing, 165–68
  in paradigms, 14
  of therapist, 168–70

beliefs (*continued*)
  in treatment paradigm, 143–44
  unconscious, 265–66
benefit from events, 295–97, 302–5

Benson, Herbert, 207
benzodiazepine, 23, 187, 203, 215
*The Big Book*, 137
biological aspect of alcoholism, 13
"bodybrain," 164
brain, relapse and, 276–77
Brestler, David, 218

caffeine, 27, 148, 194, 199
CASA, *see* National Center on
  Addiction and Substance
  Abuse
cause and effect, 169, 281–82
causes of dependency, *see*
  underlying conditions/causes
cellular communication (human
  body), 162–65
"chasing the dragon," 54
chemical imbalance, 145, 148–52,
  206–7, 209–13
Chinese medicine, *see* Traditional
  Chinese Medicine
circulatory system, 179
cirrhosis, 26
cleanses, 189
clinical psychologists, 229–35
cocaine, 22
"cold turkey," 71, 93, 203
Confucius, 172
Cousins, Norman, 167
cure:
  belief in, 160–62, 170–72
  cause and effect in, 169
  defined, 1
  possibility of, 138–40

Dalai Lama, 209
Davidson, Richard, 209
denial, 42
dependency, 22–23

on alcohol, 26–27, 28
alcoholism and addiction as, 19
from beliefs inconsistent with
  truth, 153–56
causes of, 145–48
from chemical imbalance, 148–52
as craving for emotion, 165–66
as effort to cope with life, 141
emotions in, 167
from inability to cope with
  conditions, 156–58
psychological, 26, 28
as symptom, not problem, 17–20
test for, 28–29
from unresolved events in past,
  152–53
depression, 39, 197, 199, 209–10
detoxification, 187, 188, 202–5,
  222–24
*Diagnostic and Statistical Manual of
  Mental Disorders* (DSM), 32
diet, *see* nutrition
DiCaprio, Leonardo, 48
digestive system, 180
Dispenza, Joseph, 164
distress, cause of, 308–9
dizziness, 24, 39, 267
doctors:
  medical, 188–207, 215
  of Traditional Chinese Medicine,
    182, 215–28
drugs:
  addictive, *see* addictive drugs
  prescription, abuse of, 29–33
  for psychological disorders, 33
  stacking, 33–35
  shut off body's alarm system,
    35–37
"dry drunk," 28–29
DSM (*Diagnostic and Statistical
  Manual of Mental Disorders*), 32
dual diagnosis patients, 197

Easy Sobriety®, 139
Einstein, Albert, 263

emotions:
    destructive, 208–9
    *Destructive Emotions: How Can*
        *We Overcome Them?* 208–9
    in healing, 167–68
    mind-body connection, 208–9
    power of, 164–66
endocrine system, 180
enlightenment, 312–13
ethanol, 25–26
excretory system, 180
exercise, 254–57

family therapists, *see* marriage and
    family therapists
fatigue, 39
Fava, Maurizio, 211
FDA, *see* U.S. Food and Drug
    Administration
fitness, 254–57
food allergies, 188, 193, 199, 216
Ford, Henry, 171
forgiveness, 21–22
four-minute mile, 14
four causes of dependency, 145–58
friends, healthy circle of, 270–72
future, imagining, 308–9

genetic tendencies, 146–47, 193, 195
Genova Diagnostics, 188, 195
glands, 178–79
Glenmullen, Joseph, 211–12
God, 286–87
Goleman, Daniel, 208–9
Guerrouj, Hicham El, 14
Gustafson, Paul, 246–48

half-life of drugs, 34
Hamaguchi, Lyn, 171–72
Hanaway, Patrick, 189–95
happiness, 40–41, 154, 162–63, 166,
    279–80, 294, 301, 302
headaches, 39, 228
healing mechanisms (human body),
    161–62

healing of underlying causes, 11–42,
    203
    and alcoholism/addiction as
        responses, not diseases,
        15–17
    and cycle of dependency, 31–33
    and dependencies as symptoms,
        not problems, 17–20
    and epidemic of prescription
        drug abuse, 29–31
    identification of real issues for,
        38–40
    new paradigm for, 12–15
    and psychological dependence,
        26–28
    by restoring natural state of
        balance, 40–42
    and self-punishment syndrome,
        20–22
    and stacking of drugs, 33–35
    and test for dependency, 28–29
HealthEmotions Institute, 207
Healthy Hypnosis, 246
heavy metals, 193–94, 199
herbal medicine, 220–21, 223–24
herbal teas, 215–16
heroin, 2–3, 22, 54–83 passim,
    129–32, 138
Higher Self, 259
Hippocrates, 167, 193
holistic, definition of, 176
holistic medical practitioners, 188–89,
    200
holistic recovery program, 175–277,
    *see also* treatment paradigm(s)
    choosing practitioners for, 181–83
    clinical psychologist in, 229–35
    doctor of Traditional Chinese
        Medicine in, 215–28
    healthy friends in, 270–72
    hypnotherapist in, 246–54
    knowledge of body in, 178–81
    and malfunction of ventral
        medial prefrontal cortex,
        276–77

holistic recovery program (*continued*)
marriage and family therapist in,
236–46
medical doctor in, 188–207, 215
"never again" rule in, 275–76
permanent abstinence in, 272–74
personal fitness in, 254–57
spiritual therapy in, 261–70
team for, 175–76, 185–86, 192,
196, 200, 202, 214–15
visualization and meditation in,
207, 257–61
homeopathic medical physicians,
189
homeostasis, 23
Hope, Audrey, 261–70
Hui, Kathleen K. S., 216
human body:
cellular communication in,
162–65
healing mechanisms of, 161–62
knowledge of, 178–81
hydrocodones, 22
hypnotherapists, 246–54
hypothalamus, 162–63

iatrogenic dependency, 31
I Ching, 285–88
imagining future, distress from,
308–9
immune system, 181
inability to cope with conditions,
145, 156–58
insomnia, 39
integrative medicine, 188–215

Kalin, Ned, 207
Kenworthy, MaryLou, 249–54
"kicking," 59

laboratory testing, 187–88, 193–94,
196–200, 205–6
Landy, John, 14
life path, determination of,
292–95

lifestyle, 189, 206, 270–72
liver, 26
low energy, 39
lymphatic system, 181

Mallare, Litos, 189, 195–202
marijuana dependency, 227, 234–35,
273
marriage and family therapists
(MFTs), 177, 236–46
Mayo Clinic, 26
McMullen, Keith, 230–35
MDMA, *see* Methylenedioxymethamphetamine
medical doctors, 188–207, 215
and prescription drug abuse,
31–33, 36–38
stacking of drugs by, 32–34
meditation, 207, 209, 257–61
Merck, 38
metaphysics, 168–69
methadone, 22, 87–88, 201–2, 204
methylenedioxymethamphetamine
(MDMA), 53–54
MFTs, *see* marriage and family
therapists
mind-body medicine, 207–8
mindfulness breathing, 207, 209
*The Molecules of Emotion*, 163
morphine, 22
muscular system, 179

National Center on Addiction and
Substance Abuse (CASA), 29
National Certification Commission
for Acupuncture and Oriental
Medicine (NCCAOM), 216
naturopathic physicians, 189, 200
NCCAOM (National Certification
Commission for Acupuncture
and Oriental Medicine), 216
negative reinforcement, 28
nervous system, 179–80
neurotransmitters:
defined, 193

imbalance in due to addiction,
206, 209–15
and nutritional supplementation,
214–15
rebalancing of, 214
Newton, Sir Isaac, 281
nicotine, 22, 194, 275–76
nutrition, 192–95, 198
nutritional deficiencies, 206–7
nutritional supplements, 10,
189, 196, 198, 214–15
"the observer," 161
1-800-Schedule.com, 229
one-size-fits-all treatment, 132–34
opioid dependence, 204
opportunities, obstacles as, 309–12
organs, 179–81
oxycodone, 22–23

paradigm(s), 12, 14, see also
treatment paradigm
Passages Addiction Cure Center
(Malibu, California), 1, 4–9
letters from clients, 18–19,
313–14, 319–28
community of support in,
172–73
discovering causes of addiction
at, 39–40
holistic approach at, 41
key to recovery at, 140–41
origin of, 126
treatment program at, 158
peptides, 162–63, 165
personal fitness, 254–57
personal philosophy, 279–314
based on truths of Universe,
279–82
as determinant of life path,
292–95
for difficult times, 291–95
and distress from imagining
future, 309–10
and freedom from tyranny of
events, 295–97

for healing traumas in
subconscious, 297–98
and obstacles as opportunities,
309–12
perfection of Universe in,
305–8
positive view of events in,
288–91, 300–302
and seeing benefits in all events,
302–5
wisdom from I Ching in,
285–86
Pert, Candace, 163, 164, 208
pharmaceutical industry, 36–37
philosophy of life, see personal
philosophy
positive view of events, 288–91,
300–302
powerlessness, 135–37
Prentiss, Pax, 2–4, 43–127
alcohol abuse, 96–97
and Ashley, 99–102, 106–7
development of heroin addiction,
54–57
early experience with drugs, 51–54
early life of, 43–48
jacking the dealers, 69–82
mom's help with withdrawal,
114–18
mother's addiction problems,
48–50
realization of reason for using,
121–25
in rehab, 92–95, 105–6
shooting dope, 108–13
in sober living house, 118–24
prescription drugs:
abuse of, 29–33
antidepressants, 210–13
stacking of, 33–35
Prozac, 210–13, see also
antidepressants; prescription
drugs; psychotropic
medications
"psychic need," 28

psychological dependence, 26, 28, 37
psychological disorders, 32–33
PsychologyToday.com, 229
psychotropic medications, 197, 203, 210–13
punishment, 3
 for dependency control, 131–32
 self-punishment syndrome, 20–22

Randall, Gayle Madeleine, 189, 202–15
rehab, 92–95
relapse, 138–40, 276–77
relaxation response, 207
replacement drugs, 204–5
reproductive system, 180–81
respiratory system, 180
Rothschild, Noah, 236–46
Rush, Benjamin, 13

SAMSHA, see Substance Abuse and Mental Health Services Administration
seizures, 187
self-image, 133–34
self-punishment syndrome, 20–22
Siberian addiction treatment, 131–32
skeletal system, 179
Smith, Robert, 13, 134, 138
SNRIs (selective norepinephrine reuptake inhibitors), 210–13
spiritual counseling, 261–70
spirituality, 8, 262–70
SSRIs (selective serotonin reuptake inhibitors), 210–13
stacking of drugs, 33–35
"stop mechanisms," 27
subconscious traumas, 297–99
Substance Abuse and Mental Health Services Administration (SAMSHA), 204
Supreme Being, 286–87

TCM, see Traditional Chinese Medicine
therapeutic massage, 222
therapists, beliefs of, 168–70
thoughts, power of, 164–66
thyroid, 16, 39, 147, 175, 179, 180, 199
tolerance, 23–24, 204
"tooter," 54
Traditional Chinese Medicine (TCM), 182, 215–28
traumas, 297–99
treatment paradigm(s), 129–58, see also holistic recovery program
 beliefs in, 143–44, 159–73
 discovery of underlying cause in, 140–42
 empowerment in, 134–37
 evolution of, 12–15
 one-size-fits-all, 132–33
 punishment, 131–32
 and relapses, 138–40
 and twelve-step groups, 137–38
triggers, 272
truth:
 beliefs inconsistent with, 153–56
 philosophy based on, 279–82
Tuina, 222
Turner, Erick, 212
twelve-step programs, 11–12, 134, 137–39, see also Alcoholics Anonymous

UES, see University Elementary School
underlying conditions/causes:
 alcoholism/addiction as responses to, 15–17, 175, 183–84
 of dependency, 145–58, 196, 232, 236–38
 discovery of, 140–42
 drugs that mask, 35–38, 39–40, 203

healing, *see* healing of
   underlying causes
   of medical conditions, 38–39
   in treatment paradigm, 140–42
Universal laws, 8, 153, 281–82,
   285–87
Universe, 8, 50, 154, 286, 287
   perfection of, 305–8
   personal philosophy and truths
      of, 279–82
University Elementary School
   (UES), 46–47
unresolved events in past, 145,
   152–53
U.S. Food and Drug
   Administration (FDA), 36,
   37, 38, 212, 218

Valium, 34–35
Van Lent, Mary, 271–72
ventral medial prefrontal cortex,
   276–77
Vioxx, 38
visualization, 247–61
vitamin deficiencies, 198–99

Walker, John, 14
war on drugs, 132
Weil, Andrew, 161, 181
Westside Alternative (Venice, CA),
   50–51
*What the Bleep Do We Know!?*, 164
Wilson, Bill, 13, 134, 138
withdrawal:
   from heroin, 59
   from methadone, 87–88, 204
   symptoms of, 24–25, 184, 187,
      204
   and tolerance level, 24
"workout situations," 311
workshops, 291–92
www.TheAddictionCure.com, 10,
   215, 318

X, *see* methylenedioxymethamphetamine

yoga, 177, 228

*Zen and the Art of Happiness*, 166
Zhang, Ji, 217–27

# Other Titles from Power Press

*Available from your favorite neighborhood and online bookstores:*

**Be Who You Want, Have What You Want: Change Your Thinking, Change Your Life**
*By Chris Prentiss, Trade Paperback, $15.95*

**Meditation on the Perfect You**
*Companion CD to Be Who You Want, Have What You Want*
*By Chris Prentiss, 1 CD, $9.95*

**The Little Book of Secrets: Gentle Wisdom for Joyful Living**
*By Chris Prentiss, Trade Paperback, $9.95*

**Zen and the Art of Happiness**
*By Chris Prentiss, Trade Paperback, $10.95*

**The Alcoholism and Addiction Cure: A Holistic Approach to Total Recovery**
*Audio Version, by Chris Prentiss, 10 CDs, $39.95*

**The I Ching: The Book of Answers, New Revised Edition**
*The Profound and Timeless Classic of Universal Wisdom*
*By Wu Wei, Trade Paperback, $15.95*

**A Tale of the I Ching: How the Book of Changes Began**
*An Enchanted Journey into the Origins and Inner Workings of the I Ching*
*By Wu Wei, Trade Paperback, $10.95*

**I Ching Wisdom: Guidance from the Book of Answers, Vol. I New Revised Edition**
*Practical Insights for Creating a Life of Success and Good Fortune*
*By Wu Wei, Trade Paperback, $12.95*

**I Ching Wisdom: More Guidance from the Book of Answers, Vol. II, New Revised Edition**
*Universal Keys for Creating Peace, Prosperity, Love, and Happiness*
*By Wu Wei, Trade Paperback, $12.95*

**I Ching Readings: Interpreting the Answers, New Revised Edition**
*Getting Clear Direction from the Ancient Book of Wisdom*
*By Wu Wei, Trade Paperback, $14.95*